Teaching Technology from a Feminist Perspective

THE ATHENE SERIES
An International Collection of Feminist Books
General Editors: Gloria Bowles, Renate Klein and Janice Raymond
Consulting Editor: Dale Spender

The ATHENE SERIES assumes that all those who are concerned with formulating explanations of the way the world works need to know and appreciate the significance of basic feminist principles.

The growth of feminist research has challenged almost all aspects of social organization in our culture. The ATHENE SERIES focuses on the construction of knowledge and the exclusion of women from the process—both as theorists and subjects of study—and offers innovative studies that challenge established theories and research.

ON ATHENE—When Metis, goddess of wisdom who presided over all knowledge was pregnant with ATHENE, she was swallowed up by Zeus who then gave birth to ATHENE from his head. The original ATHENE is thus the parthenogenetic daughter of a strong mother and as the feminist myth goes, at the "third birth" of ATHENE she stops being Zeus' obedient mouthpiece and returns to her real source: the science and wisdom of womankind.

Volumes in the Series

MEN'S STUDIES MODIFIED: *edited by* Dale Spender

MACHINA EX DEA: *edited by* Joan Rothschild

WOMAN'S NATURE: *edited by* Marian Lowe and Ruth Hubbard

SCIENCE AND GENDER: Ruth Bleier

WOMAN IN THE MUSLIM UNCONSCIOUS: Fatna A. Sabbah

MEN'S IDEAS/WOMEN'S REALITIES: *edited by* Louise Michele Newman

BLACK FEMINIST CRITICISM: Barbara Christian

THE SISTER BOND: *edited by* Toni A.H. McNaron

EDUCATING FOR PEACE: Birgit Brock-Utne

STOPPING RAPE: Pauline B. Bart and Patricia H. O'Brien

TEACHING SCIENCE AND HEALTH FROM A FEMINIST PERSPECTIVE:
A Practical Guide: Sue V. Rosser

FEMINIST APPROACHES TO SCIENCE: *edited by* Ruth Bleier

INSPIRING WOMEN: Reimagining the Muse: Mary K. Deshazer

MADE TO ORDER: The Myth of Reproductive and Genetic Progress:
Patricia Spallone and Deborah L. Steinberg

NOTICE TO READERS

May we suggest that your library places a standing/continuation order to receive all future volumes in the Athene Series immediately on publication?
Your order can be cancelled at any time.

Also of interest

WOMEN'S STUDIES INTERNATIONAL FORUM*

Free sample copy available on request

Teaching Technology from a Feminist Perspective

A Practical Guide

Joan Rothschild
University of Lowell, USA

PERGAMON PRESS

NEW YORK · OXFORD · BEIJING · FRANKFURT
SÃO PAULO · SYDNEY · TOKYO · TORONTO

U.S.A.	Pergamon Press, Inc., Maxwell House, Fairview Park, Elmsford, New York 10523, U.S.A.
U.K.	Pergamon Press plc, Headington Hill Hall, Oxford OX3 0BW, England
PEOPLE'S REPUBLIC OF CHINA	Pergamon Press, Room 4037, Qianmen Hotel, Beijing, People's Republic of China
FEDERAL REPUBLIC OF GERMANY	Pergamon Press GmbH, Hammerweg 6, D-6242 Kronberg, Federal Republic of Germany
BRAZIL	Pergamon Editora Ltda, Rua Eça de Queiros, 346, CEP 04011, Paraiso, São Paulo, Brazil
AUSTRALIA	Pergamon Press Australia Pty Ltd., P.O. Box 544, Potts Point, N.S.W. 2011, Australia
JAPAN	Pergamon Press, 5th Floor, Matsuoka Central Building, 1-7-1 Nishishinjuku, Shinjuku-ku, Tokyo 160, Japan
CANADA	Pergamon Press Canada Ltd., Suite No. 271, 253 College Street, Toronto, Ontario, Canada M5T 1R5

First edition 1988

Library of Congress Cataloging-in-Publication Data
Rothschild, Joan.
Teaching technology from a feminist perspective.
(The Athene series)
Bibliography; p.
Includes index.
1. Technology—Study and teaching. 2. Women in technology. I. Title. II. Series.
T56.4.R68   1987   607   87-7024

British Library Cataloguing in Publication Data
Rothschild, Joan
Teaching technology from a feminist
perspective: a practical guide.—(The
Athene series).—(Pergamon international
library of science, technology, engineering
and social studies).
1. Technology—Study and teaching
I. Title II. Series
607'.1   T65

ISBN 0-08-034234-5 (Hardcover)
ISBN 0-08-034233-7 (Flexicover)

Printed in Great Britain by A. Wheaton & Co. Ltd., Exeter

Contents

Preface/Acknowledgements

When I began teaching about women and technology in 1978, my course, although not the first, was among the earliest. Research and publication in the field were growing; so, apparently, was teaching. In the intervening period, had interest developed to explore these curriculum experiences more widely? Did faculty now want to know more about how feminist perspectives might be applied to technology courses? Although the answers appeared to be Yes, when I was approached to prepare this book, I looked to colleagues in the field for feedback. Informal discussions soon confirmed that: the number of courses had grown considerably, and the level of interest in curriculum work was high.

In the fall of 1985, we mailed a questionnaire and request for syllabi to a list composed of: members of the National Women's Studies Association, subscribers to Lehigh University's *STS Curriculum Newsletter*, members of Women in Technological History, and selected personal contacts who might not otherwise have been reached. With a few exceptions, recipients of the mailing were located in the United States. The enthusiastic response further confirmed the level of interest and activity in the field and the desire to share experiences about such teaching.

The book, therefore, is a first attempt at a "state of the art." Based largely on the syllabi received, questionnaire responses, and my own work in the field, the book has sought to analyze and synthesize curriculum experiences that apply the new research on gender and technology to technology teaching. Rather than offering a comprehensive survey, the book has sought, through examples of actual courses, to pinpoint and discuss trends, issues, and ideas of teaching in this new field. As with any initial effort, there are inevitable omissions. In this case, they have been caused variously by: faculty on leave or otherwise unavailable to respond, a net not cast wide enough to reach the variety of courses in this inter- and multidisciplinary field, the particular difficulties of locating integrative and cross-cultural courses. I hope that those who, for whatever reason, did not contribute, will make their work and experiences known so that our efforts to learn and share in this field will grow.

To those who responded this time and sent their comments and materials, I owe special thanks. There could have been no book without them. There also could have been no book without Phyllis Hall—the former editor of the Pergamon division including the Athene Series—who, with her blend of friendship and confidence in my work, urged and encouraged me to undertake the project. To Phyllis's assistant, Sarah Biondello, taking charge of the mailing and the myriad details in carrying the work through, my grateful thanks. Among those at Pergamon-Oxford, I thank Stephanie Boxall and Grace Belfiore who took on the manuscript in its final, time-pressed editing and production stages. I do not know if this is a "first," but I would also like to thank my computer. While it did not cook or clean, nor nurture my psyche as deadlines came and went, it did help me enormously to put the book together. Especially considering the subject matter, I think it deserves some recognition, whether I think it inanimate or not (see discussion, Chapter 6).

The critical function (at least for me) still lies in the human sphere. For this, I am extremely grateful to Ruth Schwartz Cowan, Stephen Cutcliffe, Daryl Hafter and Jodi Wetzel, who critically appraised the first draft of the manuscript. Their support for the work coupled with their incisive comments and constructive suggestions provided the necessary impetus for me to rethink and re-edit, and so improve and strengthen the book. However, all those named, as well as others who contributed materials and ideas, are absolved of any responsibility for what finally appears in these pages. The choices, and thus the responsibility, are mine. I hope readers will find the book's contents useful, practical, and stimulating.

Joan Rothschild
Charlestown, Massachusetts
August 1986

Chapter 1

Technology Studies and Women's Studies in the Classroom: an Idea Whose Time Has Come

Although technology in the classroom has a long history in engineering education (Layton 1971/1986; Hacker 1983), teaching *about* technology from historical, social, and philosophical perspectives is a much newer enterprise. The history of technology as a discipline dates from the late 1950s, interdisciplinary technology studies from the 1960s. The connections between women's studies and technology studies are newer still. Women's studies began in the late 1960s; teaching about women and technology began in the middle of the next decade. The purpose of this book is to describe and analyze the ways that women's studies approaches—i.e., feminist perspectives on technology—affect technology teaching in the college classroom. The focus is practical: courses taught, issues raised, methods and problems of teaching, resources used. This opening chapter will provide background and context for the development of this teaching field and offer an overview and plan of the contents of the book.

HISTORICAL DEVELOPMENT: TECHNOLOGY STUDIES AND WOMEN'S STUDIES

The interdisciplinary field of technology studies began with the founding of the Society for the History of Technology (SHOT) in 1958 which brought together the disciplines of engineering and history. In 1959, the journal *Technology and Culture* was established with the goal of reflecting the interplay of technology, society, and culture in a historical framework (Staudenmaier 1985; Rothschild

1983). With research came courses in the history of technology that began to explore social, economic, and philosophical aspects of technological development and change. Continuing this trend in the 1960s, in response to a growing social critique of the directions of science and technology and to the "two cultures" issues raised by C. P. Snow (1959, 1964),[1] interdisciplinary courses with strong social content began to emerge. Interdisciplinary science, technology, and society programs were soon established as well. Often originating on campuses with engineering colleges, these STS programs, as they came to be called, at first attracted engineering students but soon drew liberal arts and other students as well. The faculty followed a similar shift. The most recent development in technology studies education is known as the New Liberal Arts or "technological literacy," courses and programs designed to bring technological and computer literacy and quantitative skills to the liberal arts student. There are now some 100 full-fledged STS programs plus several hundred more individual courses or groups of courses in the United States.[2]

With the growth of these programs and courses came increased attention to curriculum issues. In the mid-1970s, SHOT established the Technology Studies and Education (TS&E) Interest Group as a formal sub-group to explore educational issues. Panels on teaching, curriculum, and other educational concerns became a regular feature of SHOT annual meetings. In 1977, the STS Program at Lehigh University initiated the first publication devoted to curriculum, *Science, Technology and Society Curriculum Development Newsletter*. Published six times a year, the *STS Newsletter* features an "open forum" on curriculum issues and publishes syllabi—often devoted to a single theme—and reviews recent publications. For example, the entire December 1983 issue (no. 39) was on the theme "Women and Technology." In 1983, the TS&E group of SHOT, under the editorship of Stephen Cutcliffe, compiled *The Machine in the University*, a book of sample course syllabi in the history of technology and technology studies, published by the STS program at Lehigh (Cutcliffe 1983). Reflecting curriculum trends under "New Themes," the collection included the syllabus of a course on the role of women in technological change taught by Daryl Hafter at Eastern Michigan University. A second edition of *The Machine in the University*, published in 1986, included three syllabi on gender themes (Reynolds 1987). In 1981, the *Bulletin of Science, Technology, and*

Society began publication, under the leadership of Rustum Roy. Originally published by Pergamon Press and now by the STS Press at Pennsylvania State University where Roy directs the STS program, it is described by Cutcliffe (1986) as a " 'letters' journal" that "publishes brief essays on STS questions and extensive curricular materials." The most recent addition to curriculum publications is the *NLA News*, devoted to issues in the New Liberal Arts. Begun in January 1985, it is published monthly during the academic year by the Department of Technology and Society at the State University of New York (SUNY) at Stony Brook.

Women's studies, the intellectual and academic arm of the women's movement, began with courses on college campuses in the late 1960s. Programs soon followed. Today, there are over 500 women's studies programs that offer minors, majors, and/or certificates, and, increasingly, graduate study, plus courses that number well over 20,000. In 1977, the National Women's Studies Association was founded to encourage and support feminist education in all educational settings; twelve regional associations pursue these goals in their geographic areas. Women's organizations have also been formed in most of the major disciplines. Now extending globally, women's studies was represented at the UN Decade for Women meetings in Copenhagen (1980) and Nairobi (1985) by Women's Studies International, founded in Copenhagen in 1980. Conferences at which feminist scholarship is presented within and across disciplines have been held at regional, national, and international levels since the early 1970s. *Feminist Studies* was founded in 1969, *Women's Studies Quarterly* in 1972, *Signs: Journal of Women in Culture and Society* in 1975, *Women's Studies International Forum* in 1978, to list but a few of the many journals established in the last decade and a half in which feminist research can be published and widely distributed.

Women's studies courses and programs carry into the classroom the feminist critique and analysis of traditional scholarship that began to emerge with almost explosive force in the late 1960s.[3] Not only have women been omitted from the literature; feminist perspectives have been missing as well. Feminist perspectives bring an approach to knowledge that is holistic, that is grounded in the experiential, seeking to draw on the total human experience and transcend the subject–object split of much of traditional Western scholarship. Such an approach, therefore, challenges the race and class biases of the literature as well. Thus, the purpose of feminist scholarship has been two-fold: (1) to develop a body of work about women's lives and ideas, and their contributions to society, and (2) to develop a systematic critique of existing scholarship and a distinct feminist theory and approach to knowledge.

For its first decade, women's studies research and teaching focused on these two interactive areas. More recently, a third direction has emerged, deriving directly from the first two. This is to integrate or "mainstream" women's studies teaching and scholarship into the rest of the curriculum. At a conference at Wheaton College in Massachusetts in 1983, "Toward a Balanced Curriculum," Peggy McIntosh outlined five phases of such transformation. Using the discipline of history as an example, McIntosh described the five phases: *"Phase 1*, Womanless History; *Phase 2*, Women in History; *Phase 3*, Women as a Problem, Anomaly, or Absence in History; *Phase 4*, Women as History; *Phase 5*, History Reconstructed, Redefined, and Transformed to include us all" (McIntosh 1984, 26). Much of women's studies teaching that focuses exclusively on women and is therefore woman-centered has reached Phase 4. As such, it challenges and often rejects the traditional frameworks into which Phases 2 and 3 seek to fit women. However, in order to reach toward Phase 5, to transform the disciplinary frameworks so that they are sexually, racially, culturally and socio-economically inclusive, requires a process of educational training and development that brings us back to the earlier phases. Therefore, some argue that if feminist educators concentrate only on mainstreaming, women-defined scholarship will be overwhelmed by the traditional and still powerful disciplinary canons. Speaking to this criticism, Catharine Stimpson at the same Wheaton conference advocated "both/and," that is, to keep both the more specific women's studies activities and the efforts to mainstream "as mutually enhancing activities" (Stimpson 1984, 22).[4]

As women's studies developed in the 1970s, humanities and social sciences in the liberal arts were the major focus. Disciplines such as literature, psychology, and sociology that had higher concentrations of women were soon well represented, as were history with its earlier organization of women historians[5] and anthropology with its prominent women scholars.[6] Feminist research and teaching in science and technology fields were slower to emerge and less visible than in the liberal arts for two obvious reasons: (1) there were fewer women in these fields, and (2) not only the culture, but the subject matter in these areas had strongly masculine associations. As Margaret Rossiter (1982) has pointed out, for the few women in these fields acceptance of the traditional canons and values was integral to their struggle to overcome the structural and ideological obstacles to gain entry, even to the lowest levels. Under these circumstances, they were unlikely to be inclined to challenge the methods and received wisdom of the scientific fraternity.

From a disciplinary perspective, technology fared a bit better than the scientific fields in coming under feminist scrutiny, perhaps because of ties to history, one of the first disciplines to develop strong feminist scholarship. In the early 1970s, Ruth Schwartz Cowan, a historian of science and technology, began to ask searching questions about household technology and its purported impact on women's lives. Her work on household technology was first presented at the Berkshire Conference of Women Historians and at the SHOT annual meeting in 1973, and appeared in *Technology and Culture* in 1976. That same year Women in Technological History (WITH) was formed as a sub-group of SHOT, and a panel, with presentations by Daryl Hafter, Susan J. Levine, and Martha Moore Trescott, became the first to focus on these issues, moderator Cowan asking, "Does it make a difference that the technologies discussed applied to women?"[7] Thereafter, panels and panelists on women and technology began to be included more regularly at the SHOT annual meetings. Martha Trescott's collection of articles on women in technological history appeared in 1979. Panels and workshops on feminist issues in technology—as well as in science—became a regular feature of annual meetings of the National Women's Studies Association (NWSA) starting in 1979, and in 1986 the NWSA's Task Force on Science and Technology was formed. Articles on women and technology from sociological and philosophical, as well as historical, perspectives also began to be published in a variety of journals. Judith McGaw's review of the literature on women and American technology in *Signs* in 1982 showed how far the field had come, especially in the area of women, work, and technology. A special issue of *Women's Studies International Quarterly* on "Women, Technology and Innovation" that I guest-edited was published in 1981. My collection of original articles, *Machina Ex Dea: Feminist Perspectives on Technology*, appeared in 1983. Both of these collections are interdisciplinary. An annotated bibliography on gender and technology is in preparation (Bindocci and Ochs, forthcoming).

This activity has brought feminist perspectives to technology in three ways. First, in the history of technology, it is uncovering women's contributions to invention and innovation. In so doing, it is extending the range of subject matter to include woman-associated activities and is redefining what is significant technology. Second, it is bringing research to bear on the relationship of women's traditional work—as both producers and reproducers—to technological development and change. And third, it is exploring and questioning the values and the epistemological frameworks that underlie both the study and practice of technology. In this third area lies its potential for transforming the way we think about, research, and teach about technology. It is also in this third area that feminist research follows directly in the tradition of critical inquiry that led to the rise and growth of the STS field (see Cutcliffe 1986 and above).

TEACHING ABOUT WOMEN AND TECHNOLOGY

By the late 1970s–early 1980s, a distinct field of women and technology had emerged, linked to both the history of technology and interdisciplinary technology studies. To what extent has this new field been reflected in the technology curriculum? In order to assess the state of the art of such teaching, questionnaires along with requests for syllabi were mailed to faculty in technology studies and/or women's studies. Drawing on responses to these questionnaires and the syllabi, on previously collected and published materials, and on my own experience of teaching in the field, this book addresses the question posed above. How and in what ways is the research on women and technology and the issues it raises brought into teaching about technology? An overview and chapter outline follow. Although the book draws mainly on teaching experiences in the United States, pertinent examples from Canada and the United Kingdom have been introduced where relevant.

The book is divided into seven chapters. Following this introduction, Chapters 2 through 4 discuss courses as they fall into three categories. Chapter 2 focuses on the category "women *and* technology," reviewing courses concerned with the impact of technology and technological change on women and with the variety of ways in which women and technological issues interact. Chapter 3 discusses "women *in* science and technology" courses that deal with women's roles in both science and technology, including work and career issues and courses with a practical orientation. Chapter 4 focuses on courses that seek to integrate materials on women or add them to traditional courses, a key issue being whether such courses are additive or transformational. Because conceptual gender frameworks play an important role in creating a successful course, Chapter 5 examines such frameworks as they appear in several courses that explore feminist and masculinist dimensions of approaches to technology and technological knowledge. Chapter 6 seeks to define and establish criteria for a feminist resource for technology through a feminist analysis of recent literature in the field. The final chapter summarizes the trends, the issues raised, and directions in which we need to move in order to incorporate gender further into our teaching of technology. An Appendix of syllabi, including useful resources, completes the book.

NOTES

1. For a recent reappraisal of the "two cultures" debate, see Leo Marx (1986).
2. For a comprehensive review of STS as a field of study, see Cutcliffe (1986), from which much of this historical material was drawn.
3. With roots in earlier ground-breaking scholarship as that of Simone de Beauvoir (1953).
4. See also Stimpson (1986) on the development, status, and future of women's studies in the United States.
5. The Berkshire Conference of Women Historians was founded in 1928.
6. Notably Ruth Benedict and Margaret Mead.
7. *Technology and Culture* (1977, 496–497); communication to author from Hafter, July 1986. Hafter was WITH's first chair, and Trescott WITH's first newsletter editor.

Chapter 2

Women *and* Technology

Courses that concern "women *and* technology" were among the most numerous of the syllabi received. Often having the word *women* in the title, these courses focus specifically on gender issues and technology. They tend to be sociological and/or historical in approach with a strong emphasis on *work*. Such courses, therefore, and the materials they use reflect one of the heaviest concentrations of literature in the field.

These courses further share some of the following characteristics. They are taught mainly at the upper division undergraduate level to a predominantly female audience. Their sponsorship is often the Women's Studies program in conjunction with one or more other departments or programs. Reflecting the sociological approach noted above, the co-sponsoring department is likely to be sociology. Other possible sponsors are history or history of science and an interdisciplinary STS program. Cross-listing also indicates their interdisciplinary nature. Frequently focusing on areas of work associated with women, such as housework, office work, and reproduction, the courses usually integrate theoretical and conceptual issues into their analyses of gender and technology.

One of the earliest, and most broadly conceptual, of these courses that combines many of the elements described above was started by Philip Bereano and Christine Bose at the University of Washington in 1976. Entitled "Women and Technology"* and taught by an interdisciplinary male/female team, the course was originally co-sponsored by the Social Management of Technology Program (STM) and the Sociology Department. The course was repeated in 1977, 1978, and 1980; thereafter, it was cross-listed in the Women's Studies Program as well and offered every other year (Bose et al.

---

*All syllabi included in the Appendix are designated by this symbol. They are arranged alphabetically by course title.

1982). Still under interdisciplinary co-sponsorship, the course continues to be taught by Professor Bereano of the STM Program in the College of Engineering.[1] It is an upper division course, open to graduate students and advanced undergraduates; students have been predominantly female. Among course requirements are writing a term paper, leading a class discussion, and participating actively in discussion; class participation counts heavily in the final grade.

The course is "broadly conceptual" because it places the subject of women and technology in a theoretical and values context that encompasses a variety of approaches to technology. In so doing, the course extends its subject of "women and technology" to offer a more far-reaching understanding and critique of the forces that shape our technological thinking—a point that will be discussed further in Chapter 5. The course integrates a theoretical, sociological, and historical perspective. As described by Bose et al. (1982), it "begins by setting up an analytic framework which will help [students] to understand the case studies used later" (375). This theory consists of three segments:

(a) mainstream and radical approaches to the definition of technology and its relationship to society; (b) women's relationships to technology and technological change in pre-industrial, industrializing, and industrialized societies, in order to examine how technologies have, or have not, controlled women or been controlled by women for their own needs; and finally (c) technology and values systems, specifically technocratic rationality relying on "reductionism" . . ., and feminist values emphasizing a holistic approach. . . . (Bereano and Bose 1983, 31)

The next section, a major part of the course, focuses on *the division of labor*, exploring "the impacts of technology on the home and workforce labor of women" (Bose et al. 1982, 375). Starting with the family and the relationship of family members to paid and unpaid work, the course looks historically at the development of the industrial labor force and its impact on women; the section devotes a major segment to technology and housework, a special area of research of Bose and Bereano. Biomedical technologies that particularly affect women comprise the next segment, and a new section on architecture, design, and urban planning completes the course. The 1984 syllabus for the course is included in the Appendix.

Although some new topics have been added and readings have been updated, the structure of the course and the materials used have remained essentially the same since the course was initiated a decade ago. Bereano and Bose have produced a formula that they agree is highly successful; they offer it as a model course. However, they point to some problems. Students are resistant to theory and to the amount of diverse reading required. Being more issue-oriented, students tend to prefer such segments of the course, taking longer to see the relevance of the analytic frameworks. Further, science and engineering students and women's studies students need time to get to understand each other's modes of thinking and analysis. Few men take the course, although an even gender distribution would be the ideal.

Another course entitled "Women and Technology"* that is also broadly interdisciplinary in approach, but interweaving conceptual materials throughout, was offered by Jodi Wetzel in spring 1986 at the University of Maine at Orono in the Department of Sociology and Social Work.[2] When Professor Wetzel originated the course at the University of Denver in 1980, it was an American Studies seminar, cross-listed in the Departments of English, History, and Religious Studies. The two main texts for the current version—*Machina Ex Dea* (Rothschild 1983) and Trescotts's *Dynamos and Virgins Revisited* (1979)—are supplemented by a rich and varied reading list that draws on materials in literary, historical, social scientific, architectural, geographical, biomedical, and ecological fields. As described in the syllabus, the course is

> An interdisciplinary survey of the cultural effects of technology on women's lives. Topics include the evolution of domestic technology changes in workplace technology and their relationship to women in the paid labor force; recent developments in information technology and the resulting potential for vast changes in women's lives; an historical analysis of biomedical and reproductive technology; an outline of development in architecture and design technology; and a look at the future using science fiction by women authors.

Taught to upper division undergraduates, the course combines lecture, discussion, slides, films, group projects, and fieldwork. For example, in addition to a required paper and participation in class discussion, small discussion groups are formed that are to evaluate a science fiction work from a selected list. Wetzel has taught the course to both predominantly or all-female classes as well as to classes which are half male and female. She writes that "Classes of all women are easier to work with given the subject matter. Males tend to be hostile (especially 18–22-year-old business majors). Women thrive on the informality of the discussions. . . ." The hostility of male students has been encountered also by those seeking to integrate feminist materials into other courses (see Chapter 4), an issue discussed as well in Chapter 5.

When I offered my "Technology and Gender"* course at the University of Lowell in 1983, I encountered the same resistance to theory experienced by Bose and Bereano, as described above. Students—upper division, evenly male/female, and all from liberal arts—did not become involved until we took up specific materials on gender, technology, and work. Consequently, when I adapted the course for the University of Cincinnati where I was a visiting professor in the fall of 1984, I made certain changes. After a brief introduction to the subject matter the first week, the course moved immediately to technology and work topics. Only after examining office work, blue collar and high tech occupations, and household labor in relation to women and technology, did I introduce a segment on conceptual and theoretical issues. Yet, at the end of the course, some students complained that they wanted more theory, and at the outset! Although there were a few science and engineering students and more females than males in the class at Cincinnati, the variety of students' backgrounds and unevenness of levels of preparation were similar to those at Lowell. The puzzle continues to confront me as I revise the course for its next offering, although I favor returning to the earlier conceptual model (see Chapter 5).

The original version of the "Technology and Gender" course was initiated in 1978, titled "Women, Technology, and Political Change." Cross-listed in Political Science (my discipline) and Women's Studies, the course was taught from a women's studies perspective. Concentrating on women as producers, the course explored the connections "between technology, the sexual division of labor, and social systems that support both" in an effort to "gain further insight into the how's and why's of women's position in the social order." The course began by developing frameworks for analysis from the division of labor literature. The major portion was then devoted to examining the connections of women and technology to reproduction, housework, industrial labor, and office work. It closed with exploring how feminist values might affect women, technology and society in the future.

I used a variety of books, pamphlets, and articles that drew from anthropology, history, sociology, feminist theory in several disciplines, and from science fiction. Because at that time (1978) so few fully relevant works existed and/or sources were widely scattered, I had to place a number of materials on library reserve and provide handouts. This procedure only added to student's difficulties of coping with a variety of interdisciplinary readings, a problem also shared by Bose and Bereano in their course. Many of us, however, in this new women and technology field were then working in isolation: for example, I was not to discover the Bose and Bereano work until more than a year later. Frustration over availability of materials and subsequent discovery of growing numbers of published works and work in progress led directly to efforts to collect these materials, foster new work, and make it readily available (see Rothschild 1981, 1982, 1983). Wetzel in her questionnaire also mentions the lack of texts and the scattering of materials when she initiated her course in 1980, and the welcome changes in the amount and availability of materials for teaching in just a few short years.

When I offered the course in 1983, I was able to draw on these new publications as well as on a reconceptualization of the field which had changed in the interim. Now entitled "Technology and Gender,"* the course, although still focusing on *women* and technology, applied a "gender analysis" to the study of technology. Examining the consequences for work, for invention, for technological assessment, and for future options, when the female is included instead of excluded, the course sought to fill in some of the gaps and to explore what technology would be like with feminist perspectives and values integrated. A great deal more historical material was included than previously and there was a strong emphasis on values. In addition to political science and women's studies, the course was now listed for the Technology Studies minor and approved for the values standard of the university's new core curriculum. Student projects—which included class presentation and a paper—were to be chosen from four contemporary areas: reproduction, computers/automation, war and weapons, and ecology/appropriate technology. Perhaps predictably, only the male students chose "war and weapons" and only females "reproduction," although this did not hold true for students in Cincinnati the following year (almost all of whome chose reproduction, see below). I have already noted that a number of students resisted the amount of theoretical and conceptual material, preferring concrete issues. As juniors and seniors from several liberal arts disciplines and with various levels of preparation, these students did share the fact that they had not taken the core Technology and Human Values course in the interdisciplinary Technology, Society and Human Values program at Lowell which draws more heavily on science and engineering students. The course came together best when students became involved in their projects and shared them with the class.

The following year in fall 1984 at the University of Cincinnati, I shortened the course to fit a 10-week quarter term instead of the 14–15-week semester at Lowell and, as discussed above, cut back on the theoretical component, introducing theoretical concerns later in the course sequence. As the course, still titled "Technology and Gender,"* was listed in Sociology as well as Women's Studies, I placed more emphasis on contemporary rather than historical topics. Reproductive technology had a special segment, using the new book *Test-Tube Women* (Arditti et al. 1984). This topic obviously interested students the most—or perhaps seemed most accessible to them—since almost all chose to do their papers on this subject. As at Lowell, the varied experience and backgrounds of the students—there is no interdisciplinary STS program at Cincinnati, although there is a strong women's studies program—made for uneven class discussion and participation. This confirmed my view that starting with theoretical frameworks is desirable, providing they are made accessible and relevant for the students so they have reference points for discussion.

"Women, Technology and Social Change,"* taught by Jane Peters at Portland State University in Oregon, follows this format. Cross-listed in Urban Studies, Women's Studies, and Sociology, the course was initiated in 1983 and team-taught by Jean Peters (Urban Studies) and Johanna Brenner (Sociology and Women's Studies). Continuing now to be offered by Peters, the course, as described in her questionnaire, begins by presenting the "fundamental policy issues of the technology 'triumph, threat, neutral' debate" that are found in varying ecological, engineering, political economy, and feminist perspectives. "Then we apply this analysis to 3 technological areas, workplace (with a focus on clerical work), domestic (with a spatial focus) and reproductive (looking at new technologies)." A unique feature of the course is Peters' use of the Feminist Technology Assessment Wheel as developed by Corlann Gee Bush (1981, 58). The wheel, presenting four levels of effects that can be scored for their degree of desirability, offers an innovative way to assess technological change that allows multiple effects to interact. A resource that has had greater currency in "hands on" feminist teaching about technology, the assessment wheel can also be applied in the academic classroom, a use that will be explored in Chapter 5.

The aim of the Peters course is to "set the stage," to have everyone "understand the fundamentals of the (a) social forces occurring since industrialization, (b) the issues of technology in general and (c) feminist theory." So far, the students have been drawn mainly from upper division undergraduates in the social sciences and have been almost all female. Writes Peters, "The most gratifying aspect is getting otherwise very skeptical women excited about thinking about technology as more than someone else's problem they have to try and avoid."

A course that seeks to raise women's consciousness about and encourage their practice of technology is taught by Susan Weeks and Jay McLean Riggs at Washington State University. Entitled "Gender Issues in Technology,"* the course combines mathematics with a sociological and a women's studies approach; it is taught to lower division undergraduates who are predominantly female. The course is described as

> unique in that it is designed both to provide students with a clear understanding of the role technology plays in their lives and to provide them with new skills and attitudes in mathematics. Specifically, the course addresses gender issues related to technology and mathematics and helps students overcome math anxiety by understanding its causes and consequences.

To accomplish the dual aim of the course, "approximately one-third of the semester is spent in learning and applying math and computer skills." Using an "extensive math autobiography" and through doing math problems, students' own conceptual grasp and abilities are revealed and established. Word processing is also taught. Only then, in the remaining two-thirds of the semester, does the course turn to the readings that will explore the whys of what students have experienced. Using a variety of readings, including those of Gray (1982), Rothschild (1983), and Tobias (1978), plus films, the first topics explore such conceptual themes as: "why study women and technology?," "sex role socialization," "math anxiety," "issues in technology and society," and "women as antitechnocrats." The final topics cover the specific areas of women as homemakers, paid workers, and bearers and rearers of children, ending with a look at women, technology and the future. This combining of the traditional classroom approach with the "hands on" element, and in the order presented, appears to work well, the instructors intending to increase the amount of lab and computer time the next time around.

A course at Vassar, "Women and New Technology,"* offered for the first time in spring 1986, follows in certain respects the approach of the courses described above: a theoretical framework that presents a social analysis of technology in which women and technologies are then situated. Taught by Eileen Leonard of the Sociology Department and the Science, Technology and Society Program, the course is offered by the STS Program and takes a largely sociological perspective. The course is also part of the New Liberal Arts Program in which Vassar participates. Students are upper division undergraduates, predominantly female. After examining social contexts and perspectives of technology in the first weeks of the term, the course, writes Leonard, "explores the relationship between women and technology by focusing on three types of technology of particular concern to women: reproductive technology, household technology and office automation." Ethical dimensions and control of technology are examined in the final section. The format is discussion, class presentation, and some lectures, with a paper required of each student. The reading list is comprehensive.

Another new course, focusing specifically on reproductive and health issues in relation to women and technology, is taught by Kathleen Doherty Turkel at the University of Delaware. Entitled "Body Politics"* and offered as a senior seminar in Women's Studies, the course is particularly concerned with the ways that law and public policy shape women's choices. The course examines "the historical context as well as the contemporary practices and debates surrounding issues ranging from contraception, to reproductive technologies, to occupational health." The three texts—Ehrenreich and English's *For Her Own Good* (1979), Arditti et al.'s *Test-Tube Women* (1984), an Wendy Chavkin's *Double Exposure* (1984)—are supplemented by library readings that focus particularly on conceptual and authority issues. Taught in a seminar-discussion format, students are required to write two "reaction papers" that evaluate the assigned materials in light of related readings, to participate in a group project, and to prepare a final paper on some aspect of the group's chosen topic.

At Eastern Michigan University, Daryl Hafter of the Department of History and Philosophy, has developed a graduate level course entitled "Technology, Social Change and the Role of Women."* Cross-listed in History and Women's Studies, the course is part of a new Master's Program in Women's Studies, and draws female students predominantly. Starting with pre-industrial Europe and placing the analysis within the history of technological change, the course traces the interaction of changing technology and the changing roles of women through the Industrial Revolution to the present, including both domestic technology and high tech. Values, problems, and goals of technology, especially as they emerge today, are explored against the historical backdrop. Readings combine standard works in the history of technology with the newer feminist sources. A research paper is required that is presented in class. The course combines lectures and seminar-format discussion. Hafter writes that students like the readings and the chronological approach, with interest high when topics touch closely on their own perspectives, such as domestic technology and women working in a high tech society. The choice of interviewing someone working with technology for their paper has proved very popular, the students combining oral history and the history of technology. Students also "enjoy presenting their papers in class and hearing what others have done."

A field of growing interest in women and technology—that of the built environment—is represented by a graduate seminar taught at the Massachusetts Institute of Technology (MIT) by visiting professor of architecture Leslie Kanes Weisman. Entitled "Architecture and Planning in a Feminist Society"* and offered in the spring of 1986, the course was listed in the Departments of Architecture, Planning, and the Women's Studies Program. It combined feminist perspectives in the disciplines of architecture, planning, environmental psychology, and cultural geography. As described in the syllabus, the seminar studies "society's buildings and spatial organization in terms of their social consequences from a feminist perspective," directing the disciplines of architecture and planning

> toward understanding why the acts of building and controlling space have been a male perogative, how the built landscape shapes social experience and personal identity, and how we can begin to design and plan new housing, public buildings, communities, and urban space that challenge the patriarchal forms and values embodied in the "man-made" environment.

Combining a weekly lecture and discussion format, the course is divided into three major segments—plus a final segment for term projects—that moves from conceptual formulations to issues of space and power to specific plans and feminist visions for social change in the built environment. For example, the first segment, "Architecture, Symbols, and Social Values," opens with an overview on "The Spatial Dimensions of Feminism," followed by lectures and discussion on "Bodyscape As Landscape" and "Female and Male Principles in Architecture." The next segment, on "Spatial Dominance and Social Control," explores power issues through such subjects as the "sexual geography" of the "territorial imperative" as in buildings and urban parks, "sheltering women from rape and battering," cross-cultural examples of the "spatial caste system" in housing, and environments for "re-designing childbirth." The third segment, "Housing, Communities, and Social Change," after discussing how "discrimination by design" keeps "women house poor," explores a variety of feminist design, space, and housing alternatives that included "Feminist Fantasies and Future Realities." In addition to attending and fully participating in class meetings, students were expected to prepare a term project to be presented to the class in the final weeks of the term. Using a special issue of *Heresies* (1981), a feminist publication on art and politics, as the basic text, the course draws on a wide variety of feminist writings in the fields of planning, design, geography, and housing, as well as in social theory and analysis. Combined with a recommended reading list supplied, the course readings constitute a basic bibliographic introduction to feminist design, planning, and architecture literature.

Another area of increasing importance, yet apparently still under-represented in course work (see discussion in final chapter), is that of women, development and technology. In 1981–82, through a cooperative effort of the Technology Education Department and the Women's Studies Program at West Virginia University, planning was begun to develop a course to integrate materials on technology, women, and international development. The result was "Women in International Development."* The course is offered each year in the spring semester through the Technology Education Department and cross-listed with Women's Studies; spring 1986 marked its fifth consecutive year. Originally team-taught by the three planners, Judith Stitzel, Coordinator of Women's Studies, Ed Pytlik, Director of Graduate Programs in Technology Education, and Kate Curtis, graduate student in the Masters Program in Technology Education, the course is now taught by Professor Pytlik—at whose impetus the course was originally developed—with Professor Stitzel offering guest lectures.

In published reports describing the course (Stitzel et al. 1985a, 1985b), the three planners and coteachers show how women's studies and technology education enhance each other to build a course on women and development. This interaction can enrich courses in other areas as well:

> Since Women's Studies and Technology Education both approach their subjects from an interdisciplinary perspective—including aspects of economics, education, geography, history, political science, sociology and anthropology —together they can enrich an investigation of women and development. Technology Education contributes . . . an awareness of the complex relationships of technology to other aspects of culture, including patterns of social organization. Since economic development usually involves technological change, this awareness is very important; the human costs of new technology's disruption of the social equilibrium are well documented in the literature of change. Women's Studies contributes an awareness of the variables that determine women's status in particular societies and insures a feminist perspective on the ways in which women and their activities have been subordinated. (Stitzel et al. 1985a, 1)

As described in the syllabus, the course has five objectives: to "examine cultural diversities in the definition of women's roles and status," to "study women's contributions to the formal and informal [economic] sectors," to "investigate women's access to education, health, income, credit, and technology," to "analyze the impact of socioeconomic development on women" evaluating "distribution of resources not only *across* households, but *within* households," and to "understand how women are left out of development planning, how they can be included, and why they should be." In seeking to fulfill these objectives, the course sequence "leads the students from a general overview of related topics to more specific and complex ones as the semester progresses" (Stitzel et al. 1985a, 3). The introductory sections include a discussion of the advantages of a dual perspective of Technology Education and Women's Studies (see above), the problem of definitions such as "first," "second" and "third" worlds, development strategies, and use of women's studies methodology. Using a "local" development project—a woman's cooperative quilting project in Appalachia—to bring these concepts "home," the course seeks to sensitize students to these issues. In the next section, discussion of the impact of colonialization on sex-stratification in different societies completes the background for students to then examine a case-study of a large-scale development project. In the course as offered in 1983 when honoraria were provided by the administration, the second half of the semester featured guest speakers from several developing countries who focused on such topics as women's access to education, income, credit and technology, on food and agriculture production, and on fertility and family planning. Videotapes were made of these lectures so they could be incorporated into subsequent offerings of the course. In this manner, although changes have occurred, the course has retained its original scope, direction, and content. There has been some shift in the readings. When initiated, the course drew particularly on reports and documents from government agencies and organizations involved in international rural development and women in international development. Still used to update readings for the course, these publications are housed in the Technology Education Research and Resource Center at the University. While strong on statistics and description, such documents were weak in theory and critical analysis, which were supplied through a "packet" of readings drawn from a variety of scholarly and other sources. In the intervening time, as has occurred for other areas in the women and technology field (as noted above), materials providing such analyses have markedly increased in the women and development area. Thus, in recent versions of the course, Charlton's *Women in Third World Development* (1984) plus the Dauber and Cain collection (1981) have been introduced, substituting for a number of the "packet" readings.

Taught at the upper division undergraduate and graduate levels, the course is an approved elective for the major in international relations and for the general education requirement in the social sciences. Attracting students from a variety of fields, and more women than men, the course has combined a unique mix of American and international students. Many of the latter hold significant positions in their countries in the developing world to which they return after graduate study. Professor Stitzel has remarked that it has been gratifying to learn of the impact of the course on these students and their work at home, as they have indicated in follow-up communications.[3]

At Worcester Polytechnic Institute in Massachusetts, at which the vast majority of students are engineering majors, a significant number of student Interactive Qualifying Projects have been developed in recent years on issues related to women and technology. Under the "WPI Plan" initiated in the early 1970s, all students must spend a year of intensive independent study, usually in teams of two or three people, examining an issue that demonstrates the interaction of technology and society. As Iris Young of the Humanities Department points out, the subject of women and technology is found in the Interactive Qualifying Project rather than in specific courses "partly because so much teaching activity at WPI takes place in project rather than course format."[4] Professor Young has identified some 44 such projects devoted to issues about women and technology, plus another dozen concerning minorities and the handicapped and technology, that were undertaken during the period 1978–86. Projects in these areas are being specifically encouraged and expanded at WPI. The women and technology topics include women in engineering and other non-traditional occupations, medical and health technologies related to women, health issues and VDTs and the automated workplace. The list of project topics relating to women is included in the Appendix.

A course on "Women Writers" taught by Annette Kolodny at Rensselaer Polytechnic Institute includes a two-week segment on women and technology. Approached through two utopian novels, Charlotte Perkins Gilman's *Herland* (1979) and Marge Piercy's *Woman on the Edge of Time* (1976), the segment also includes a list of leading works in the women/science/technology field that have been placed on library reserve for use by the student panel taking on the topic. This technology section, as well as the other segments of the course, is presented within the context of Carol Gilligan's *In a Different Voice* (1982) which forms the main conceptual framework for the course. Although not having technology as the central focus, the course does indicate how materials on women and technology can be incorporated into another discipline, in this case literature.

While resources for the courses described in this chapter range widely, many titles and authors recur, both for technology generally and specifically for women and technology. For example, Ruth Schwartz Cowan's work is well represented, especially her "'Industrial Revolution' in the Home" (1976) and "Virginia Dare . . . Virginia Slims" (1979) articles, as are essays from Martha Trescott's collection *Dynamos and Virgins Revisited* (1979) and from mine, *Machina Ex Dea* (Rothschild 1983). The Arditti et al. collection, *Test-Tube Women*, published in 1984, was used in four of the courses, and Joann Vanek's "Time Spent in Housework" (1974) and the Baxandall et al. article, "The Working Class Has Two Sexes" (1976) were used in three. Work by Roslyn Feldberg and Evelyn Glenn (1983), and by Corlann Gee Bush (1983) was listed frequently, as was that of Carolyn Merchant (1980, 1983), Sally Hacker (1979, 1981), Marge Piercy (1976), Shulamith Firestone (1971), Linda Gordon (1977), and Dolores Hayden (1981). Alternative technology and ecological issues were represented not only by feminist authors such as Judy Smith (1978), but also by David Dickson (1975) whose work was used in several courses. Other critics or commentators on technology appearing frequently for course readings were Harry Braverman (1974), Jacques Ellul (1964), Lewis Mumford (1963), and Daniel Bell (1973).

The recurrence of titles and authors apparently reflects two factors: the sociological and critical (though not necessarily negative) approach of these courses to their subject matter, and the emergence of a body of ideas and framework for analysis in what is still a very new field. Such materials and the ideas they represent can contribute markedly to the task of building conceptual gender frameworks, which is addressed in Chapter 5.

NOTES

1. Professor Bose now teaches at the State University of New York (SUNY) Albany.
2. In July 1986, Professor Wetzel became Director of the Institute for Women's Studies and Services at Metropolitan State College in Denver.
3. Telephone conversation with author, July 21, 1986.
4. Letter to author, January 19, 1986.

Chapter 3
Women *in* Science and Technology

"Women *in* Science and Technology" courses share popularity and some characteristics with courses discussed in the previous chapter. As in the "Women *and* Technology" category, *work* is frequently a major topic, encompassing scientific, engineering, and other technical fields, as well as medicine, mathematics, and computers. Offered in interdisciplinary women's studies programs usually in conjunction with another program or department, the courses will combine approaches, including sociological, historical, scientific, and philosophical. Classes tend to be small in size, using a seminar format. The subject matter of the "women *in*" courses focuses on the traditional exclusion of women from science and technology, women's roles in and contributions to these fields, and the implications of and reasons for gender differences and segregation that exist. In exploring the *whys* of gender bias in these traditionally male fields, the courses demonstrate the conceptual links between science and technology, especially attitudinally and ideologically. Included also in this chapter are "hands on" courses or course segments that are devoted to having women gain scientific and technical skills and knowledge.

Viewing syllabi for these courses, one is struck by certain commonalities. The courses bear almost identical titles: variations of "Women, Science and Technology," even though specific course content and intent may be different. Each course includes empirical material about women in scientific and technical fields, as well as conceptual and theoretical perspectives. While the mix will vary, significantly, among courses reviewed for this category, almost all include at least some conceptual material that is central to the course, no matter what the degree of empirical content. The reasons why are fairly obvious. As suggested above, the purpose of these courses is not a serial rendering of women's experiences in scientific and technological professions and occupations. Rather, given the empirical evidence—and uncovering new evidence overlooked by traditional scholarship about women in these fields—the courses start from the question, "Why?": Why do the numbers of women remain small? Are the answers to be found in the sciences and in the technical fields themselves? Do answers lie in differing female and male perspectives on science and technology? What are the ideological factors? the structural factors? the epistemological and philosophical? No matter how practical the focus—e.g., to draw women into these fields—each course seeks to set the role of women in scientific and technological fields in a larger social, and often historical and theoretical, context. This approach is strongly feminist.

At Simon Fraser University in British Columbia, Canada, a women's studies course, "Women, Science, and Technology,"* while illustrating these points, offers contrasting approaches when taught by two different instructors. Starting from the premise that ours is "a society increasingly dependent on science and technology" in which "interest has grown in investigating the different ways that women and men relate to these areas," the course description states that it will "examine both the nature of science/technology and aspects of the above differences." The course seeks to combine historical, demographic, psychological, sociological and scientific approaches.

As taught by Hannah Gay, from the History Department, the course first builds its conceptual framework by exploring the topics: the nature of science, particularly the nature of scientific theories and beliefs; the nature of technology and how we are affected by technological innovation; and gender bias in scientific theory and belief. Proceeding from this framework, the course looks at women in scientific and technical jobs. It closes with the questions, "Do men and women have different scientific and technical aims? What might be the consequences of parity in the scientific/engineering workplace?" The course thus moves from the theoretical to the empirical, joining the two in exploring the questions raised at the end.

As taught by Margaret Benston, from Women's Studies, the course has a more heavily practical aspect, emphasizing math and computers. Opening with a "general considerations" section that explores social, ideological, scientific, and gendered views of women, science and technology, the course in Part Two takes up barriers to the practices of math and science. As the major part of the course, this section combines practical and theoretical work. The course ends with further "considerations" about issues of feminism and scientific rationality and objectivity, returning to the conceptual themes. Using a variety of readings to set the framework—including Tobias' *Overcoming Math Anxiety* (1978), Horwitz and Ferleger's *Statistics for Social Change* (1980), and Fields' *About Computers* (1973)—Part Two develops practical projects that provide "skills maps" in statistics, computers, calculus, and automobile mechanics. Bearing some resemblance to the Weeks and McLean–Riggs course described in Chapter 2, although having a different mix, the purpose here is to "allow students to assess their own changing attitudes and reactions to these areas as they gain understanding of them." In combining the theoretical and practical in this manner, the course seeks to expose sources of internalized gendered attitudes and practices in science and technology and to explore ways to break out of these patterns. More mathematical and scientific than technological in focus, the course nevertheless reveals conceptual linkages of gendered scientific and technological attitudes.

At Stanford University, Londa Schiebinger's course, taught in the Values, Technology, Science and Society (VTSS) Program, is more ambitious in scope. Although titled "Women, Science and Technology in Europe and America, 17th Century to the Present,"* the course uses a topical rather than a chronological approach, drawing on history to support the topical discussions. Originally planned to cover only women and science, in response to a departmental suggestion to include the history of technology as well, the course as developed seeks to interweave science and technology, and to combine the theoretical and empirical. The choice of readings reflects this mix, the books including: Margaret Rossiter's *Women Scientists in America* (1982), Ruth Bleier's *Science and Gender* (1984), Evelyn Fox Keller's *Reflections on Gender and Science* (1985), *Machina Ex Dea* (Rothschild 1983), and Rita Arditti et al.'s *Test-Tube Women* (1984). The course starts by exploring the experiences of women scientists and the institutional barriers to women's participation in science and technology. Turning to the conceptual, the course examines the ways in which science has been used to support sexist beliefs and practices, drawing on both contemporary and historical examples. Historical contributions of women to science and technology in the next section are followed by feminist theories of science and gender and by feminist scientific alternatives. Attention next focuses on the sexual division of labor and technology, the course closing with an examination of the implications of reproductive technologies, relating the ideology and reality of power. Although these last two course topics—the sexual division of labor in the workplace, home, and reproduction—concern the impact of science and technology *on* women, the major focus of the course remains women *in* science and technology, placing it here rather than in Chapter 2. Reading requirements for the course are extensive, including a number of books and articles in addition to the books listed above; each student is required to undertake a research project. Students are predominantly female upper division undergraduates. The course is also listed in the History of Science and Feminist Studies departments.

"Women/Science/Technology,"* offered by Ruth Schwartz Cowan at the State University of New York (SUNY) at Stony Brook, also examines women scientists' experiences and theoretical issues of gender and science. Taught as a History of Science colloquium and listed in the History and Women's Studies departments, the course combines historical, sociological and philosophical approaches. The upper division undergraduates are predominantly female. The course starts with autobiographical accounts of women scientists, and examines issues of gender and work and of discrimination against women in the sciences. Using Rossiter's *Women Scientists in America* (1982), the course next takes up historical perspectives. Philosophical, ideological, and biological dimensions of gender and science are then explored using Keller's *Reflections on Gender and Science* (1985) and Bleier's *Science and Gender* (1984). Turning to technological topics in the final sections, the course asks "Why are there so few women engineers?" It considers women and microelectronics, and women and household technology in "Women, Machines and Work," using Cowan's history of household technology, *More Work for Mother* (1983), for the final topic. The course draws on a number of guest lecturers, mostly in the sciences and from other departments, with some outside speakers included as well. As in other courses in this category, there is an emphasis on both the experiential and the ideological: to expose the predominantly female student class to the experiences of other women and to show how the gender ideology of science reflects and influences scientific practice. The inclusion of a strong emphasis on science in these courses—the largest component in Cowan's course—reflects in turn the importance of the interplay of the ideological and material in explaining the exclusion of women from science, an interplay that also underpins the problematic relationship of women and technology.

With the title "Women in Science, Technology, and Management,"* a course offered by Jaynor Johnston in the College of Technology at Eastern Michigan University has a strong career and business orientation. In this, it differs somewhat from the courses described so far in this category. As outlined in the syllabus, the course has three objectives: to familiarize students with technological concepts especially as they relate to women's issues, to probe the nature and origins of problems that women face in taking leadership positions in technological society and technology-based fields, and to present women's roles, impacts, and problem-solving strategies in selected non-traditional (for women) fields, including telecommunications, science and technology R&D, and industrial management. Divided into two units, the course in Unit I explores "Women and Issues in Technology and Science," interweaving conceptual and experiential materials. Topics include: definitions and approaches, cultural and historical perspectives, gender differences and implications for industry, feminist critiques of science and technology, and the experiences of a female engineer (Lillian Moller Gilbreth) and geneticist (Barbara McClintock). Focusing more closely on concrete workplace experience in Unit II, "Women and Management Issues," the course examines the implications of the technological transformation of the workplace for women in professional and managerial occupations, strategies and behaviors for change, and problems and solutions of structural and institutional barriers for professional and managerial women. The course features several outside speakers drawn from business and industry, academe, and government. The course, listed in both the Department of Interdisciplinary Technology and the Women's Studies Program, is open to both undergraduate and graduate students. Building on the conceptual base from the first section of the course, the second, more practical section on "management" maintains the links through the technological nature of the workplaces and society explored.

For the above courses, there is considerable overlap of reading materials used, shown particularly in the courses of Cowan and Schiebinger. Among the authors whose works appear on the reading lists of most, if not all, of these course syllabi are: Margaret Rossiter (1982), Ruth Bleier (1984), Evelyn Fox Keller (1985), Ruth Hubbard (e.g., Lowe and Hubbard 1983), Carolyn Merchant (1980, 1983), Joan Rothschild (1983), Sally Hacker (1981), Rita Arditti et al. (1984), Elizabeth Fee (1983), and Corlann Gee Bush (1983). Representing a range of fields, including the physical sciences, sociology, and the history and philosophy of science and technology, these authors and their works further illustrate the growing numbers of resources to draw from and the interdisciplinary nature of teaching in this field.

Courses that are principally or entirely "hands on" are often situated in special educational settings, such as continuing, community, or other adult education programs. One example is a series of 15 courses administered by Renée LoPilato, Coordinator of Industrial Technology Programs and Women's Programs at Lane Community College in Portland, Oregon. The courses are listed under both the Industrial Technology Programs and the Community Education Division. Covering such topics as "Careers/Trends in Robotics,"* Auto Tech for Beginners," "Introduction to Machine Shop," "Introduction to Electronics," "Introduction to Construction" and "Introduction to Bricklaying," the courses consist of 80 percent practical or hands on instruction in the lab and 20 percent devoted to lectures on theories and concepts. Attracting predominantly female students, the courses are "designed specifically for those with no entry skills, especially women." Continues LoPilato, textbooks, course guides, films, etc. "use gender inclusive language"; she seeks to "hire all women as role models/instructors."

In the United Kingdom, a growing interest in women and technology issues is reflected in teaching activities and projects of the Technology Faculty, one of six faculties, at the Open University. As described by Ruth Carter, staff tutor in technology, the Open University, begun in 1970, is a "national distance-teaching university providing adults with the opportunity to study part-time for a degree" (Carter 1985). It now enrolls about 18,000 adult students per year; almost half of the students are women. Courses are taught by printed text sent by mail, through TV and radio, plus a one-week summer school (Bruce et al. 1984). Spurred in part by the declaration in the United Kingdom of 1984 as Women Into Science and Engineering (WISE) year, which sought to publicize the need for and to encourage more women and girls into science and engineering careers, a working group of the Technology Faculty was formed "to investigate the problem of very low numbers of women students in our courses" (Carter 1985). Among the results were facilitating changes toward more woman-oriented approaches and content in "Living with Technology," the initial, year-long Technology Foundation Course required of all students pursuing a technology degree program. An "introduction to technological decision-making," concerned with "shelter, communications, energy, natural resources, food and health," rather than an introduction to engineering science (Carter 1985), the course content has been adaptable to this more woman-oriented focus. Facilitating measures have included appointing more women teaching staff, preparing an audiotape for Foundation Course tutors, holding special meetings for women at summer school orientations, and expanding funding for women to study technology courses.

Another project at the Open University, undertaken by members of the Technology Faculty and the Institute of Educational Technology, was to introduce a women and technology component, particularly focused on feminist technology assessment, into the interdisciplinary women's studies course, "The Changing Experience of Women". As described by the three faculty involved, Margaret Bruce, Gill Kirkup, and Chris Thomas, in their report, *Teaching Technology Assessment to Women* (Bruce et al. 1984), this was done through offering a five-hour optional technology module during the week-long summer school scheduled for the course. There were three aims: first, the theoretical, to "demonstrate that technology is not value-free or genderless"; second, the practical, to "teach a few basic skills of Technology Assessment and attempt to produce female sex-role impacts of technology"; and third, the "affective . . . to build confidence in the women students, so that they could use the Technology Assessment skills and their own experience to evaluate aspects of technology that are specially relevant to them" (Bruce et al. 1984, 47).[1] Sharing the aims of other practically-oriented efforts described in this section, this course activity, it was hoped, "would help demystify technology, in the sense of laying open its main principles, modes of operation and systems of social control" (Bruce et al. 1984, 47).

An issue that surfaces in this category of courses is the extent and nature of gender differences in attitudes and approaches to science and technology. Educational efforts to explain and correct gender imbalances in scientific and technological pursuits accept the fact that such differences exist, no matter what the origins or cause. It is usually agreed, too, that women may need special approaches initially to overcome blocs to scientific and technical knowledge. Further, among those who seek change, there is obvious agreement that such gender differences in knowledge and skills are not immutable, but amenable to change. But, as to whether women learn differently from men, whether there are distinct gender-based cognitive styles requiring different methods of teaching, there is far less agreement. While not necessarily ruling out socialization and cultural factors, those who find this distinction argue that teaching methods and approaches in mathematics, science and technology are so geared to male learning styles that women are inevitably disadvantaged. The remedy is to develop different, woman-oriented ways of teaching such subjects to women.[2]

One adherent of this view who is working in the technology education field is Deborah Brecher, co-founder of the Women's Computer Literacy Project in 1982, and author of *The Women's Computer Literacy Handbook* (1985). The Project has developed intensive two-day computer courses for women that have been conducted in a number of cities in addition to the home-base of San Francisco, including New York, Anchorage, Los Angeles, and Washington, DC. The course, limited to twelve women per class with one computer per student, covers the following topics: concepts and terminology of computer hardware and software, computer languages and programming, operating systems, data base management/ electronic filing and word processing. Aimed at women who know nothing about computers as well as those who want to understand the machines they use, plus those who need new workplace skills or want to reorganize their own work, the course uses practical and familiar analogies such as bathtubs, typewriters, and file cabinets, in addition to humor, to explain complex subjects. In this manner, but without talking down, the course provides students with a mix of explanation and hands on experience. Brecher has found the method successful, strengthening her view that there are distinct learning—and thus teaching—styles for women and men.[3] While a detailed exploration of feminist pedagogy is beyond the scope of this book, the discussions of feminist approaches and method in Chapters 5 and 6 speak further to this issue of gender-based teaching and learning.

NOTES

1. See Chapter 5 for further discussion of the development of "feminist technology assessment," its use at the Open University, and its wider applications.
2. For example, Adrienne Rich argues that "the underlying mode of the feminist teaching style is . . . by nature antihierarchical" (1979, 145).
3. Conversation with author, June 1986.

Chapter 4

Gender and Technology: Integration or "Add Women and Stir"?

Up to this point, we have considered courses that focus specifically on women. But, as discussed in the opening chapter, feminist perspectives on education involve not only courses about women and a particular subject area but also courses that integrate the new scholarship on women into the disciplines. Only a decade after the first women's studies courses were introduced on college campuses, the first national convention of the National Women's Studies Association (NWSA) in 1979 featured a number of panels on curriculum integration. Such panels reflected the early and growing commitment that feminist research and education had a broader goal than research and teaching on women. That goal was, and is, transforming the traditional bodies of knowledge and curricula themselves. In panels such as these, feminist educators were more clearly defining the goals of integration and transformation, and asking *how*?

Speaking to these issues at the first NWSA convention's closing session, Charlotte Bunch cautioned that feminist educators should not settle for "add women and stir."[1] In so doing, we risk losing and/or diluting the impact of feminist scholarship. To make explicit her culinary metaphor: if one adds a new ingredient to the beef stew without changing the basic recipe, the flavor or consistency might change somewhat, but we still have only a variation of the same beef stew. Or, if one adds a salad to a meal of meat, potatoes, and pie *à la mode*, one has merely added a course, and not appreciably changed the dietary balance of the menu. In the latter case, the new element can be easily isolated and dispensed with. In both examples, the new ingredient or menu item at best serves as a novelty, a diverting change, but without any lasting impact on the whole. In technology

30

studies, for example, one might add a few women inventors to a history of invention or include a segment on household technology in a course on work and technological change without affecting the approach, structure and format of the course in any meaningful way. What feminist educators such as Bunch argue is that women's studies is something other than a diverting new ingredient. Rather, the new feminist research questions much of traditional scholarship itself and thus courses based on such scholarship. The aim, therefore, is integration of the new research and transformation of the traditional curriculum. In the 1980s the efforts at curriculum integration have also been termed "mainstreaming."[2]

To what extent is an integrative and transformational approach occurring in technology studies? Both my own experience teaching in an interdisciplinary STS program and the sample syllabi I have received indicate that, to the degree that material on women is included in traditional courses, "add women and stir" rather than an integrative approach is the norm. However, there are integrative attempts, and I will start the discussion with those. I will then move to those courses that tend to compartmentalize or isolate materials on women rather than integrate them. In an effort to illuminate some of the problems of technology studies in incorporating feminist perspectives, the chapter will end with application of the five phases of curriculum integration, as mentioned in Chapter 1, to such courses.

In addition to differences in content and approach, courses that either attempt to integrate work on women or to include such material within a traditional course differ from the women/technology courses discussed in the two previous chapters in two other ways: in origins and audience. Rather than arising in or being strongly tied to a women's studies program, the courses originate from or are linked primarily to other departments and/or programs, including STS programs. Reflecting these origins (as well as course content), course titles tend to use words such as *society* or *values* rather than *women*, or to be gender inclusive in language, such as using both *feminine* and *masculine*. And, instead of generally being predominantly female, the classes may have half or even a majority of the students male.

At the University of Delaware in a course entitled "Society, Nature, and Technology,"* Kathleen Doherty Turkel has sought specifically "to 'mainstream' feminist material into a course that is not explicitly a Women's Studies Course." Listed in the departments of Philosophy and Sociology, in the Center for Science and Culture, and in the University Honors Program, the course is taught from an "interdisciplinary social science perspective" to upper division undergraduates equally divided between males and females. The course examines a "variety of perspectives toward technology," focusing on "issues regarding the ways in which technology has shaped human social relations and consciousness." These issues include: the "question of value neutrality in science and technology," the "question of 'expertise' and the layperson/expert dichotomy," "images of nature," "implications for citizenship and political participation," and "rationalizations of inequality: questions of social class, race and gender."

The course starts with a conceptual framework on nature, ideology, and politics that draws heavily on political and social theory. As such, the framework sets the stage for weaving gender, race, and class analysis into subject areas within a broader context of power, authority, and ideology. Specific areas include: scientific objectivity, Social Darwinism and sociobiology, work and workers: including scientific management and health and safety, reproductive technologies, the environment and politics, and alternative conceptions of technology and political and social organization. The course covers materials on science as well as technology, reflecting the course's conceptual nature that necessarily links science and technology. In addition to Marian Lowe and Ruth Hubbard's *Woman's Nature* (1983) and Michael Brown's *Laying Waste* (1979), a wide variety of library reserve readings is used. Turkel reports male students' resistance to the feminist readings, a difficulty her course shares with a number of others, although in contrast to the experience of the two courses discussed immediately below.

At the State University of New York at Stony Brook, Ruth Schwartz Cowan and Elizabeth Garber co-teach an introductory course in the history department, entitled "Science, Medicine and Technology in Western Civilization." Although the title and syllabus do not immediately reflect the course's integrative nature, Cowan shows how the course does integrate feminist materials and perspectives. "How do we do it?" she asks.

First, by choosing a Western Civ text which is integrative (McKay, Hill and Buckler [1983]) and second—and most importantly—simply by integrating, . . . without saying that we are doing anything feminist. When we talk about Aristotle, for example, we lecture about his ideas about scientific method as well as his ideas about reproductive biology. When we talk about the scientific revolution we talk about the death of nature—as if it were simply (which it is) part of received wisdom on the subject. Industrialization means talking about the "home" as well as the "workplace"; World War II means talking about the home front as well as the battlefront. When we lecture about physics in the early 20th century we talk about the experiences of Irene Curie and Lise Meitner as part of the international effort to build the bomb. When we talk about Darwinism and Freudianism we talk about their implications for the understanding of sexual differences and sexuality.

Cowan and Garber have found no hostility to their approach, from males or females. Cowan explains that this is because "students do not know they are getting an "approach.' We do not make an issue of it; we just do it, as if talking about long standing myths about sexuality has always been a part of Western Civ courses."[3]

In a contrasting approach, the title of John Staudenmaier's course at the University of Detroit, "Technology, USA Style: Masculine–Feminine Imbalances,"* reflects its major conceptual focus on gender. The course applies the masculine–feminine theme to the history of American technology. Taught in the History Department as a seminar to a combination of graduate and undergraduate students equally divided between males and females, the course includes historical, philosophical, psychological, and sociological perspectives. A unique feature of the course is the use of the Edison Institute facilities in Dearborn, consisting of the Henry Ford Museum, Library, and Greenfield Village, for student research projects, which comprise a significant portion of the course's activities and requirements. Of two course themes developed at the outset, technological momentum vs progress, and gender and technology, the gender theme is more pervasive. In the first of four goals, the course aims to "explore the ways in which men and women and what are often called 'masculine and feminine' traits as they have influenced—and been influenced by—America's technological style." To achieve this thematic goal as well as the course's research goals, the following issues are pursued:

What are the commonly accepted stereotypes of "male and female" in our culture?
How have male–female relationships, especially as related to the technologies of work and homelife, changed during the shaping period of our culture (roughly 1700 to 1930)?
How are these relationships reflected in and influenced by technological designs?

After introducing the conceptual themes and discussing the gender and work impact of the Industrial Revolution, the course proceeds historically to develop the gender "imbalances" around certain topics: categories of female and male rhetoric in such areas as etiquette, dress, work, money; advertising; 18th and 19th century contrasts of work and male–female relationships; 20th century contrasts of male and female relationships to technology; and recent feminist research on gender and technology. Included early in the course is an all-day tour of the Edison Institute complex to familiarize students with the facilities for their research projects. These projects attempt to link students to the historical and conceptual nature of the course by requiring them to interpret the historical and social meaning of a particular technology of their choosing, paying attention to the course's basic theme of "Masculine–Feminine Relationships and Values." Students are also required to prepare short papers on the weekly readings. Staudenmaier found the experience "extraordinary." Students "formed a strong community, discussed issues vigorously, and . . . learned a great deal about the complexities of gender in America . . . research papers . . . were exceptional."

A much different approach is taken at the University of Lowell in the STS Program's core course, "Technology and Human Values,"* at least one unit of which has been offered almost every semester since the program's inception in 1977. The course is team-taught by two to four faculty members—two or three the most usual number—course content varying between fall and spring terms and also according to the individuals teaching. Teams balance liberal arts and engineering and/or science faculty and include both males and females, the balance more often male since engineering/science faculty participating are all men while the liberal arts faculty are both sexes. Typically, a three-person team will consist of an engineer, a social scientist, and a humanities faculty member—or possibly two social scientists; a two-person team of an engineer and a humanities or social science faculty, almost always gender balanced.

Although integrating feminist materials has not been a major focus, faculty of both sexes—whether feminist or no—have been committed to include some materials on women and technology in at least one segment of each course given. For example, in the fall semester course, usually devoted at least in part to the theme of work and the Industrial Revolution, a segment on the family had often been included that developed changing relationships between home and work and discussions of housework and household technology. However, experience showed that this treatment and topic arrangement tended to ghettoize the subject of women and technology.

Subsequent versions of the course have incorporated the topics of family, home, work, and technology into a segment on the Lowell mills, usually comprising the opening segment of the course.

The course as offered in the fall of 1985 went further perhaps than previously to try to counteract ghettoization of women and technology topics and to integrate them into the course, both through readings and lecture organization. Taking Lowell and the Lowell mill women as a case study to develop issues about technology, society and values in the early Industrial Revolution, the course used Thomas Dublin's *Women at Work* (1979) and also assigned visits to the Lowell Historic Park, students then reporting on the mills, mill workers and their lives. The next section, "Technology and the Global Economy," included a slide-lecture on technological development in the Third World, strongly focused on women, and a segment on multinationals that used Fuentes and Ehrenreich's *Women in the Global Factory* (1983) as the reading, which introduced issues of race and class, as well as gender. Using Kurt Vonnegut's *Player Piano* (1952) to underscore the transition from the industrial age to the electronic age, the course explored family issues in this connection. The final section, "Computers," included discussion of gender, class and race implications of the changing structure of work. Despite the topical integration of material on women, there was no conceptual integration. That is, the course did not attempt to build a conceptual framework about gender roles and practices in which to place discussions about women and technology.

The spring semester of the course, which usually has a heavier science focus than the fall, covering topics such as the Scientific Revolution and war and weapons, has often included a segment on reproductive technologies and/or genetic engineering. When the focus is almost exclusively on women's concerns and reactions to such technologies, students tend to be less receptive even to the point of active dislike. This is similar to their response to any segment that seems to focus exclusively on women. Since the student body in this course is usually about two-thirds male, the reaction is not unusual, especially given that the course is in no way advertised as focusing on gender issues. Originally designed under a National Endowment for the Humanifies grant to develop social and values issues about technology for engineering and science students, this core course—as well as most courses in the program—draws students mainly from the still heavily male Colleges of Engineering and of Pure and Applied Science, plus to some extent from Management Science which has a better sex balance. The subject matter, too, seems to attract more males than females, and the course is usually taught at the campus on which the male student population is clustered. The format is a large lecture of anywhere from 60 to 120 students—depending on number of instructors—meeting twice a week, plus a weekly discussion section with about 30 students each. My own attempts at various times in discussion sections to introduce conceptual gender issues have met with discomfort and resistance. While the Lowell experience has moved beyond the "add women and stir" stage in some respects to integrate materials about *women* and technology, the courses do not necessarily do so from *feminist* perspectives. Having a conceptual framework may be critical here, to be discussed further below and in the following chapter.

At Bloomsburg University in Pennsylvania, an Interdisciplinary Studies course taught by William Baillie of the English Department has begun to include feminist materials, although such concerns do "not yet permeate the course." Entitled "Science, Technology, and Human Values,"* the course includes the disciplinary perspectives of philosophy, history, literature, and physics. The course seeks to compare "the interaction of science and technology with human values" through studying "representative past, present, and future technological developments and their impact on personal and social values." Like the Lowell core course, particular topics differ each semester. As taught in fall 1984 the course started with five questions: 1. What is a value? 2. Where in the world are we? 3. How do we know? 4. What is technology? 5. Is technology the enemy? Specific topics were then grouped under three major headings: "The Industrial Revolution," "The Uncertainty Principle" and "Planning the Future." Five course sessions covered topics relating to women, drawing on readings from *Machina Ex Dea* (Rothschild 1983). Women and Science, Women and Technology, and Women and Work were taken up under "The Uncertainty Principle" dealing with scientific revolutions and principles of knowing. Considerations of Genetic Engineering—Technics, and Women and Genetics, opened the section on "Planning for the Future." Other books assigned were Pirsig's *Zen and the Art of Motorcycle Maintenance* (1975), Skinner's *Walden Two Revisited* (1976), and Teich's *Technology and Man's Future* (1981), plus a number of handouts and films. Students were lower division undergraduates and predominantly female. In view of this sex distribution and that "the female students tend to be less comfortable with technology-and-values issues than males," Baillie is "especially concerned that females and males see some of the issues in relation to feminist perspectives." Thus, more coverage and integration of feminist materials apparently are planned.

Two courses which fall under the "Women *and* Technology" category discussed in Chapter 2, that of Daryl Hafter at Eastern Michigan University and that of Eileen Leonard at Vassar, in some ways fit the integration category even though their central focus is on women. In the case of Hafter, her graduate level course, "Technology, Social Change and the Role of Women,"* starting from classic readings in the history of Western technology, such as Burke and Eakin (1979), Kranzberg and Pursell (1967) and Jean Gimpel (1977), seeks to integrate the new feminist historical research. Drawing on the works of, for example, Trescott (1979), McGaw (1979), Hafter (1979), Scott and Tilly (1975), and Cowan (1976, 1979), the course enlarges on and expands the traditional subject matter through the feminist materials and perspectives that are brought to bear. Leonard in her course "Women and the New Technology"* does something similar for a traditional approach to the sociology of technology. Her feminist texts and analysis are integrated with the classic social analyses of Ellul (1964) and Braverman (1974) and ethical discussions of, for example, Paul Goodman (1967), Fromm (1968), Kranzberg (1964), and the Hastings Center (Annas 1981). That courses focusing specifically on women can constitute an important and necessary stage in the integration process is discussed in the final sections of this chapter.

At Rensselaer Polytechnic Institute a course taught in the Science and Technology Studies program by John Schumacher deals with a philosophical issue central to the study of technology: the relationship of human beings to nature. Entitled "Metaphysic," the course asks:

> What is nature? Are we separate from nature? What is body? Are we separate from body? What are our extraordinary powers to know and control nature? Do we possess any extraordinary powers?

Using Carolyn Merchant's *The Death of Nature* (1980) as one of seven books assigned, Schumacher writes that the course "includes a female perspective with others in the course." The "others" include a Native American perspective (Boyd 1976), those of Descartes, Newton, and Bishop Berkeley, of Carlos Castaneda (1973), and of Zukav (1980) on the new physics. Although the course draws primarily on Merchant's discussion of the organic rather than the female image of nature and thus does not fully develop a *feminist* approach to nature, in exploring various dimensions of mind/body and human/nature dualisms, it goes well beyond the oppositional "man/nature" conceptualization that generally prevails (see critique in Chapter 6).

A course taught as a combined lecture and seminar in the Values, Technology, Science and Society (VTSS) Program at Stanford by Donald Jordan of the History Department adds some feminist materials for discussion, but does not reconceptualize or otherwise change the basic framework of the course. Entitled "Technology and Science in Contemporary Society," the course is organized topically around such subjects as progress and religion, culture, gender, war, work, art, and ethics and values. Using readings from *Machina Ex Dea* (Rothschild 1983), which is one of eight books assigned, the course adds a feminist reading to two of the ten weekly seminars. In a third, on "Technology and Gender," there is a guest lecturer (female) and all five readings assigned are on women and technology. In introducing materials on women in this manner, the course provides an example of the additive rather than integrative approach.

A recurrent concern of courses seeking to integrate feminist materials, or even to introduce topics about women, into a traditional curriculum, is that expressed by Kathy Turkel at the University of Delaware. "Most of the problems," she writes in her questionnaire, "had to do with the resistance of students (primarily male students) to feminist scholarship and arguments. . . . Some of the male students consistently questioned the credibility of feminist authors and dismissed their arguments out-of-hand as 'hysterical,' 'irrelevant,' etc." I have had a similar experience in the core course at Lowell, as noted above. Yet, Cowan and Garber at Stony Brook have not encountered student hostility when incorporating feminist materials, and John Staudenmaier at the University of Detroit found receptivity and increased gender awareness among students from his approach.

A further issue arises, linked to this concern. What kind of course and approach best integrates feminist materials into technology studies? How explicit should the feminist approach be? Should the focus be on gender balance or on women and feminist issues to demonstrate the imbalance? Is there perhaps no one "best way," the approaches needing to vary depending on the subject matter and situation? Applying the five phases of curriculum integration proposed by Peggy McIntosh can shed light on these questions and concerns.

Phase 1, we will recall, omits women and represents the traditional or mainstream curriculum. Much of technology studies teaching appears still to be in this phase. Such courses and approaches are the starting points for the critiques and challenges developed in later phases. Phase 2, in which examples of exceptional and/or elite women are added to a traditional course—such as, including a few outstanding women inventors—corresponds to "add women and stir." Illustrated by the Jordan course at Stanford, this approach, however limited, is a first step toward a more inclusive curriculum, according to the McIntosh developmental model. Hostility to the new materials is less likely in such courses since traditional views about gender, and about the field itself, are not questioned.

Controversy and problems—for faculty and students—begin to surface in Phase 3. Difficulties occur because Phase 3 "—women as a problem, anomaly, or absence in the structures of knowledge—raises questions of how the systems of reality got defined in such a way that women's realities got left out." Such questioning extends to "all lower-caste people," asking how most men as well as women who are neither white nor elite "got left out of the definitions given to us by the main structures of knowledge" (McIntosh 1984, 26–27). As women "are studied as victims, as deprived or defective variants of men, or as protestors, with 'issues,' " and start to be viewed in a "systemic context" of "class, race, and gender" (Rosser 1986, 9),[4] the categories of analysis begin to be questioned and the disciplines challenged. For faculty, this means a disturbing process of overturning accepted canons even as excitement builds through exploring new materials and ways of teaching. For students, Phase 3 courses mean unsettling new ideas about women and men as the once accepted gender hierarchies and values are undermined.

Some of the courses discussed in this chapter take up women as a special case and examine "women's issues," thus seemingly fitting into Phase 3. But, where there is no accompanying feminist conceptual framework that asks "Why does this situation exist?," there can be little or no questioning of the traditional context or framework in which the course is presented. If this is the case, while moving beyond the additive approach, the course will not go far enough to fully constitute Phase 3. The core course, "Technology and Human Values," at Lowell, and "Science, Technology, and Human Values" at Bloomsburg may be described in this way, since women's issues are explored without being set in a feminist framework. On the other hand, Turkel's "Society, Nature, and Technology" at Delaware does implicitly critique and challenge traditional conceptualizations. However, because it, too, does not fully articulate a feminist framework, the course also falls short of Phase 3. In Phase 3, a feminist critique of traditional approaches must be developed in order for transformational concepts to begin to be formulated in the next phase.

Phase 4 moves toward such transformation. It constitutes a radical shift in the basis for knowledge, upending many of the frameworks still used in Phases 1, 2, and 3. No longer merely questioning the traditional structures and their supporting systems of power, Phase 4 holds that since women account for half of life's experiences, those experiences should become at least half of human history (Rosser 1986, 9). Since the formerly invisible majority of the have-nots and powerless have been providing the basis for civilization, their skills and experience must be key to creating radically altered bases for knowledge (McIntosh 1984, 27). A Phase 4 course would be one in which the categories of analysis were "racially inclusive, multifaceted, and filled with variety," demonstrating and validating "plural versions of reality" (Rosser 1986, 9). The course would draw on a range of evidence and materials, often new to the academic world, that would reflect such reconceputalization. Phase 5, the final phase, completes the epistemological transformation of the disciplines so that all of humanity is included, an achievement that is still far off.

To some extent, all courses that seek to integrate feminist materials into technology studies at a level that goes beyond "add women and stir" will draw on elements from Phase 3 or Phase 4. The Cowan and Garber course is a case in point. In developing the sex difference implications of Aristotle's biology and Freud's psychoanalytic theories, the course implicitly questions the standard interpretations. This is Phase 3. In balancing home and workplace in the Industrial Revolution and the homefronts and battlefronts in World War II, the course seeks to show women's experiences as a vital part of Western scientific and technological history. Phase 4 is addressed here. However, because the implied critique of standard interpretations is not presented as feminist—and purposely so—and because the balancing of women's and men's experiences does not necessarily question the conceptualization of "Western Civilization" itself—which Phase 4 must begin to do—the course does not quite fit into either Phase 3 or Phase 4. In terms of this developmental model, the course does not appear to provide a basis for framing transformational categories in the history of technology that would lead to reconceptualization of the discipline in Phase 5. The Staudenmaier course also falls between two stools when this integrative model is applied. Focusing specifically on gender, the course both questions stereotypical frameworks (Phase 3) and seeks to call attention to female–male "imbalances" (Phases 3 and 4). But, in stressing contrast and difference, the conceptual framework—although useful, as will be discussed in Chapter 5—also does not help us to create inclusive transformational categories. Does this mean that these two courses are not appropriate for integrating feminist materials into the technology curriculum, despite their success in the classroom?

Let us look more carefully at the McIntosh integration scheme. Critical to the scheme is that the phases are conceived of developmentally. Each stage is necessary to the next. The level of feminist awareness grows through the experience and discovery taking place in each phase, the increased awareness leading to new approaches and ways of thinking. Feminist thinking eventually becomes the catalyst for re-evaluating and recasting the epistemological underpinnings of the discipline. Although the ultimate goal is integrative in this sense of being transformational, the route to that goal is through focusing on *female* experience. If one is to understand the distortions and imbalances that have existed in order to build a feminist critique, then one must focus on what is missing: on women, race, and class. Only then can feminist analysis begin to search for new, inclusive categories of analysis, and begin to think of integrating the varied strands of human experience into a transformed basis for knowledge. In the McIntosh developmental scheme such integration cannot begin until well into Phase 4. Until that point, through Phase 3 and into Phase 4, feminist curricular development focuses on women and women's experiences, in their class, multiracial and multicultural dimensions.

Viewing the integrative process in this way casts women/technology courses in a new light. Such courses as those in Chapters 2 and 3 (including Hafter and Leonard above), rather than being ghetto-ized as "women only" courses, become part of the integrative process. They become important vehicles for curriculum integration. That is, in their focus on women and feminist perspectives, women/technology courses, as they explore the reasons for women's special situation, gain the insights and awareness at this Phase 3 stage to lead to reconceptualization of categories in Phase 4. The Bose and Bereano course described in Chapter 2 is a good example. Critically exploring implications of female, as well as race and class, relationships to technology, the course meets the criteria of Phase 3. In the way it develops an integrated conceptual framework in the opening segment (see also Chapter 5), it also begins to frame the categories of analysis characteristic of Phase 4.

Where does this emphasis on women/technology courses as integrative vehicles leave the courses that are designed to be integrative, courses that stress incorporation and balance? As Rosser has pointed out (1986, 9–10), one particular value of the developmental approach is that it can demonstrate the consequences of bypassing one or more feminist curricular stages. There is a distinct danger that feminist perspectives will not be developed or incorporated if integration is attempted before an adequate feminist critique and careful feminist conceptualizations have been developed. This is the real problem with the technology and values courses at Bloomsburg and Lowell. Having no developing feminist critique, these courses attempt to leap over a critical integrative stage. Although they have included feminist issues, these courses do not provide sufficient basis on which to build the feminist content further, or perhaps even to sustain it. The integration process could flounder and stop. When integrative courses build on models such as the Bose and Bereano course, feminist content is more likely to be sustained and developed as integration proceeds.

What emerges from this analysis is not that many integrative courses lack usefulness and validity. This is not the case. Rather, the point is demonstrated that a feminist conceptual framework is critical for successful curriculum integration and that integrative courses should explore ways and means to construct such frameworks. I would argue further that such frameworks should be explicit rather than implicit, particularly at this stage of curriculum integration in technology studies. It is important to speak to Cowan's apparently opposing view.

Cowan argues, " 'don't talk about it, do it'." In their course at Stony Brook that integrates feminist materials, Cowan and Garber do not indicate that they are "doing anything special," much less "doing anything feminist." Rather, they proceed as described earlier in this chapter. They develop feminist perspectives on science, medicine and technology from Aristotle to Freud by presenting feminist ideas and analysis as an accepted part of human history. They have met no resistance from students of either sex because, having not been told they are getting a special approach, students don't find anything untoward in the course content. Cowan's point is well taken. The method has obviously worked well with their students at Stony Brook. But, I question whether the course provides an effective model for integration that could be used by others. As Cowan herself indicated to me, she did not submit the syllabus originally or think it would be useful to include in the Appendix (it isn't) because the syllabus does not reveal the course's feminist content. There *is* a feminist framework, but it is not made explicit. Rather, the feminist approach depends largely on the instructors and how they present the material. To teach in this way requires a high level of feminist consciousness—what one could call Phase 4 thinking. How many of those teaching traditional courses share this level of feminist consciousness with Cowan and Garber? Because of the late start that technology studies has had in women's studies, the still relatively small numbers of women and feminist scholars in the field, and the questionnaire responses I received to prepare this book, I suspect that faculty with this level of feminist awareness are few. Thus, at this stage of curriculum integration in technology studies, it may be difficult and impractical to advise other faculty in the technology field to just "do it," following the Cowan and Garber lead. Do *what, with* what? faculty may well ask. The result might be just another version of "add women and stir."

I also question whether masking the feminist approach best serves the interest of students in the long run. Might it not encourage today's often complacent students further in thinking that there no longer is a "problem," while the realities of most university teaching—particularly in the scientific and technical areas—and of patriarchal society are otherwise? Even at the risk of meeting resistance and losing some students, should we not consciously try to shake them up and raise their level of gender awareness? I do not suggest that students necessarily leave the Cowan and Garber course unchanged and unmoved just because they are not expressing resistance to the material. But, we might think about the fact that resistance to feminist thinking is probably to be expected, and may not be a bad thing.

Making gender content and objectives explicit need not automatically bring such resistance; it may even help counteract it. For example, a stated focus on gender issues did not seem to turn off male students in Staudenmaier's course, although the small class size and upper level of the course may have produced a self-selected group with better than average training in critical thinking. Kathy Turkel's course may have suffered from not framing its feminist objectives clearly from the outset. Had these objectives been worked into the course's overall conceptual framework, the feminist materials might have met less resistance, the students knowing what to expect and having a frame of reference in which to place the new materials. However, would such students have enrolled if a feminist framework had been explicit? It is a Catch-22 situation. A course that is truly integrative and one that would hope to draw in students not attracted to an explicitly feminist course, might bear a title and course description so general as to not immediately reveal the gender elements. Then, when feminist issues are introduced, student hostility can result. But, if one is clear about the feminist content, the audience may remain limited and the integration process limited as well. To counteract resistance by limiting the audience is no solution. On the plus side, it has been my experience that when male students do sign up for a course with "gender" or other indication of feminist content in the title or advertised course description, they enter openly and are willing to learn, even if they do not have a raised gender consciousness.

Therefore, courses seeking the "best way" to bring gender materials to technology studies need to explore how to develop feminist conceptual frameworks. This means course conceptualizations in which the feminist elements have been clearly articulated. Such frameworks can take many forms. Their dimensions are the subject of the next chapter.

NOTES

1. Author's notes at National Women's Studies Association First Annual Convention, Lawrence, Kansas, May–June 1979. As noted by Bunch, the phrase was first developed in conversation with Mary E. Hunt. See Charlotte Bunch (1981).
2. See, for example, Spanier et al. (1984) and Stimpson (1986).
3. Letter to author, July 1986.
4. For an application of the McIntosh phases to the discipline of biology, see Rosser (1986, Chapter 1).

Chapter 5

Feminine–Masculine: Developing Conceptual Frameworks

The previous chapter proposed that feminist conceptual frameworks need to be developed to successfully integrate gender materials into technology teaching. This means creating *gender* frameworks. Women's studies makes an important analytical distinction between *gender* and *sex*. *Sex* is a descriptive category used to designate female and male. *Gender* is a social category. The biological sexual division of the species is transformed through the "sex–gender system" (Rubin 1975) into the gender categories of femininity and masculinity. These categories are reflected in behaviors, beliefs, and social organization. When we identify the newborn as a girl or boy, we are signifying *sex*; when we buy that child a doll or truck, we are signifying *gender*.

Because of the pervasiveness and power of gender categories and the sex–gender system, women's studies holds that gender analysis must inform all scholarly inquiry. Creating a gender framework for incorporating feminist materials into technology studies means showing how and why gender is a necessary category of analysis for thinking and studying about technology. For some, this can mean explicitly contrasting masculinist and feminist categories and approaches; for others, it can mean concentrating on feminist aspects, the contrast with the dominant and masculinist approach thereby implied; for still others, it can mean developing a distinctly feminist mode of analysis of technology. Creating these gender frameworks is often not a simple task, for a number of reasons.

Part of the problem stems from there being no single, agreed-to feminist theoretical perspective on the nature and origins of gendered characteristics, on their relationship to sex difference, and how such gender dualisms affect our approaches to knowing. For example, feminist theory will vary considerably on the degree to which nurturance and life-generation are female and aggression and destruction are male, on where these attributes come from, and whether they have any biological, physiological, psychic, or cognitive basis or effects. Radical feminists, viewing such differences as fundamental and psychically-rooted (though not necessarily genetic), will affirm and reinforce what is female even to rejecting what is male. In socialist and liberal feminism, the social basis of gender difference is stressed; gender characteristics are viewed as socially constructed and thus subject to material and ideological transformation. Still other feminist approaches describe a more nearly androgynous human model, to the extent often of denying gender difference and acknowledging only physiological differences of sex.

A further problem arises from the multidisciplinary and multifaceted nature of the research and literature on sex and gender difference. Extending beyond its home discipline of psychology, the subject is explored in the biological sciences, and its effects examined in such disciplines as sociology, anthropology, and philosophy.[1] The research may also be informed by different schools of psychological and psychoanalytic thought as well as by different feminist theoretical perspectives. While it is not necessary to be fully acquainted with the entire range of this literature in order to build a conceptual framework on gender useful for technology teaching, awareness of and sensitivity to the basic ideas and positions in the field are certainly called for.

Another problem is that of conveying the subject of gender dualism in its complex and controversial dimensions to an audience with little or no previous background in feminist theory and/or women's studies. Students often lack experience with theory generally and thus lack a context or framework for integrating these new ideas. Response to such ideas can range from resistance and denial, discomfort, even hostility, to sheer lack of comprehension. The issues are often perceived simplistically, or even literally, students' failure to understand the distinctions between *gender* and *sex* leading to their applying gender characteristics universally, on the one hand, and individually and personally on the other. Contributing as well are the intensely personal feelings, accompanied by heightening of emotional tensions, when gender issues are raised.

My own course, "Technology and Gender,"* points up one aspect of the problem of how to present conceptual materials, given the frequent resistance of students to theory, especially at the undergraduate level. As explained in Chapter 2, when I offered the course at Lowell in the fall of 1983, I started with conceptual frameworks in order to provide an overview and context for what feminist perspectives on technology might mean. Contrasting socially constructed female and male values, the section explored their effects on scientific objectivity, on the subject matter of technology, and on technological inquiry. The course then developed segments on women and work and women and invention, returning to conceptual issues in Part IV to consider various aspects of gender dualism. Specific topics such as reproduction, computers and automation, war and weapons, and ecology and appropriate technology were taken up next through the students' research projects, the course ending with future visions of science and technology in feminist utopias. Partly because my students—mostly juniors and seniors and political science or other social science majors—balked at having theory placed first and at the amount of theory, I changed this component for the version taught at the University of Cincinnati as a visiting professor in the fall of 1984. At Cincinnati, I reduced the theory segment and did not introduce it until one-third of the way through the term. Evaluating the course at the end of the term, the brighter students said they would have preferred *starting* with theory to set the context for the specific topics discussed! Although this was a more diverse group of students than those at Lowell in terms of their majors, their general levels of knowledge and backgrounds were not that different. Obviously, this illustrates that there is no one, or perfect, way to present conceptual and theoretical materials, especially to undergraduates, and that we must try a variety of approaches. The various efforts to build such frameworks that are described in this chapter offer some choices and models.

In view of this complex of problems, it is significant—and probably healthy for the field—that some of the most interesting and forthright attempts to deal with gender issues have been by male faculty members who have developed masculinist–feminist conceptual frameworks. That they have sought to build gender-balanced frameworks is perhaps not surprising. Confronting and working with gender issues can be more problematic for men in our society than for women, requiring men to work through the contradictions. For male academics (who are predominantly white as well), feminist perspectives present a challenge to the received wisdom and approaches to thought that have been an unquestioned part of their intellectual heritage. In the process, men's concepts of masculinity and male identity may also be challenged, and even threatened. Thus, moti-

vated at an emotional level that can also lead to questioning the
rational–emotional split, males may need to focus on and understand
gender dualism in both its male and female dimensions as applied to
their fields of study. Women, brought up in the same masculinist
intellectual tradition, will also be challenged by feminist approaches
to knowledge. But, for women, the emotional content will lie in a
sense of "coming home" as they realize the degree to which "human"
thought and history had excluded, submerged, or denigrated *their*
experiences. For women, therefore, exploring and explaining gender
dualisms may mean greater attention to the female dimension as they
seek not only to restore the ideological and empirical balance to
human knowledge but also to search for meaning in their own
neglected female heritage.

The attempt to build conceptual gender frameworks for technology
studies courses is, therefore, a critique of the existing literature, and
of approaches to and content of the field. In the discussion that
follows, the efforts will be grouped according to type: a social science
critique, a combined philosophical and sociological critique, or a
combined philosophical, psychological and women–nature critique.
The chapter will end with discussion of a conceptual framework built
on a feminist assessment of technology.

An example of a conceptual framework that employs a social
science critique is in the course developed at the University of
Washington, originally by Christine Bose and Philip Bereano, as
discussed in Chapter 2. Although this course is entitled "Women *and*
Technology,"* devoting most of its subject matter to that interaction, the entire first month is spent on building a conceptual
framework. This framework is not exclusively a gender framework.
Rather, it is a sociological, values, and political analysis of technology
and technological society into which feminist perspectives have been
introduced and integrated. For example, the first part, "Technology
and Social Change," offers "Mainstream" and "Radical" views of the
effects of technological and industrial change on society. This is
followed by readings on "Women, Technology and Society" that
show the special ways that women have been affected by such
changes in both the developed and developing worlds. The next part,
"Technology and Values," first explores different views on the nature
of rationality, followed by a "Feminist Sensibilities" section that
extends the discussion to include biological, psychological, environmental and ecological aspects of sex differences. The final part of this
opening conceptual segment works a feminist critique of the

"experts" into a discussion of "The Technological Elite." In this manner, in the opening section, the course has developed a theoretical framework that has included and integrated feminist social, values, and political perspectives into a broader social science critique and analysis. Describing the success of this approach, Bose and Bereano write that

> the course has fully integrated a mass of theoretical and substantive reading from several disciplines. A feminist and anti-reductionist view towards technology has also been developed and supported. Students have both read much and done some original research and synthesis of materials. (Bose et al. 1982, 376)

Although they report that students are at first resistant to theory, in the end the approach works as its relevance is demonstrated in the rest of the course material. This integrative conceptual approach may also be particularly appropriate for sociologically-oriented courses in which the feminist social and political analyses that are used may seem less threatening (than, for example, the psychological critiques) and thus can be more easily integrated. This kind of model can also help to legitimize women and technology as a field of study.

An integrative conceptual approach that combines a philosophical and sociological critique lies in John Staudenmaier's course at the University of Detroit, "Technology, U.S.A. Style: Masculine–Feminine Imbalances"* (See Chapter 4). Focusing on contrasting masculine and feminine perspectives in the history of American technology, the conceptual materials—that is, the ideas and ideology —on gender are interwoven with and illustrated by examples from the readings and the students' research projects. Background readings in the first three weeks on the Industrial Revolution point out both its differential gender effects and the male aspects of its underlying ideology. The next six weeks are spent specifically contrasting male and female rhetoric and images about technology and customs, work, money, advertising, housework and consumption, using readings that are both empirical and descriptive, and philosophical and analytical. Not until the tenth week does the course focus on the research of current feminist scholars such as Gilligan (1982), Keller (1980) and Chodorow (1974), exploring their theories of gender differences in relation to human behavior, thought, and morality. Such placement puts this research in historical context. It also locates this feminist theoretical material in the broader masculine–feminine context that has already been built, perhaps thereby making it more accessible and acceptable to students who may resist feminist analysis. Because these gender theories are controversial even among feminists, it is difficult to present them and important to find ways to do so that show their relevance within a larger body of thought. This course, therefore, may provide a useful model. The final weeks are devoted to synthesis and presentation of student projects that were to develop historical and social meanings of a specific technology within the context of masculine–feminine relationships and values.

The course taught by Susan Weeks and Jay McLean Riggs at Washington State University, discussed in Chapter 2, also offers a conceptual framework that is philosophical and sociological in its critique. As noted in the earlier discussion, this course, "Gender Issues in Technology,"* devotes its first segment to "hands on" exercises before moving to explanatory theories. Building on students' experiences, the course examines how sex role socialization "affects female career patterns, life choices and attitudes toward math and technology," using readings such as Gray's *Patriarchy as a Conceptual Trap* (1982). Research and attitudes on female–male abilities in math are explored next with Tobias' *Overcoming Math Anxiety* (1978) as the main text. "Technology's place in the larger society, especially as an instigator of social change" is then focused upon, showing how a feminist assessment of technology (Bush 1983 and below) might influence that interrelationship. With this material as a base, the feminist critique of science and technology is presented in the next section, "Women as Antitechnocrats." Using such readings as Turkle (1984b), Lowe (1981), Keller (1983b) and Merchant (1983), the section explores such issues as the relationship between gender and science, the effect of gender on computer programming, and the historical association of women with nature. The rest of the course looks at specific technological areas within this framework of theory that began from experience. The course thus provides an interesting and innovative mix of the theoretical and experiential, a model of a conceptual framework that might be especially applicable for a predominantly female classroom.

Another integrative conceptual framework that is both sociological and philosophical is found in Jodi Wetzel's course. "Women *and* Technology,"* taught most recently at the University of Maine (see Chapter 2). Following a topical format, the course combines conceptual and empirical readings for each topic. For example, the segments on "Domestic Technology" and on "Technology and the Third

World," dealing with technology and women's labor, combine theoretical readings on the division of labor by sex and on work and family with examples of women in particular work and technology situations. Readings for the "Domestic Technology" segment include Bose (1979), Cowan (1976), Hayden (1984) and Kamerman (1979); for the "Third World" section, Leacock (1981), Papanek (1977), and Tinker (1979). The segment " 'Appropriate Technology': Values" includes a slide show on "Cultural Images of Women (and Men) in Technology" and theoretical readings about women and nature (Merchant 1983; King 1983; Keller 1983b). The assignment for groups to evaluate a selected feminist science fiction work also carries out this approach since science fiction describes a concrete situation within a broader conceptual and values framework. Taught since 1980, the course seems to work well using this integrative approach.

At the University of Sussex in England, Brian Easlea of the Science Studies Group offers two courses that develop philosophical and cultural critiques of science and technology within an overall gender perspective. One is an undergraduate seminar in humanities entitled "Man and His Image of Nature: Gender-Related Perspectives on Science and Technology,"* open to students taking degrees in the School of Culture and Community Studies; the other, "Progress, Technology and Gender, or, Imperatives of Technology,"* is for graduate level students in science and technology policy. In each, conceptual frameworks based especially on feminist gender analysis are developed.

Using *Machina Ex Dea* (Rothschild 1983) as the text for the undergraduate course, supplemented by a number of readings, mostly by feminist scholars, "Man and His Image of Nature . . ." presents eight seminars that develop and compare masculinist and feminist philosophic and psychological ideas linking the themes of sexuality and nature. Starting with "The Place of Sexuality, Reproduction and Science in Feminist Utopias," the course systematically develops the feminist critique of the invasive, destructive power of science and technology as deeply imbedded in psycho-sexual origins—extending from the bedroom, to nature, to the nuclear arms race, to the control of reproductive technology. Easlea writes that although students find the course's "wide-ranging nature difficult to encompass at first," because they "do not submit their assessment essays for nearly a year, they have sufficient time to put the topic they wish to focus on into a meaningful historical and cross-disciplinary perspective." Thus, he finds the course "works well."

The "Progress, Technology and Gender . . ." course also draws on this psychosexual and philosophical critique. Directed, however, at science and technology policy students at the graduate level, the course ties in more closely with the themes of progress and technological imperatives, linking the psycho-sexual with Marxist analysis to build an explanatory framework for exploitation and violence against humanity and nature. Starting with Marx vs Freud on the "Realm of Freedom," the course next develops the ideas of "male culture as transcendence" and "female nature as immanence" through the work especially of de Beauvoir (1953), Ortner (1974) and Dinnerstein (1976), to complete the theoretical base. It then takes up "The witch-hunting imperative: generalised fear and hatred of the dangerous feminine?" with a number of historical and philosophical works on witchcraft including those of Easlea (1980) and Merchant (1980). "The scientific imperative: culture's conquest of 'female' Nature?" includes the work of Leiss (1972), Merchant (1980), Easlea (1983), Keller (1985), Bernal (1970), and Dinnerstein (1976), plus Elshtain's (1984) critique of Chodorow and Dinnerstein. "The gestational imperative: replacement of the feminine?" segment, after providing a feminist overview with Mary O'Brien's *The Politics of Reproduction* (1981), presents contrasting views on the new reproductive techniques: against current trends (Hanmer 1983; Rowland 1984) and in favor of "positive eugenics" (Fernbach 1981). "The weapons imperative" covers "neomarxist, psychosexual and feminist perspectives" through such authors as MacKenzie (1983), Easlea (1983), Strange (1983), Caldicott (1984), and Ruddick (1984). "Sadomasochistic imperatives" develops "origins and implications" in writings by de Beauvoir (1953), Eisenstein (1984), Benjamin (1980) and others. The course ends with "insights from science fiction," including the writings and critiques of Schweickart (1983), Le Guin (1975), Piercy (1976), Gearhart (1979) and Callenbach (1978), to move "towards the just and peaceful society."

In contrasting feminine and masculine approaches, the conceptual frameworks of both of Easlea's courses are rooted in an important, but controversial, body of feminist thought that explores the philosophical and psychosexual roots of gender dualism and their impact on scientific and technological thought and practice. Thus these courses and the frameworks they embody represent a significant attempt to make an aspect of feminist thought, critical for scientific and technological analysis, available in the college classroom.

Another course using the feminist philosophical and pyschological critique of nature and human nature is taught by Mary Anderson of the Lyman Briggs School at Michigan State University. Entitled "Women, Nature, and Science/Technology,"* and combining the disciplinary perspectives of science and technology studies, psychology, philosophy, and literature, the course is largely conceptual. It focuses on "the symbolic and historic association made between women and nature," analyzing "some dominant value premises of Western culture," questioning "to what extent these reflect a distinctly male perspective," and discussing "their implications relative to issues of scientific objectivity and the direction of technological development." The conceptual framework offers three components. It starts with a discussion of "Is Female to Male as Nature Is to Culture?" using readings from Aeschylus (1959), de Beauvoir (1953), Merchant (1980) and Ortner (1974). The course then uses Dorothy Dinnerstein's *The Mermaid and the Minotaur* (1976) plus the work of Nancy Chodorow (1978) and Jane Flax (1983) to analyze feminist sociological and psychological theories for their impact on the organization and use of science and technology. The feminist critique of scientific objectivity and the role of gender in scientific inquiry follows, using works of Keller (1983b) and readings from Harding and Hintikka's *Discovering Reality* (1983). Implications for women in science and women and technology are then explored. The course ends with a look at feminist utopias and a return to conceptual themes. Taught to upper division undergraduates, the class has at different times been predominantly female or split evenly between females and males. Unlike Easlea's course which employs the feminist analysis of nature and human nature as a powerful critique of technological thought and policy, Anderson's course represents a more neutral stand. Pointing out that "there is by no means complete agreement among feminists on what the association of women and nature means or should mean," Anderson writes that the "course aims to synthesize different perspectives on how society might achieve a more inclusive understanding of human nature and a more liberated science." As such, the course presents an alternative model for dealing conceptually with these loaded gender issues.

   As discussed in the previous chapter, gender frameworks seek to move beyond critique to reconceptualize approaches and categories of analysis. In so doing, feminist perspectives can begin to suggest what a feminist science and technology would look like. For example, some of the courses that deal with conceptual issues discuss feminist research method, a method that challenges and cuts through the traditional concept of "objectivity" to link subject and object. As described by Keller in her biography of Barbara McClintock, aptly titled *A Feeling for the Organism* (1983a), an involved, interactive approach to subject matter is not only feminist, but good scientific practice. Whether in the sciences, humanities, or social sciences, this feminist method, discussed further in the next chapter, applies to all areas of research, including technology. The method is key in the long-range endeavour to bring feminist perspectives to bear to transform epistemological categories. When feminist method informs research on gender dualism and on the impact of gender analysis, new analytic tools are fashioned that will change the questions and eventually the categories. For example, feminist ways of looking at nature when joined with a feminist critique of the relationship of *man*, technology, and nature demand that we frame both philosophical and empirical questions differently. In the process, we can create alternative feminist approaches that will modify or reshape our research and teaching on technology.

One recently developed alternative feminist approach is in the area of technology assessment. The approach is both conceptual and practical. Technology assessment (TA), as it has developed especially in connection with policy-oriented studies, maps social consequences of a particular technology using a system of a numbered order of effects, arranged in linear sequence. The aim is to assess the risk–benefits of that technology and thus provide information that can direct social choices. Feminists have joined others in pointing out that "non-experts" who are nevertheless affected are usually excluded from the TA process and that those with vested interests in the outcome often have undue say. But feminist critics have shown specifically that most TA starts from the premise that technology and its effects are gender neutral: it assumes that women and men will be affected in the same way (Bruce et al. 1984). Contraception and microwave ovens are obvious examples that such is not the case. Through focusing on gender questions—What is the impact of a technology on women, on men, on gender-roles? How are options, opportunities, distribution of social and economic benefits for each sex affected?—feminist technology assessment has developed.

Corlann Gee Bush, for example, offers a dramatically different technology assessment model. Called an *Effects Wheel*, it is described by Bush in *Taking Hold of Technology* (1981), a Topic Guide for teaching sponsored by the American Association of University Women. To envision her reconceptualized model, imagine a wheel diagram drawn two-dimensionally, the technology whose effects are to be assessed at the wheel's hub. Spokes radiate outward to carry four primary effects to their second, and then third, and outermost, levels, each represented by a concentric circle. As the segments within the circles expand to include additional effects at each level, multiple effects can be incorporated. When the wheel diagram is completed, instead of a linear progression that can move only from one order of effects to another without being able to show how the orders or the effects could interact, a visual representation has been created that allows one to "contemplate several different variables or relationships at the same time" (Bush 1981, 57; see also Bush 1983).

The Wheel has been used as a conceptual tool in women and technology courses, such as that of Jane Peters at Portland State University (see Chapter 2). It has also been particularly useful in more practically-oriented courses, such as those discussed in Chapter 3. Part of the above discussion of technology assessment was drawn from Bruce et al.'s report, *Teaching Technology Assessment to Women* (1984), in which their work at the Open University in the United Kingdom is described (see Chapter 3). The Wheel figured prominently in the experimental technology module the authors introduced into the summer school session for "The Changing Experience of Women" course. Combining the use of "brainstorming" and the Effects Wheel to develop a feminist assessment of contraception, the authors report that students generated a list of sex-role impacts that revealed the women's broader concerns as consumers of these technologies. Thus a conceptual tool also became a practical means for women to develop technology assessment skills that would be relevant to them and their own experience.

Although the Effects Wheel has been applied primarily to technologies as they affect women and used mainly in teaching to women, the concept of the wheel is readily applicable to the field of technology assessment generally and to teaching about it. In addition to building feminist criteria into a model for technology assessment, the Wheel's ability to allow multiple variables to be assessed and interact recommends its use as a conceptual and teaching tool. It offers an alternative, and perhaps substitute, model for technology assessment. In this manner, a feminist reconceptualization can influence and transform our approaches to technology teaching.

NOTE

1. For a representative sampling, see Maccoby and Jacklin (1974), Tavris and Offir (1977), Gilligan (1982), Hubbard et al. (1982), Rosaldo and Lamphere (1974) Gould (1983), and Fausto-Sterling (1986).

Chapter 6

Passing the Litmus Test: What is a Feminist Resource on Technology?*

Resource materials for gender and technology continue to grow, in numbers and variety. Many of these books, articles, and other works have been mentioned in reviewing courses in the previous chapters. The syllabi in the Appendix, which include additional materials, show further how resources can be used in teaching technology from feminist perspectives. The "References" section stars works of particular value for teaching, and an "Additional Resources" listing is also included.

The works cited are of several different types. Some do not relate to technology specifically, but develop feminist theories—as de Beauvoir (1953), Dinnerstein (1976) or Gilligan (1982)—that are useful for creating conceptual frameworks that incorporate feminist perspectives. Other works are feminist critiques of science—such as those of Fee (1983), Bleier (1984), or Keller (1985)—which are relevant for understanding feminist theoretical perspectives as they relate to both science and technology. There are also theoretical and philosophical works dealing with such subjects as reproduction (O'Brien 1981) or human nature (Jaggar 1983) that provide further feminist theoretical perspectives, plus feminist philosophical works that consider technological issues (Merchant 1980; Gray 1981). Finally, there are those works, many drawn from history and sociology, that focus specifically on women and technology topics, such as women and invention, housework, reproduction, factory work, office

*Portions of this chapter appeared in: Joan Rothschild, "Turing's Man, Turing's Woman, or Turing's Person?: Gender, Language, and Computers," Working Papers Series No. 166 (Wellesley, MA: Wellesley College Center for Research on Women, Spring 1986). Copyright © Joan Rothschild 1986.

work, and other kinds of women's labor, as well as on such issues as weapons, ecology, and the environment, and their relationship to women.

For all of these resources, one might assume that as long as the words *women* or *female* or an equivalent are included or implied in the title and women are central to the subject matter, the work is somehow *feminist*. But this is not always the case: *woman* and *feminist* are not necessarily synonymous. Conversely, a work that is not explicitly about women may be a feminist work. How, then, do we establish criteria to answer the question: "What is a feminist resource for technology?" Just as courses might only pay lip-service to the relationship of women and technology or even include substantial materials on women and technology without making the methodological and conceptual changes a feminist approach entails, so printed and audio-visual materials about women can similarly fail to incorporate a feminist approach. On the other hand, courses can be feminist in method and outlook without focusing centrally on women; this can also be true for resources.

One way to approach this issue is through language. As demonstrated in a well-developed body of feminist scholarship (e.g. Kramer 1975; Miller and Swift 1980; Vetterling-Braggin 1981; Thorne et al. 1983; Spender 1985), gendered language reveals gender biases. Far from being the neutral gender-free convention claimed, use of male pronouns and such words as *mankind* to stand for all human beings in reality excludes the female, literally and philosophically, from human experience and discourse. As pointed out in the Introduction to *Machina Ex Dea*, almost two decades ago Lynn White, noting how such usage underscored women's sense of being secondary, still failed to change the language in his own work (Rothschild 1983, x)! Drawing examples as well from articles in *Technology and Culture*, the Introduction went on to show how use of male language forms reflected an exclusively male view of technology, that the "prototype—the inventor, the user, the thinker about and reactor to technology—is male" (1983, xix), the analysis further suggesting how deeply intertwined are language and gender perspectives. Many of the examples used were drawn from the 1960s and 1970s. Examination of later works reveals, unfortunately, that little may have changed—at least in some writings about technology.

Two recent books about computers and human culture differ markedly in their use of gendered language and thus in their gender perspectives. A comparison of their language and their styles reveals

these differing perspectives. The comparison will also suggest feminist criteria for examining a technology resource. The two books are:
J. David Bolter's (1984) *Turing's Man: Western Culture in the
Computer Age* and Sherry Turkle's (1984a) *The Second Self: Computers and the Human Spirit*. The way each book describes Turing's
test, as to whether computers can think,[1] suggests the differences
between them:

> Turing envisioned a game in which a human player is seated at a teletype
> console, by which he can communicate with a teletype in another room.
> Controlling this second console would be either another human or a digital
> computer. The player could ask any question he wished through his console in
> order to determine whether he was in contact with a man or a machine. (Bolter,
> 191)
>
> . . . Turing proposed a contest. You enter a room and see two terminals. One is
> connected to a computer and the other to a person who can speak through it
> from another room. You may type questions, assertions, insults, anything you
> wish, at either terminal, and you may do so for as long as you like. Your goal is
> to decide which of the terminals is connected to a computer and which to a
> person. . . .
>   Turing suggests that if under these circumstances you cannot decide which is
> the computer and which is the person, you will have to conclude that the
> machine is intelligent. (Turkle, 264)

The two descriptions differ factually. The second quoted, Turkle's,
with the person having choice of two terminals, is correct. But they also
differ in their use of language. While Bolter starts his account with a
"human player," he switches to a male pronoun when referring to that
player in the rest of the passage and to the human at the other end of
the terminal. Turkle, on the other hand, adopting the device of the
second person, "you," for the human player, avoids gendered language or repitition of "he or she," "her or his," etc. These patterns
characterize language usage throughout both books.

The two passages reveal a further difference. Bolter, using the third
person, remains outside, distanced from his subject, leaving the
reader distanced as well. Turkle, choosing the second person, projects a more conversational, interactive atmosphere, drawing the
reader into her description. Again, the styles—one distanced, the
other interactive—are characteristic of both books.

These differences in language use and style reflect the authors'
profound difference in approach to their subject matter that goes
beyond differences that might stem from such factors as disciplines or
scope and purpose of each book. That difference lies in the awareness

of gender. Their two approaches illustrate a fundamentally different understanding of the role of gender in human interaction not only with computers but with technology generally in a cultural context. Bolter's book follows the dominant male tradition in the technology literature. Turkle's book is feminist. After a brief summary of the books' contents and arguments, these gendered differences and their significance will be illustrated.

In exploring the meanings and dimensions of the human–computer relationship, both books take up the age-old, and ultimately metaphysical analogy between human beings and machines. Does the computer affect, change, or extend this analogy? If so, in what ways? The authors differ as to how such questions are framed and how they are answered.

For Bolter, a classicist by training, the computer is the "defining technology" of our age, that is, a technology that "defines or redefines man's role in relation to nature" (13). To understand this role of the computer today, he explores the computer's relationship to the defining technologies of earlier ages of Western culture: to the spindle and potter's wheel of the ancients whose world was cyclical, finite, animistic and organic; to the clock that came to represent the mechanistic world-view of the Scientific Revolution; and to the steam and the heat engine that ushered in a dynamic and infinite world-view and the power over nature of the industrial age. Choosing component elements of the computer—mathematics, logic, space, time, language, memory, and creation—through which to compare the computer with the defining technologies and world-views of these prior ages, Bolter finds that, in combining elements from the past, the computer emerges as something new, and potentially dangerous. A machine that behaves like a tool, the computer has no moving parts; but it is a tool of the mind, not hand (though activated by touch). Finite and superficial like the ancients, having its own rules in a world of its own like the mechanistic age, the computer in the electronic age calls forth "Turing's man." Instead of man as a clay vessel animated by divine breath, or man as a clock, man is cast in the image of the computer. He is an "information processor" and nature is "information to be processed" (13). Rejecting the premises and goals of artificial intelligence researchers, Bolter fears a loss of our history and our very humanity as we come to identify too closely with machines and we *all* become "Turing's men." He advocates instead a partnership between "man and computer."

Turkle, too, sees the computer as a unique entity. It is more tool than machine, but a tool that is an extension of self. For Turkle, the computer exists on the border between the inanimate and the animate, between a machine or thing and an entity with seemingly human qualities. A social psychologist whose work has focused on the cultural context and implications of psychological phenomena,[2] Turkle is concerned with the psychological, cultural, and ultimately metaphysical dimensions of the human interaction with this inert yet somehow living object. For Turkle, the computer is an "evocative object," drawing a new set of responses and thoughts about ourselves and the world that begin to constitute a computer culture. Divided into three parts, the book probes the dimensions of these interactions and contexts. In the first part, based on interviews and observations of children, Turkle describes three developmental stages of children's interactions with computers: metaphysical, mastery, and identity. Using these stages as organizing themes to examine how adult computer relationships are played out, she looks at "The New Computer Cultures" of hackers and those in artificial intelligence in Part II, and the wider implications for us generally in "Into a New Age" in Part III. For Turkle, the most important implication is that, as we begin to see ourselves as emotional machines, we exhibit a "deeply felt tension" revealing that "the question of mind in relation to machine is becoming a central cultural preoccupation" (313).

How may language usage be contrasted in the two books? Bolter's language does not totally exclude the female. When used in a particularized sense, the language attempts to be inclusive. For example, when referring to *people* who are engaged in various human activities, the author uses such terms as "men and women," or "he and she," to indicate that both sexes are involved. But, when referring to human beings in the generic or abstract sense, he uses the male indefinite noun and male pronouns almost exclusively. Thus we find throughout: *Turing's Man, mankind, layman, craftsman*, the *programmer . . . he*. Even when the terms *human* or *human beings* or *men and women* are used, *he* or *him* generally follows, as in the passage on the Turing Test quoted above. This admixture is not just stylistically jarring. In causing errors and distortions, it has a contrary effect of making the gender bias in subject matter, argument, and cultural and philosophical perspectives even more glaring than if the author had used male language throughout. A few examples will illustrate.

In showing computer technology as "team technology," Bolter
writes that,

> It was born through collective projects at such universities as Pennsylvania,
> Cambridge, and Harvard, where *men and women* with varied backgrounds in
> science and engineering were united by the common vision of creating a logic
> machine. (35, italics added)

While some women were involved—albeit largely hidden from history—the computer culture was and remains almost exclusively male
(Levy 1984; Turkle 1984a). Masculine forms are appropriate here,
not gender inclusiveness.

Characterizing "dynamic technology since the Middle Ages" as "a
quest for power, an obsessed effort from which there was no turning
back," Bolter continues,

> Western *men and women* tackled all problems, literary or technological, with
> the same determination to pursue the ever-receding limit of the ultimate. Even
> the *businessman* of the nineteenth and twentieth century, who has pursued
> wealth beyond all proportion, sometimes to the ruin of his health and family, is
> an expression of the same Faustian urge. (223, italics added)

Despite the use of *men and women*, Bolter presents a male model.
The "Faustian urge," pursuit of the "ultimate," or the "quest for
power" have not historically described a female quest. If the activity
does not apply to women, gender inclusive language is both inap-
propriate and inaccurate.

Further distortions occur when the female is excluded from generic
usage. Although he names the spindle and potter's wheel as the
defining technologies of the ancient world, in exploring their social
and cultural meanings, Bolter does not use female language forms to
refer to those who spin. It is the "the craftsman . . . he," whether the
material worked is flax, wool, wood, or clay (180), even though
spinning threads and using the spindle have been traditional female
activities in a high proportion of cultures.

In the ancient Greek world, Bolter finds the creative process
embodied in Plato's creator deity of "a craftsman, a metaphysical
potter or carpenter. . . ." (181)

> . . . the idea of imposing patterns upon shapeless materials, influenced by the
> working methods of potters and carpenters, was central to both Plato's and
> Aristotle's thinking and therefore to the thinking of the ancient world. (182)

Spinning—the work of women—and the spindle metaphor are lost.

Nor does Bolter associate the circular and cyclical imagery of the spindle and the potter's wheel with the female.

If there is no female spinner—or female weaver—neither are there any female poets, philosophers, farmers, clockmakers, programmers—even the file clerk is "he" (169). When Bolter's generic man interacts with nature, nature is "she," following the usual convention. Blurring the distinction between generic and gender-specific use of masculine forms, Bolter adopts the view of man and nature as adversaries, with technology as the mediating factor:

> In the Middle Ages, the accomplishments of technology . . . fostered a new view of mankind versus the forces of nature. The discoveries of the Renaissance and the Industrial Revolution moved men closer to nature in some respects and separated them even more radically in others. . . . Yet the desire to master nature—to harness her more efficient sources of power in steam and fossil fuels and to mine her metals for synthetic purposes—grew steadily throughout this period. (9)

A central thesis of the book is that Turing's man in the computer age is even more separated and isolated from nature than Renaissance or Industrial man. In order to prevent electronic man from becoming the human prototype, Bolter calls on "humanists"—in the tradition of the Greeks and the Romantics—to rekindle a "sensitivity to nature" and "define a new relationship to nature" (228). Bolter's humanist poets and philosophers, like his "man as computer," are, generically and specifically, all men. His language reveals a failure to recognize the gender dualism implicit in the empathic–rationalist oppositions of human nature he describes, and in the pitting of "man" against nature, although such dualisms have been widely discussed by such authors as de Beauvoir (1953), Ortner (1974) and Merchant (1980).

When gender dualism is ignored in the discussions of creation and creativity, the book's most serious distortions and contradictions occur. Comparing the relationship of the creator to the thing created using various technologies in different ages, the author moves from potter to clockmaker to engineer, and finally to programmer. He concludes that the programmer, although accepting the limits of the computer and its rules, "is farther removed from his materials than anyone before in the history of technology" (185). Using male examples and masculine language forms, Bolter warns that this extreme separation from his materials and from nature itself, can result in the programmer playing God. Turing's man as the grand programmer may fashion a new creation myth, making "the world not once and for all but many times over again, rearranging its elements to suit each new program of creation" (187–88). In the person of the artificial intelligence researcher, he may seek to so improve upon nature as to create "an electronic man" (201), Turing's man operating within the narrow confines of computer logic, space and time.

At this point at which creation for Bolter becomes *procreation*—although he does not use the term, nor even suggest its application to world-creation myths—we have something more than a one-sided, male view of the creative process vis-à-vis technology. As he traces "The Technology of Making Man" (201) from the animistic Pygmalion myth to the alchemists' attempts to create an "artificial man, the homunculus" who is "found in the Jewish cabalistic tradition as the golem" (203), to the mechanical automata of the eighteenth century, Bolter introduces the section with the following sentence:

> There was perhaps never a moment in the ancient or modern history of Europe when no one was pursuing the idea of making a human being by other than the ordinary reproductive means (201).

No *one*? No *man* is what is meant. Although the prototype of the horror story about artificial procreation was written by a woman, Mary Shelley ([1818], 1965), *Frankenstein* is a critique of the hubris of a man who fails to take responsibility for and nurture his creation. Making humans artificially is an unlikely pursuit for woman, or women. Possessing the power to give birth, women, for most of human history, have been far too busy doing just that, willingly or unwillingly, and taking on the consequences. His language acting as both trap and mask, Bolter ignores the fact that attempts at and fascination with artificial procreation are male myths and male endeavors (Easlea 1983). Appalled that the "homunculus that results" from the artificial intelligence laboratory is "not a whole man," but a "calculating engine" without emotions (209–10), Bolter writes,

> The attempt to make man over, with whatever available technology, is an attempt to circumvent or reverse the process of nature. Man the artificer and man the artifact merge, but on the artificer's terms. In bypassing the ordinary sexual process of reproduction, man achieves a new freedom from nature; computer technology offers a path to this new freedom. (209)

". . . and to *power*" he might have added. That this would mean for *men* new freedom from, and power over, the one power *women* possess that men do not—the power to reproduce—[3] cannot enter his discussion. Also precluded from the "artificer" and "artifact" merging is the concept of male–female fusion in the process of procreation (Keller 1985). Loss and denial of the female role in procreation mark a final level of distortion of reality which such language usage reflects.

Turkle's language contrasts with that of Bolter. Not only is the language gender-neutral, but this neutrality has been achieved without jarring or unfelicitous phrasing, such as over-use of "his or her" or using "humankind" or the third person indefinite "one." Turkle has made a conscious effort to accomplish this (a point confirmed to me by the author). The method works. As shown in the passage about the Turing Test quoted above, Turkle has accomplished her task by turning sentences around as needed, using the second person or plural forms where feasible, and generally being able to devise alternative phrasing that avoids awkward locutions. The result is a model for successful use of non-sexist language in a book whose major focus is not gender issues nor a feminist critique of the emerging computer culture.

Just as Bolter's use of gendered language revealed gender bias and an unawareness of gender dualism in our culture, so Turkle's use of gender-neutral language reveals not only a lack of gender bias but also a sensitivity to gender issues. For example, Part I discusses her research with children of both sexes. In the course of observations and interviews, she found distinct differences between boys and girls in both style and interplay with the computer, especially in the ways those of the middle years sought mastery, and how children identified with the computer during early teens. These differences, although not specifically sought out, emerged in the course of her inquiry into how children think about computers and interact with them. In Part II, again, without making this her central point, she notes that the computer hackers and artificial intelligence people she is discussing are almost all men. Functioning within a male-oriented culture, they reflect some of the distinctively male patterns of computer interaction she had found among children. In both instances, awareness of gender factors is revealed not only through content but also in the way that content is expressed. An author aware of gender as a factor in human thought and development cannot write "the child . . . he" and the "computer hacker . . . he" if both sexes were meant in the first case and only one sex in the second.

But, using gender-appropriate language does more than erase confusion and ambiguity, enabling an author to be gender-specific when called for and gender-neutral when both sexes are meant. In revealing sensitivity to gender issues, such usage presents a more nearly objective picture of the subject described than the claimed objectivity and comprehensiveness of the model that would use the word "mankind" to represent the whole human race. When Bolter follows the latter format, he obscures the fact that his subject is "man," literally, in a Western *male* culture. The Turkle model breaks us out of that bind to be able to focus on *human*–computer interaction with a depth not possible in Bolter's framework—even though the intent of his book is far more global than hers.

Bolter's detached style and method also reflect a male cultural perspective. Bolter leaves the reader outside, even though the author's intent is the opposite: to engage us with his concerns. In seeking to show where the artificial intelligence mentality will lead, Bolter tries to alert his readers to the dangers of identifying so closely with machines that we become like them, losing what makes us human. But what does make us human? For Bolter, it is the pursuits and qualities of the humanist in our society. The model is not just male, but the detached, intellectualized, white Western male, who objectifies reality. Bolter addresses the central concern of his book—the relationship of human beings to machines, as revealed by computers—in oppositional terms, between man and machine. In limiting his concept of *human* not only to *man* literally, but to Western humanist man, Bolter has set up a narrow, two-dimensional framework for his argument. Although his humanist man encompasses Romantic attributes and sensitivity to nature missing from computer man, humanist man still exists separately from mature and from machines. Computer or Turing's man is merely humanist man shorn of his literary and philosophic sensibilities. With a truncated view of what is human, Bolter cannot deal adequately with the complexities of human–computer relationships, leaving the reader perhaps aware of dehumanizing possibilities, but unconvinced of the dangers of our becoming "Turing's men." There is more here than the alienation of the female reader who is left out of Bolter's humanity. The view of technology and culture is incomplete as well. The reader is not engaged partly because the alarm has been sounded before, and also because the picture of the way in which technologies define our culture does not square with or include much of human and cultural experience. Bolter's book, subtitled *Western Culture in the Computer Age*, attempts a broad canvas that is not realized.

This style and method contrast with that found in Turkle's book, which can be characterized as "inside", or interactive. It is an approach that engages the reader, producing a multifaceted inquiry into the human–computer relationship. Turkle and Bolter agree that the computer is, indeed, a new breed of machine. But, as Turkle emphasizes, it is a machine that "talks" to us, that responds to us visually and, increasingly, audibly. Not only is it a machine we communicate with through our minds, it is a machine about which we have feelings. Combining the methodology of observation and analysis with an interactive approach, Turkle systematically discovers and conveys a variety of dimensions and levels of human responses to the computer. Her language both reflects and reinforces this approach. When she uses the second person and avoids sexist, depersonalized abstractions to refer to human beings, she not only involves the reader; she has also found a means of expression that is consistent with and appropriate for her subject matter. Her language and style support her philosophical premise, enabling her to explore complexities of human–machine interactions.[4]

Turkle's approach may be called female in the sense that Bolter's is male, reflecting certain socially-defined gender attributes. In our present cultural and social framework, the detached and distant have been identified as male, the interactive and connective as female. Embodying these and other so-called male attributes, the male model has become the accepted tradition of intellectual inquiry,[5] a tradition that excludes or distorts the female and subordinates female attributes. Set against this is not only feminist scholarship but a feminist mode of inquiry. In this sense, Turkle's book is feminist.

Although she does not focus on sex differences nor on a feminist critique, Turkle's book is feminist because her mode of inquiry, or *method*, is feminist. Feminist method is inclusive, not exclusive. Recognizing gender as a necessary category of analysis provides tools for an enlarged, holistic view of human beings and the universe studied. But the prism or vantage point remains experiential (Reinharz 1979; Smith 1979). In the social sciences, feminist method brings to traditional "objective" and empirical methodology an interactive approach that acknowledges and gains from involvement with the subject of study.[6] Just as interaction and connectedness are components of "good science" (Keller 1985), so are they necessary for good scholarship in the social sciences. Turkle's book is feminist not only by virtue of language and gender awareness, but also because her method enables her to generalize from a particular that does not limit, but enlarges, human experience. Although exploring a smaller universe than Bolter's, Turkle's book succeeds in both personalizing and universalizing the complexities of our evolving relationship with computers as machines.

What can we draw from the above comparison of the Bolter and Turkle books that will help to establish criteria for assessing a feminist resource on technology?

First, there is the important issue of language: its usage and the way in which such usage reflects gender perceptions and biases. Gender-exclusive language, the use of male pronouns and indefinite nouns to stand for all human beings, acts to exclude the female. But, as we saw with Bolter, attempts at gender-neutral or gender-inclusive language can also be exclusionary if such usage does not reflect changes in content and perspectives. The anthology of readings on technology and society edited by Albert Teich provides a further example. Published in its first three editions (1972, 1977, 1981) as *Technology and Man's Future*, the book in its fourth and most recent edition (1986) bears the title *Technology and the Future*. The change, however, is only title-deep, as immediately reflected by the cover. Instead of the figure sculpture reproduced on the cover of the first three editions, Ernest Trova's "Study: Falling Man (Wheel Man) 1965," the fourth edition substitutes a NASA photograph of a spaceman walking on the moon. True, we have had women in space, but the image conveyed is still male. Although the editor has changed organization and content to reflect a currently "balanced set of readings on technology and society" that explore "many differing views" related to "policy perspectives" (1986, x), critical issues relating specifically to women are still conspicuously absent; nor is there any sign of the growing feminist analysis and critique of technological development—present, past, or future. Among the additions are articles on military technology and on biotechnology (legal and commercial issues of recombinant DNA); there is none on reproductive technologies. For Teich, explaining the new cover, "Space is the new frontier" (1986, x).

Thus, looking critically at language usage teaches us to go beyond language to examine content and perspectives. While, as we have seen, gender-neutral language does not always signify gender awareness, such usage is still a necessary condition for a feminist resource. We should seek such usage in all resources we use (as well as employing gender-neutral language ourselves and encouraging it among our students), whether we are teaching an explicitly feminist course or not. The Turkle book provides an important example here. It is a non-sexist, feminist book that is NOT about "women and computers" nor making an intended *feminist* analysis or critique of computers and culture. It also provides a model of successful use of non-sexist language.

Second, comparison of the Bolter and Turkle books shows us the importance of style and method. Demonstrating the difference between a feminist experiential, interactive and holistic approach and the traditional male approach that is distanced, detached, and exclusionary, the comparison showed how the latter approach failed in its inclusive goal to address the significance of the *human*–computer relationship in *Western culture*. This is critical because of the claim made by such traditionally-oriented scholarship to be *humanistic*, to be inclusive. When combined with language usage, an approach that is removed from human experience in this way not only omits issues of gender, but also those of race, class, and multicultural perspectives, and the connections among them. Feminist analysis allows for such inclusion and connections but without, at the same time, making global claims for any single work.

The last point brings us to the heart of what gender analysis and feminist perspectives are all about,[7] and thus to framing criteria for a feminist resource on technology. When it is argued that gender is a necessary category of analysis for all scholarly inquiry, the statement is based on the premise that omission of the female and feminist perspectives is not accidental. Rather, it reflects a power imbalance in the history of Western scholarship that in turn reflects an ideological and societal power imbalance. A white male elite has controlled society and scholarship, setting the framework and the categories for analysis, legitimizing what is a proper subject for study. Women are the Other who are to be repressed and controlled, as are the poor (who are more female than male), and as are the races and cultures that are not of the white race and dominant cultures. A feminist resource, therefore, must reflect the consciousness of the Other so as to raise and change the consciousness about who and what is studied.

What specific criteria are suggested?

— Is the language gender-neutral?
— If so, does the language reflect gender awareness, or is the language superficial reflecting no change in approach or thought?
— Are women included, if they should be, in the subject matter?

— If so, how are they included? Are they appendages, or are they integrated into the subject matter? Do they appear only in stereotypical roles? Are their traditional roles accepted uncritically?

— If women are the main focus of the study, how are they treated? Are they symbols or a category apart, or do they emerge as real and diverse human beings?

— Does the study question or lead to questioning of the traditional approaches to the study of technology that have omitted feminist perspectives? Does it build gender awareness and present a diversified approach?

These criteria can be useful in analyzing technology materials not only to locate feminist resources but also to build a feminist critique of all technology resources. While works on gender and technology are subject to review in both technology and feminist journals and writings, the rest of the technology literature usually receives appraisal only in the technology field. It is rarely measured against feminist criteria.[8] Thus, anthologies such as the one by Teich mentioned above continue to be compiled, re-edited and re-issued, devoid of any gender analysis or perspectives. Histories of technology continue to be written and used that ignore or pay lip-service to women and gender issues. Films and TV programs on science and technology, using male narrators, continue to depict the worlds of discovery and invention as male creations. A Naisbitt (1982) can fashion a set of roseate "megatrends" that have little relationship to the lives of real women, present or future. On the other hand, Arnold Pacey's recent *The Culture of Technology* (1983) draws on the new feminist research to show how feminist values and women's experiences can contribute to a critique of contemporary technology. Although there are occasional lapses in language usage—for the most part, it is gender-neutral—and although the impact of feminist ideas is not developed far enough, the book is significant as an attempt of mainstream literature to integrate and interweave feminist perspectives with other beliefs and values. Yet, how many faculty might think to use the Pacey book in this integrative way? We need a systematic feminist critique of the technology literature not only to reveal shortcomings but also to identify useful resources.

One way to introduce feminist analysis, and to build gender awareness in the process, is to engage in such critique in the classroom. Although these pages may appear to imply that the technology literature has no redeeming intellectual value, such is obviously not the case. There is no intent to dismiss summarily over 2,000 years of recorded thought and scholarship because it does not pass the feminist litmus test (Rich 1979). The argument, rather, is that a work is necessarily distorted and incomplete if woman is an ignored or demeaned Other. We must analyze, select, and build a more inclusive literature. The classroom, it seems to me, is one place to do this. Choosing a work appropriate to the course subject matter from the technology literature, faculty can subject it to a feminist analysis using the criteria suggested above. This can be done through lectures or as a class exercise in which students apply gender analysis to a work or works in their papers and projects. A three-fold purpose would be served. (1) More works would undergo a gender critique. (2) Feminist criteria and tools of gender analysis would be developed among both faculty and students. (3) These criteria and tools could be applied to other areas and meshed with other critiques to foster a broader, more diversified approach.

Therefore, we need not rely exclusively on feminist resources in order to bring feminist perspectives to our technology teaching. By critically examining the prevailing technology literature in our fields, we create further feminist teaching methods and resources. In this way, not only are the male biases of technology and the approaches to technology revealed to students, but the ideological, social, and cultural contexts in which such biases exist and flourish can be exposed as well.

NOTES

1. The test or "game" was devised by mathematician Alan Turing in 1950 (Turing 1950).
2. See Turkle (1978).
3. For a description of a future society in which women voluntarily give up their power to procreate so as to equalize power between the sexes, see Piercy (1976).
4. Turkle's description of her method as ethnographic (see endnotes, 1984a, 315–323) supports my view of her method as interactive and relational.
5. For a perceptive discussion of the effects of this intellectual tradition on women's education, see Martin (1985).
6. See Westkott (1979), for example, on *intersubjectivity*, and Duelli Klein (1983) on *conscious subjectivity*.
7. See also discussion at the beginning of Chapter 5.
8. There are two points here. One is that mainstream journals in technology, as well as other fields, generally do not include feminist critiques of traditional works. Feminist scholars are called upon to review books about women or "women's subjects" (e.g. textile workers, reproductive technology). Rarely are they asked to review other works in their fields. At the same time, books concerning women may

be reviewed by non-feminist scholars who have expertise in the particular field (e.g. in labor history, in biology).

The second point is that feminist journals also do not offer feminist critiques of mainstream works. This has much to do with the way in which women's studies has developed. When women's studies began in the late 1960s, building on a few earlier feminist critical works (see Chapter 1), it began as a critique of male scholarship. Male scholarship was *the* dominant and predominant model, the mainstream that feminists found unsatisfying and were reacting against. Kate Millett's explosive analysis of male authors in *Sexual Politics* published in 1969—based on her Ph.D. dissertation in literature at Columbia University—was among the first of the intense, incisive critiques that were to follow in the humanities and social sciences in the next several years. But, as the 1970s advanced and women began to discover their own past and find their own voice, feminist scholarship stopped reacting and began to act in its own behalf. A rich outpouring of literature, drawing on the new feminist research, expressed this new-found voice. The tremendous growth of women's studies courses and programs at this time and their emphasis on *women's* experiences, as noted in Chapter 4, further reflected and encouraged this direction for research and writing. The review sections of women's studies journals and separate feminist review publications that began to appear have devoted themselves almost exclusively to this women's studies literature. Perhaps in part because of the overwhelming volume of feminist writing and because of no perceived need to engage in such critique, feminist journals have generally not dealt with mainstream literature.

Thus, on both counts traditional works escape feminist scrutiny. Whether there will be any change in the mainstream journals is hard to predict. In women's studies, perhaps as the focus on integration grows, in an effort to build more inclusive disciplines, there may be renewed interest in developing a systematic critique of mainstream scholarship.

Chapter 7

Looking Ahead: Teaching Technology from a Feminist Perspective

The material in this book has been based in large measure on responses to questionnaires mailed to faculty in technology studies and women's studies, and related fields. I also drew on my own research and teaching experience, and on association with colleagues in these areas. As revealed in the preceding chapters, these questions arise: What are the ways that feminist perspectives are being introduced to technology teaching? What is the state of the art? What is now included in such teaching? What is still missing? What are the pressing issues and problems, and what practical suggestions have emerged? What are the resources, what are the needs? Finally, in what directions do we move to foster a healthy, supportive relationship between women's studies and technology studies in the classroom? In summing up in this closing chapter, these questions will be addressed and explored.

After a brief history in Chapter 1, Chapters 2, 3 and 4 grouped the courses viewed into three categories: "Women *and* Technology," "Women *in* Science and Technology," and courses that sought to add materials on women and technology or to integrate gender perspectives into general courses. Chapter 5 dealt with conceptual frameworks, drawing on courses reviewed in the preceding chapters as well as examining new ones. Chapter 6 sought to answer the question, "What is a feminist resource for technology?"

The largest group of courses looked at were in the "Women *and* Technology" and "Women *in* Science and Technology" categories, discussed in Chapters 2 and 3. Although admitting of considerable variety, they tended to draw on a number of the same materials and also to be taught from sociological and/or historical perspectives.

They often were located, at least partly, in a women's studies rather than an STS program (although this was not true, for example, of the Bereano course at the University of Washington nor the Schiebinger course at Stanford). The courses discussed in Chapter 4 that sought to include or integrate feminist materials into general courses varied in approach and emphasis. While some sought merely to add a segment or segments on women without making other changes in the course, others attempted integration, drawing on feminist conceptual materials. Application of the McIntosh developmental model of curriculum integration demonstrated the need for successful courses to be built on a feminist critique and to include a conceptual gender framework. As discussed in Chapter 5, the presence of a conceptual framework containing a clearly articulated gender analysis not only gave a course internal coherence. It also provided intellectual support and legitimacy for the introduction of feminist perspectives that were controversial, and even threatening, for some students, particularly males. Several examples were discussed, including a model for a feminist assessment of technology. Through comparing two recent books on computers and culture as a point of departure, Chapter 6 suggested criteria for appraising a feminist resource for technology that included language, style and method, and analysis of how women and gender issues are treated.

The subject matter of the courses reviewed has tended to be Western, and especially American, reflecting a primary focus of the technology studies field. With the exception of the "Women in Development" course at West Virginia University, and segments in Wetzel's course as taught at the University of Maine and Bereano's at the University of Washington, cross-cultural and development issues have not been widely represented. These issues are of growing concern in women's studies. Although arising in an American context, women's studies has now developed internationally, with an impressive literature in cross-cultural and development studies. To the extent that gender and technology issues are addressed in this literature, however, the research will usually be part of the broader field of "women and development" (see Bourque and Warren 1987). Therefore, to seek out how women, technology, and development materials might be applied in the curriculum would mean extending the call for syllabi more widely than could be done for the present book. It is critical, however, that cross-cultural research on gender, technology, and development finds its way into the technology classroom and that we explore current teaching in the field. From hauling the water, to growing the food, to bearing the children, to nurturing and caring for their families, women do two-thirds of the world's work. Theirs has been a long and continuing relationship with technology and technological change that spans time and cultures—a relationship that a Western solipsism has long neglected, especially for women in the Third World. Perhaps women's studies can be the cutting edge to bring a global perspective to technology studies that is sensitive to the "Others" of culture, race, class, and gender.

The teaching of practical aspects of technology, known as "hands on" courses, received brief attention, mainly in Chapters 3 and 5. Although many of these courses take place in settings not traditionally academic, such as continuing, community, or other adult education programs, they are very much a part of feminist education because they seek to empower women.[1] A key element in this process is demystification. Combining the theoretical and practical—the mix depending on educational setting and audience—courses try to dispel the mysteries and taboos surrounding areas from which women have been alienated and denied access, such as the technical and technological. Through enlightenment can come confidence, then mastery and empowerment. This model can be applied in other than an exclusively female setting.

It can be applied very well, for example, to teaching in the New Liberal Arts. Directed at liberal arts students of both sexes, technological literacy courses and programs have as their aim technological empowerment. The rationale for the New Liberal Arts is that students in non-scientific and non-technical fields will be *dis*empowered if they do not overcome their alienation and antipathies and gain the requisite knowledge and skills of things mathematical, scientific, and technological to function in a technologically-oriented world. While an exclusively hands-on model may not be appropriate for an academically-oriented classroom, the mix which seeks to integrate hands on and theoretical and conceptual materials—as in the Peters and Benston courses referred to in Chapters 2 and 3—may be a useful model for technological literacy courses. If, however, the feminist dimension of this model is not transferred as well, the course may end up empowering only men. More than one faculty member has remarked that it is often much more difficult to gain and keep the interest of female students in technological literacy courses, even when they number half or a sizable plurality of the students (and therefore have been initially attracted to the course). It is critical in these courses to speak specifically to the female dimensions of technological alienation and disempowerment, and to do so both conceptually and in practice. Many of the courses described in this book provide materials to help accomplish this aim. The experience of Deborah Brecher's Women's Computer Literacy Project, described in Chapter 3, may be particularly instructive.

Although teaching at the primary and secondary levels was beyond the scope of this book, the importance of feminist perspectives in technology teaching from earliest schooling through high school needs to be addressed by educators. To the stereotypes of girls' disenchantment with math and science and things technical starting in junior high have been added the picture of boys'—as opposed to girls'—fascination with computers starting in the early primary grades. Attitudes and practices are set long before students enter our college classrooms. Clearly, it is important to build gender awareness early about technology and technological issues, conceptually as well as practically. Materials used in courses discussed in this book could well be useful in the high school classroom along with the examples of how to present the subject matter. A systematic survey of the extent to which feminist perspectives on technology obtain at the pre-college level might also be useful so that concrete recommendations could be made. (See, for example, Diane McGrath (1986) who has probed not only attitudes but how and why priorities are set.)

Other kinds of curriculum information at the college level also need systematic study. Among the courses reviewed, most were at the upper division undergraduate level, having no prerequisites (save being an upper division student), and offered as lecture-discussions or seminars; students were predominantly female. Although the questionnaire did not ask specifically about class size as well, among the respondents who volunteered this information, many reported a small class emphasizing discussion, as might befit an upper division and even graduate (for some) course. Ruth Cowan's comment that her women/science/technology course "worked superbly well—with 10 students. I shudder to think of how to manage it with a large group that would require lecturing and defeat discussion" reflects my own thinking and experiences about such courses. A number of others reviewed, such as Staudenmaier's at the University of Detroit, Bereano's at the University of Washington, and Hafter's at Eastern Michigan University, clearly depended on a small group seminar format. What *would* happen if these classes were larger? Are large classes that successfully use feminist perspectives more numerous than the responses received indicate? The factor of class size needs to built into any further curriculum study on gender and technology. So, too, the question of whether the course is elective or required should be asked; although not specifically addressed, most of the courses reviewed appeared to be electives. Therefore, systematic study would be appropriate that would add questions about course size and elective–required status to those about course level, sex ratio format, prerequisites, disciplinary perspectives, department or program location of course, and type of institution, correlating the responses.

This kind of information and understanding is critical if we are to bring feminist perspectives to a wider range of technology courses. From the survey of courses represented by the syllabi discussed in this book, it would appear that concentrated attention to gender issues or concerted efforts to integrate gender tend to occur in selective, specialized courses with a selective clientele. Two areas need more focus: (1) larger, more standard technology and STS courses, for example, in the history of technology and technological change; and (2) women's studies courses that until recently have been focused almost entirely in the humanities and social sciences. In the first area, for example, the aim would be to integrate feminist materials into required, or otherwise well populated, core or survey courses in STS programs. In the second area, an aim would be to integrate scientific and technological issues into required introductory courses in women's studies programs.

Moving in these two directions for curriculum change to reflect feminist perspectives can enlarge the learning compass and positively influence gender imbalances in the classroom. Together with a third direction—to integrate feminist perspectives into the New Liberal Arts—such recommended changes can also speak to the relationship of gender to the two cultures debate. When feminist perspectives are successfully brought into an STS survey or core course, male students, who may constitute a majority, will gain insights about the importance of gender factors for technology, as will female students. But, because the content now speaks to *them*, more females are likely to be drawn to the course and their interest in things technical sustained and encouraged. When technology studies are introduced into the women's studies curriculum, through presenting feminist perspectives on technology, the scope of women's studies is broadened to encompass a previously distant terrain, and students can expand their range of knowledge in new direction. When gender perspectives are integrated into technological literacy courses and programs, the gender stereotypes about technical vs non-technical thinking can be challenged and rethought. But so, too, can the humanistic–scientific, or two cultures, split. As noted in Chapter 5 and above, technological literacy courses and programs are aimed at the liberal arts student, male or female, who is ignorant of and/or turned off from quantitative and technical thinking. What happens under these circumstances, to assumptions that non-quantitative and non-technical modes are associated with the female, while mathematical, scientific and technological thinking is male? As pointed out in this book, feminist perspectives on technology are not confined to *female* and *women's* issues, but speak to the broad concerns and values of technology study and practice. Applying feminist perspectives, faculty have an opportunity to explore the gender dimensions of the two cultures argument so as to further explain it and transcend it.

In addition to the recommendations outlined above, what else will aid in bringing feminist perspectives to the technology classroom? Clearly, more resources are needed. A great many materials have been published since the late 1970s, making an increasing amount of relevant feminist research available. But, the widespread use of reading packets containing selected articles and the frequent assignment of library readings indicate a continuing need to synthesize materials and also to explore more areas in depth, as in the works on household technology (Cowan 1983; Strasser 1982) and on reproductive technology (Arditti et al. 1984), which are extremely popular. Many more materials on women, technology, and development, and cross-cultural perspectives generally, are also needed (see Bourque and Warren 1987). While some films have become available, particularly focusing on technology, work and/or health issues,[2] audio-visual resources are still far too few. Especially because such resources are highly effective teaching tools for students of the TV generation, there is a need for films, slide-tapes, and other visuals on a range of technological subjects that incorporate feminist perspectives. As remarked in Chapter 6, the current film image is of a world of science and invention literally "man-made." Film-makers should be encouraged to correct this imbalance. It would also be useful to establish resource centers to collect curriculum materials on gender and technology and place them on-line, readily available to all who needed them.

None of this can happen without people and without finding more ways for those of us engaged in this enterprise to talk to each other. I would encourage more workshops and working conferences, both regionally and nationally, to discuss gender and technology curriculum issues. Faculty development programs are a must. A project to develop course segments and course materials might also be useful. These proposals would need both institutional supports and outside funding of the kind that has been forthcoming for integrating women's studies into the liberal arts curriculum and for the New Liberal Arts programs. The need now is for support to integrate feminist research and perspectives on technology into the technology and the liberal arts curricula.

Preparing this book has been a learning experience for me: from the range and variety of course offerings to the extent of shared resources and approaches, from the many positive experiences to the issues and problems faced. It is encouraging to learn how far the curriculum work has come. Yet, it is clear there is much more innovative thought and action to take. I have sought in these last pages to outline the needs and the directions this work should go. Needless to say, I see it as a worthwhile endeavor.

NOTES

1. See, for example, the work of the Women's Resource Center in Missoula, Montana, especially in the area of appropriate technology (Smith 1978; *Conference Proceedings* 1979).
2. See, for example, recent films such as *Terminal* (1985), *The Electronic Sweatshop* (1985) and *The Global Assembly Line* (1986).

References

All works mentioned in the text are cited below. Those particularly useful as feminist resources are marked with an asterisk (*).

Aeschylus. 1969. *The Eumenides: the Oresteian trilogy*. Trans. Philip Vellacott. New York: Penguin.

Annas, George. 1981. Contracts to bear a child: compassion or commercialism? *The Hastings Report* (April): 23–24.

*Arditti, Rita, Renate Duelli Klein and Shelley Minden, eds. 1984. *Test-tube women: what future for motherhood?* London: Routledge & Kegan Paul.

*Baxandall, Rosalyn, Elizabeth Ewen and Linda Gordon. 1976. The working class has two sexes. *Monthly Review* 28, no. 3 (July–August): 1–9.

*de Beauvoir, Simone. 1953. *The second sex*. Trans. and ed. H. M. Parshley. New York: Alfred A. Knopf.

Bell, Daniel. 1973. Five dimensions of post-industrial society. *Social Policy* (July–August): 103–110.

Benjamin, Jessica. 1983. Master and slave: the fantasy of erotic domination. In *Powers of desire: the politics of sexuality*, ed. Ann Snitow, 280–299. New York: Monthly Review Press.

*Bereano, Philip and Christine Bose. 1983. Women and technology: a university course and an annotated bibliography. *Science for the People* (May–June): 31–34.

Bernal, J.D. [1929]1970. *The world, the flesh and the devil: an inquiry into three enemies of the rational soul*. London: Jonathan Cape.

*Bindocci, Cynthia Gay, and Kathleen Ochs, comp. and ed. (forthcoming) *Gender and technology: an annotated guide to historical and contemporary works*. New York: Garland Publishing

*Bleier, Ruth. 1984. *Science and gender: a critique of biology and its theories on women*. New York: Pergamon Press.

Bolter, J. David. 1984. *Turing's man: Western culture in the computer age*. Chapel Hill: University of North Carolina Press.

*Bose, Christine. 1979. Technology and changes in the division of labor in the American home. *Women's Studies International Quarterly 2*, no. 3: 295–304.

*Bose, Christine, Philip Bereano and Ivy Durslag. 1982. Teaching women and technology at the University of Washington. In *Women, Technology and Innovation*, ed. Joan Rothschild, 374–377. Oxford: Pergamon Press.

*Bose, Christine, Philip Bereano and Mary Malloy. 1984. Household technology and the social construction of housework. *Technology and Culture* 25, no. 1 (January): 53–82.

*Bourque, Susan C. and Kay B. Warren. 1987. Technology, gender, and development: Incorporating gender in the study of development. *Daedalus: the Journal of the American Academy of Arts and Sciences* 116, no. 4 (Fall): 173–197.

Boyd, Doug. 1976. *Rolling thunder*. New York: Dell Publishing.

Braverman, Harry. 1974. *Labor and monopoly capital: the degradation of work in the twentieth century*. New York: Monthly Review Press.

*Brecher, Deborah. 1985. *The women's computer literacy handbook*. New York: New American Library.

Brown, Michael. 1979. *Laying waste*. New York: Washington Square Press.

*Bruce, Margaret, Gill Kirkup and Chris Thomas. 1984. *Teaching technology assessment to women*. Milton Keynes, England: The Open University.

Bulletin of Science, Technology and Society. 1981–. State College, PA: STS Press, Pennsylvania State University.

Bunch, Charlotte. 1981. *Feminism in the 80s: facing down the right*. Denver, CO: Inkling Press.

Burke, John G. and Marshall C. Eakin, eds. 1979. *Technology and change*. San Francisco: Boyd & Fraser.

*Bush, Corlann Gee. 1981. *Taking hold of technology: topic guide for 1981–83*. Washington, DC: American Association of University Women.

*Bush, Corlann Gee. 1983. Women and the assessment of technology: to think, to be; to unthink, to free. In *Machina ex dea*, ed. Joan Rothschild, 151–170. New York: Pergamon Press.

*Caldicott, Helen. 1984. *Missile Envy: the arms race and nuclear war*. New York: William Morrow.

Callenbach, Ernest. 1975. *Ecotopia*. New York: Bantam Books.

*Carter, Angela. 1983. Anger in a black landscape. In *Over our dead bodies: women against the bomb*, ed. Dorothy Thompson, 146–156. London: Virago Press.

*Carter, Ruth. 1985. Affirmative action for women engineers and technologists at the Open University in the United Kingdom. *SWE Newsletter* 16 (December). Baltimore–Washington Section.

Castaneda, Carlos. 1973. *Journey to Ixtlan*. New York: Simon & Schuster.

*Charlton, Sue Ellen. 1984. *Women in third world development*. Boulder, CO: Westview Press.

*Chavkin, Wendy, ed. 1984. *Double exposure: women's health hazards on the job and at home*. New York: Monthly Review Press.

*Chodorow, Nancy. 1974. Family structure and feminine personality. In *Woman, culture, and society*, ed. Michelle Zimbalist Rosaldo and Louise Lamphere, 43–66. Stanford, CA: Stanford University Press.

*Chodorow, Nancy. 1978. *The reproduction of mothing: psychoanalysis and the sociology of gender*. Berkeley: University of California Press.

Conference proceedings: women and technology: deciding what's appropriate. 1979. Missoula, MT: Women's Resource Center, April.

*Cowan, Ruth Schwartz. 1976. The 'Industrial Revolution' in the home: household technology and social change in the 20th century. *Technology and Culture* 17, no. 1 (January): 1–23.

*Cowan, Ruth Schwartz. 1979. From Virginia Dare to Virginia Slims: women and technology in American life. *Technology and Culture* 20, no. 1 (January): 51–63.

*Cowan, Ruth. Schwartz. 1983. *More work for mother: the ironies of household technology from the open hearth to the microwave*. New York: Basic Books.

Cutcliffe, Stephen H. and the Technology Studies and Education Committee of the Society for the History of Technology, comp. and ed. 1983. *The machine in the university: sample course syllabi for the history of technology and technology studies*. Bethlehem, PA: Science, Technology and Society Program, Lehigh University.

Cutcliffe, Stephen H. 1987. The emergence of STS as an academic field. In *Research in Philosophy and technology IX*, ed. P. Durbin. Greenwich, CT: JAI Press.

*Dauber, Roslyn and Melinda L. Cain, eds. 1981. *Women and technological change in developing countries*. Boulder, CO: Westview Press.

82   Teaching Technology from a Feminist Perspective

Dickson, David. 1975. *The politics of alternative technology*. New York: Universe Books.

*Dinnerstein, Dorothy. 1976. *The mermaid and the minotaur: sexual arrangements and human malaise*. New York: Harper & Row.

*Dublin, Thomas. 1979. *Women at work: the transformation of work and community in Lowell, Massachusetts, 1826–1860*. New York: Columbia University Press.

*Duelli Klein, Renate. 1983. How to do what we want to do: thoughts about feminist methodology. In *Theories of women's studies*, eds. Gloria Bowles and Renate Duelli Klein, 88–104. London: Routledge & Kegan Paul.

*Easlea, Brian. 1980. *Witch-hunting, magic and the new philosophy*. Brighton, Sussex: Harvester Press.

*Easlea, Brian. 1983. *Fathering the unthinkable: masculinity, scientists and the nuclear arms race*. London: Pluto Press.

*Ehrenreich, Barbara and Deirdre English. 1979. *For her own good: 150 years of the experts' advice to women*. Garden City, NY: Anchor Press/Doubleday.

*Eisenstein, Hester. 1983. *Contemporary feminist thought*. Boston: G. K. Hall.

The Electronic Sweatshop. 1985. *Les productions du regard et les productions contre-jour*. San Francisco: California Newsreel (film/video).

Ellul, Jacques. 1964. *The technological society*. Trans. John Wilkinson. New York: Vintage Books.

Elshtain, Jean Bethke. 1984. Symmetry and soporifics: a critique of feminist accounts of gender development. In *Capitalism and infancy: essays on psychoanalysis and politics*, ed. B. Richards. Free Association Books.

*Fausto-Sterling, Anne. 1986. Myths of gender: biological theories about women and men. New York: Basic Books.

*Fee, Elizabeth. 1983. Women's nature and scientific objectivity. In *Woman's nature: rationalizations of inequality*, ed. Marian Lowe and Ruth Hubbard, 9–27. New York: Pergamon Press.

*Feldberg, Roslyn L. and Evelyn Nakano Glenn. 1983. Technology and work degradation: effects of office automation on women clerical workers. In *Machina ex dea*, ed. Joan Rothschild, 59–78. New York: Pergamon Press.

Feminist Studies. 1969–. College Park, MD: Women's Studies Program, University of Maryland.

Fernbach, David. 1981. *The spiral paths: a gay contribution to human survival*. Boston: Alyson Publications.

Fields, Craig. 1973. *About computers*. Boston: Little, Brown.

*Firestone, Shulamith. 1971. *The dialectic of sex: the case for feminist revolution*. New York: Bantam Books.

*Flax, Jane. 1983. Political philosophy and the patriarchal unconscious: a psychoanalytic perspective on epistemology and metaphysics. In *Discovering reality*, eds. Sandra Harding and Merrill B. Hintikka, 245–281. Boston: D. Reidel.

Fromm, Eric. 1968. *Revolution of hope*. New York: Bantam Books.

*Fuentes, Annette and Barbara Ehrenreich. 1983. *Women in the global factory*. New York: Institute for New Communications; Boston: South End Press.

*Gearhart, Sally Miller. 1979. *The wanderground: stories of the hill women*. Watertown, MA: Persephone Press.

*Gilligan, Carol. 1982. *In a different voice: psychological theory and women's development*. Cambridge, MA: Harvard University Press.

*Gilman, Charlotte Perkins. [1915–1916] 1979. *Herland*. New York: Pantheon Books (originally published as a serial in *The Forerunner*).

Gimpel, Jean. 1977. *The medieval machine: the Industrial Revolution of the Middle Ages*. Harmondsworth, England: Penguin Books.

The Global Assembly Line. 1986. Wayne, NJ: New Day Films (film/video).

Goodman, Paul. 1967. The morality of scientific technology. *Dissent* (January–February): 41–53.

*Gordon, Linda. 1977. *Woman's body, woman's right: a social history of birth control in America*. New York: Penguin Books.
*Gould, Carol C., ed. 1983. *Beyond domination: new perspectives on women and philosophy*. Totowa, NJ: Rowman & Allanheld.
*Gray, Elizabeth Dodson. 1981. *Green paradise lost*. Wellesley, MA: Roundtable Press.
*Gray, Elizabeth Dodson. 1982. *Patriarchy as a conceptual trap*. Wellesley, MA: Roundtable Press.
*Hacker, Sally. 1979. Sex stratification, technology and organizational change: a longitudinal case study of AT&T. *Social Problems* 26, no. 5 (June): 539–557.
*Hacker, Sally. 1981. The culture of engineering: woman, workplace, and machine. *Women's Studies International Quarterly* 4, no. 3: 341–353.
*Hacker, Sally L. 1983. Mathematization of engineering: limits on women and the field. In *Machina ex dea*, ed. Joan Rothschild, 38–58. New York: Pergamon Press.
*Hafter, Daryl M. 1979. The programmed brocade loom and the "decline of the drawgirl". *Dynamos and virgins revisited*, ed. Martha Trescott, 49–66. Metuchen, NJ: Scarecrow Press.
*Hanmer, Jalna. 1983. Reproductive technology: the future for women? In *Machina ex dea*, ed. Joan Rothschild, 183–197. New York: Pergamon Press.
*Harding, Sandra and Merrill B. Hintikka, eds. 1983. *Discovering reality: feminist perspectives on epistemology, metaphysics, methodology, and philosophy of science*. Dordrecht: D. Reidel.
*Hayden, Dolores. 1981. *The grand domestic revolution: a history of feminist designs for American homes, neighborhoods, and cities*. Cambridge, MA: MIT Press.
*Hayden, Dolores. 1984. *Redesigning the American dream: the future of housing, work, and family life*, New York: W. W. Norton.
*Heresies. 1981. 3, no. 3, issue 11.
Horwitz, Lucy and Lou Ferleger. 1980. *Statistics for social change*. Boston: South End Press.
*Hubbard, Ruth, Mary Sue Henifin and Barbara Fried, eds. 1982. *Biological woman—the convenient myth*. Cambridge, MA: Schenkman Publishing.
*Jaggar, Alison M. 1983. *Feminist politics and human nature*. Totowa, NJ: Rowman & Allanheld.
*Kamerman, Sheila B. 1979. Work and family in industrialized societies. *Signs: Journal of Women in Culture and Society* 4, no. 4: 632–650.
*Keller, Evelyn Fox. 1980. Baconian science: a hermaphroditic birth. *Philosophical Forum* XI, no. 3 (Spring): 299–308.
*Keller, Evelyn Fox. 1983a. *A feeling for the organism: the life and work of Barbara McClintock*. San Francisco: W. H. Freeman.
*Keller, Evelyn Fox. 1983b. Women, science, and popular mythology. In *Machina ex dea*, ed. Joan Rothschild, 130–146. New York: Pergamon Press.
*Keller, Evelyn Fox. 1985. *Reflections on gender and science*. New Haven: Yale University Press.
*King, Ynestra. 1983. Toward an ecological feminism and a feminist ecology. In *Machina ex dea*, ed. Joan Rothschild, 118–129. New York: Pergamon Press.
*Kramer, Cheris. 1975. Women's speech: separate but unequal. In *Language and sex: difference and dominance*, eds. Barrie Thorne and Nancy Henley, 43–56. Rowley, MA: Newbury House.
Kranzberg, Melvin. 1964. Technology and human values. *Virginia Quarterly Review* 10 (Autumn): 578–592.
Kranzberg, Melvin, and Carroll Pursell, Jr, eds. 1967. *Technology in Western civilization I*. New York: Oxford University Press.
Layton, Edwin. 1971. *The revolt of the engineers: social responsibility and the American engineering profession*. Baltimore, MD: Johns Hopkins University Press (reissued 1986, with new introduction).

*Leacock, Eleanor. 1981. History, development, and the division of labor by sex: implications for organization. *Signs: Journal of Women in Culture and Society* 7, no. 2: 474–491.

*LeGuin, Ursula K. 1974. *The dispossessed*. New York: Avon Books.

Leiss, William, 1972. *The domination of nature*. New York: George Braziller; 1974. Boston: Beacon Press.

Levy, Steven. 1984. *Hackers: heroes of the computer revolution*. Garden City, NY: Anchor Press/Doubleday.

*Lowe, Marian. 1981. Cooperation and competition in science. *International Journal of Women's Studies* 4, no. 4: 362–367.

*Lowe, Marian and Ruth Hubbard, eds. 1983. *Woman's nature: rationalizations of inequality*. New York: Pergamon Press.

*Maccoby, Eleanor M. and Carol N. Jacklin. 1974. *The psychology of sex differences*. Stanford, CA: Stanford University Press.

MacKenzie, Donald. 1983. Militarism and socialist theory. *Capital and Class*, no. 19 (Spring); 33–73.

*Martin, Jane Roland. 1985. *Reclaiming a conversation: the ideal of the educated woman*. New Haven: Yale University Press.

Marx, Leo. 1986. The origins and present state of the debate. Unpublished paper delivered at Colloquium Series "The Two Cultures: Controversy Revisited," Cambridge, MA: Massachusetts Institute of Technology, 26 February.

*McGaw, Judith A. 1979. Technological change and women's work: mechanization in the Berkshire paper industry, 1820–1855. In *Dynamos and Virgins Revisited*, ed. Martha Trescott, 77–99. Metuchen, NJ: Scarecrow Press.

*McGaw, Judith A. 1982. Women and the history of American technology, review essay. *Signs: Journal of Women in Culture and Society* 7, no. 4 (Summer): 798–828.

*McGrath, Diane. 1986. The politics of technology in education. Paper delivered at Eighth Annual Convention, National Women's Studies Association, Champaign-Urbana, IL.

*McIntosh, Peggy. 1984. Interactive phases of curricular re-vision. In *Toward a balanced curriculum*, ed. Bonnie Spanier et al. 25–34. Cambridge, MA: Schenkman Publishing.

*McKay, John P., Bennett D. Hill and John Buckler. 1983. *A history of Western society*, 2nd ed. Boston: Houghton Mifflin.

*Merchant, Carolyn. 1980. *The death of nature: women, ecology, and the scientific revolution*. New York: Harper & Row.

*Merchant, Carolyn. 1983. Mining the earth's womb. In *Machina ex dea* ed. Joan Rothschild, 99–117. New York: Pergamon Press.

*Miller, Casey and Kate Swift. 1980. *The handbook of nonsexist writing for writers, editors and speakers*. New York: Harper & Row.

*Millett, Kate. 1969. *Sexual politics*. New York: Doubleday.

Mumford, Lewis. 1963. *Technics and civilization*. New York: Harcourt Brace Jovanovich.

Naisbitt, John. 1982. *Megatrends*. New York: Warner Books.

NLA News. 1985–. Stony Brook, NY: Department of Technology and Society, State University of New York.

*O'Brien, Mary. 1981. *The politics of reproduction*. Boston: Routledge & Kegan Paul.

*Ortner, Sherry B. 1974. Is female to male as nature is to culture? In *Woman, culture, and society*, ed. Michelle Zimbalist Rosaldo and Louise Lamphere, 67–87. Stanford, CA: Stanford University Press (originally published in *Feminist Studies*, no. 2 (Fall 1972): 5–31).

*Pacey, Arnold. 1983. *The culture of technology*. Cambridge, MA: MIT Press.

*Papanek, Hannah. 1977. Development planning for women. *Signs: Journal of Women in Culture and Society* 3, no. 1: 14–21.

*Piercy, Marge. 1976. *Woman on the edge of time*. New York: Alfred A. Knopf.

Pirsig, Robert M. 1975. *Zen and the art of motorcycle maintenance*. New York: Bantam Books.

*Reinharz, Shulamit. 1979. *On becoming a social scientist*. San Francisco: Jossey-Bass.

Reynolds, Terry S. and the Technology Studies and Education Committee of the Society for the History of Technology, comp. and ed. 1987. *The machine in the university: sample course syllabi for the history of technology and technology studies*, 2nd ed. Bethlehem, Pa: Lehigh University; Houghton, Mich: Michigan Technological University.

*Rich, Adrienne. 1979. Toward a woman-centered university. In *On lies, sekrets, and silence: selected prose 1966–1978*, 125–155. New York: W. W. Norton.

*Rosaldo, Michelle Zimbalist and Louise Lamphere, eds. 1974. *Woman, culture, and society*. Stanford, CA: Stanford University Press.

*Rosser, Sue V. 1986. *Teaching science and health from a feminist perspective: a practical guide*. New York: Pergamon Press.

*Rossiter, Margaret W. 1982. *Women scientists in America: struggles and strategies to 1940*. Baltimore: Johns Hopkins University Press.

*Rothschild, Joan, guest ed. 1981. Special issue. *Women's Studies International Quarterly* 4, no. 3.

*Rothschild, Joan, ed. 1982. *Women, technology and innovation*. New York: Pergamon Press.

*Rothschild, Joan, ed. 1983. *Machina ex dea: feminist perspectives on technology*. New York: Pergamon Press.

*Rowland, Robyn. 1984. Reproductive technologies: the final solution to the woman question? In *Test-tube women*, ed. Rita Arditti et al. 356–69. London: Pandora Press.

*Rubin, Gayle. 1975. The traffic in women: notes on the "political economy" of sex. In *Towards an anthropology of women*, ed. Rayna Rapp Reiter, 157–210. New York: Monthly Review Press.

*Ruddick, Sara. 1984. Preservative love and military destruction: some reflections on mothering and peace. In *Mothering*, ed. J. Trebilcot. Totowa, NJ: Rowman & Allanheld.

*Schweickart, Patrocinio. 1983. What if . . . science and technology in feminist utopias In *Machina ex dea*, ed. Joan Rothschild, 198–211. New York: Pergamon Press.

Science, Technology and Society Curriculum Development Newsletter. 1977–. Bethlehem, PA: STS Program, Lehigh University.

*Scott, Joan and Louise Tilly. 1975. Women's work and the family in nineteenth-century Europe. *Comparative Studies in Society and History* 17 (January): 36–64.

Signs: Journal of Women in Culture and Society. 1975–. Chicago: University of Chicago Press.

*Shelley, Mary. [1818] 1965. *Frankenstein*. New York: New American Library.

Skinner, B. F. 1976. *Walden Two Revisited*. New York: Macmillan.

*Smith, Dorothy. 1979. A sociology for women. In *The prism of sex: essays in the sociology of knowledge*, ed. Julia A. Sherman and Evelyn Torton Beck 135–188. Madison: University of Wisconsin Press.

*Smith, Judy. 1978. *Something old, something new, something borrowed, something due: women and appropriate technology*. Missoula, MT: Women and Technology Network (originally published by Butte, MT: National Center for Appropriate Technology, 1978).

Snow, C. P. 1959. *The two cultures and the scientific revolution*. Cambridge: Cambridge University Press.

Snow C. P. 1964. *The two cultures: and a second look*. rev. ed. Cambridge: Cambridge University Press.

*Spanier, Bonnie, Alexander Bloom and Darlene Boroviak, eds. 1984. *Toward a balanced curriculum*. Cambridge, MA: Schenkman Publishing.

*Spender, Dale. 1985. *Man made language*. 2nd ed. London: Routledge & Kegan Paul.

Staudenmaier, John M., S.J. 1985. *Technology's storytellers: reweaving the human fabric*. Cambridge, MA: MIT Press.

*Stimpson, Catharine. 1984. Where does integration fit: the development of women's studies. In *Toward a balanced curriculum*, eds. Bonnie Spanier, Alexander Bloom and Darlene Boroviak, 11–24. Cambridge, MA: Schenkman Publishing.

*Stimpson, Catharine with Nina Kressner Cobb. 1986. *Women's studies in the United States*. A Report to the Ford Foundation. New York: Ford Foundation.

*Stitzel, Judith, Ed Pytlik and Kate Curtis. 1985a. "Only connect": Developing a course on women in international development. Working Paper #83 (April). East Lansing: Michigan State University.

*Stitzel, Judith, Ed Pytlik and Kate Curtis. 1985b. "Only connect": developing a course on women in international development. *Women's Studies Quarterly* XIII, no. 2 (Summer): 33–35.

*Strange, Penny. 1983. *It'll make a man of you: a feminist view of the arms race*. Nottingham, England: Peace News/Mushroom Books.

*Strasser, Susan. 1982. *Never done: a history of American housework*. New York: Pantheon Books.

*Tavris, Carol and Carol Offir. 1977. *The longest war: sex differences in perspective*. New York: Harcourt Brace Jovanovich.

Technology and Culture. 1959–. Chicago: University of Chicago Press.

Teich, Albert H., ed. 1972. *Technology and man's future*. New York: St Martin's Press.

Teich, Albert H., ed. 1977. *Technology and man's future*. 2nd ed. New York: St Martin's Press.

Teich, Albert H., ed. 1981. *Technology and man's future*. 3rd ed. New York: St Martin's Press.

Teich, Albert H., ed. 1986. *Technology and the future*. 4th ed. New York: St Martin's Press.

Terminal: VDTs and women's health. 1985. Granada Television (G.B.) San Francisco: California Newsreel (film/video).

*Thorne, Barrie, Cheris Kramarae, and Nancy Henley, eds. 1983. *Language, gender, and society*. Rowley, Mass: Newbury House.

*Tinker, Irene. 1979. Women, technology, and poverty: some special issues. *Social Education* 43, no. 6: 444–445.

*Tobias, Sheila. 1978. *Overcoming math anxiety*. New York: W. W. Norton.

*Trescott, Martha Moore, ed. 1979. *Dynamos and virgins revisited: women and technological change in history*. Metuchen, NJ: Scarecrow Press.

Turing, Alan. [1950]. Computing machinery and intelligence. *Mind* 59: 433–460; repr. 1964. *Minds and machines*, ed. Alan Ross Anderson, 3–30. Englewood Cliffs, NJ: Prentice-Hall.

Turkle, Sherry. 1978. *Psychoanalytic politics: Freud's French Revolution*. New York: Basic Books.

*Turkle, Sherry. 1984a. *The second self: computers and the human spirit*. New York: Simon & Schuster.

*Turkle, Sherry. 1984b. Women and computer programming: a different approach. *Technology Review* (November–December): 48–50.

*Vanek, Joann. 1974. Time spent in housework. *Scientific American* 231, no. 5 (November): 116–120.

*Vetterling-Braggin, Mary, ed. 1981. *Sexist language: a modern philosophical analysis*. Totowa, NJ: Rowman & Littlefield.

Vonnegut, Kurt. 1952. *Player Piano*. New York: Dell Publishing.

*Westkott, Marcia. 1979. Feminist criticism of the social sciences. *Harvard Educational Review* 49, no. 4: 422–430.

Women's Studies International Forum. 1978–. Oxford: Pergamon Press (formerly *Women's Studies International Quarterly*).

Women's Studies Quarterly. 1972–. New York: The Feminist Press.

Zukav, Gary. 1980. *The dancing Wu Li masters*. New York: Bantam Books.

Additional Resources

(Some of these titles appear in the syllabi in the Appendix. Because full citations are not always given, the works are included here.)

Books

Abbott, Edith. 1918. *Women in industry: a study in American economic history*. New York: D. Appleton.

Arms, Suzanne. 1975. *Immaculate deception: a new look at women and childbirth in America*. Boston: Houghton Mifflin.

Baker, Elizabeth Faulkner. 1964. *Technology and women's work*. New York: Columbia University Press.

Barr, Marleen S., ed. 1981. *Future females: a critical anthology*. Bowling Green, OH: Bowling Green State University Popular Press.

Blewett, Mary H. 1988. *Men, women and work: a study in class, gender and protest in the 19th century New England shoe industry*. Urbana, IL: University of Illinois Press.

Boserup, Ester. 1970. *Women's role in economic development*. New York: St Martin's Press.

Brighton Women and Science Group, eds. 1980. *Alice through the microscope: the power of science over women's lives*. London: Virago Press.

Chapkis, W., ed. 1981. *Loaded questions: women in the military*. Amsterdam: Transnational Institute.

Chapkis, Wendy and Cynthia Enloe, eds. 1983. *Of common cloth: women in the global textile industry*. Amsterdam: Transnational Institute.

Cockburn, Cynthia. 1983. *Brothers: male dominance and technological change*. London: Pluto Press.

Corea, Gena. 1985. *The mother machine: reproductive technologies from artificial insemination to artificial wombs*. New York: Harper & Row.

Crompton, Rosemary and Gareth Jones. 1984. *White-collar proletariat: deskilling and gender in clerical work*. Philadelphia: Temple University Press.

Davies, Margery W. 1982. *Woman's place is at the typewriter: office work and office workers 1870–1930*. Philadelphia: Temple University Press.

D'Onofrio-Flores, Pamela and Sheila M. Pfafflin, eds. 1982. *Scientific–technological change and the role of women in development*. Boulder, CO: Westview Press.

Ehrenreich, Barbara and Deirdre English. 1973. *Witches, midwives and nurses: a history of women healers*. Old Westbury, NY: Feminist Press.

Enloe, Cynthia H. 1983. *Does Khaki become you? The militarization of women's lives*. Boston: South End Press; London: Pluto Press.

Faulkner, Wendy and Erik Arnold, eds. 1985. *Smothered by invention: technology in women's lives*. London: Pluto Press.

Foner, Philip S. 1977. *The Factory Girls*. Urbana, IL: University of Illinois Press.

Frederick, Christine. 1915. *Household engineering: scientific management in the home*. Chicago: New School of Economics.
Future, technology and woman. 1981. Proceedings of the Conference. San Diego, CA: San Diego State University, 6–8 March.
Hartmann, Heidi I., Robert E. Kraut and Louise A. Tilly, eds. 1986. *Computer chips and paper clips: technology and women's employment*. Vol. I. Washington, DC: National Academy Press.
Himes, Norman E. [1936] 1970. *Medical history of contraception*. New York: Schocken Books.
Holmes, Helen B., Betty B. Hoskins and Michael Gross, eds. 1980. *Birth control and controlling birth: women's perspectives*. Clifton, NJ: Humana Press.
Holmes, Helen B., Betty B. Hoskins and Michael Gross, eds. 1981. *The custom-made child? Women's perspectives*. Clifton, NJ: Humana Press.
Howe, Louise Kapp. 1977. *Pink collar workers*. New York: Avon Books.
Hudak, Leona M. 1978. *Early American women printers and publishers 1639–1820*. Metuchen, NJ: Scarecrow Press.
Huws, Ursula. 1982. *Your Job in the Eighties: A Woman's Guide to New Technology*. London: Pluto Press.
Jensen, Joan and Sue Davidson, eds. 1984. *A needle, a bobbin, a strike: women needleworkers in America*. Philadelphia: Temple University Press.
Josephson, Hannah. 1949. *The golden threads: New England's mill girls and magnates*. New York: Duell, Sloan & Pearce.
Kennedy, David M. 1971. *Birth control in America: the career of Margaret Sanger*. New Haven: Yale University Press.
Kraft, Philip. 1977. *Programmers and managers*. New York: Springer.
Leacock, Eleanor, Helen I. Safa and contributors. 1986. *Women's work: development and the division of labor by gender*. South Hadley, MA: Bergin & Garvey.
Malcolm, Shirley et al. 1985. *Science, technology and women: a world perspective*. Washington, DC: American Association for the Advancement of Science.
Marschall, Daniel and Judith Gregory, eds. 1983. *Office automation: Jekyll or Hyde?* Cleveland: Working Women Education Fund.
Matrix Collective. 1984. *Making space: women and the man made environment*. London: Pluto Press.
Mazey, Mary Ellen and David R. Lee. 1983. *Her space, her place: a geography of women*. Washington, DC: Association of American Geographers.
McIntyre, Vonda N. and Susan Janice Anderson, eds. 1976. *Aurora: beyond equality*. Greenwich, CT: Fawcett.
Mozans, H. J. 1913. *Woman and science*. New York: D. Appleton.
Office work in America. 1982. Cleveland: Working Women.
Pinchbeck, Ivy. 1930. *Women workers and the Industrial Revolution 1750–1850*. London: George Routledge & Sons.
Race against time: automation of the office. 1980. Cleveland: Working Women, National Association of Women Office Workers, April.
Reuther, Rosemary Radford. 1975. *New woman new earth: sexist ideologies and human liberation*. New York: Seabury Press.
Rich, Adrienne. 1976. *Of woman born: motherhood as an experience and institution*. New York: W. W. Norton.
Rich, Adrienne. 1979. Toward a woman-centered university. In Rich, *On lies, secrets and silence*. New York: W. W. Norton, 125–155.
Rodriguez-Trias, Helen, M. D. 1978. *Women and the health care system. Sterilization abuse*. Two lectures. New York: The Women's Center, Barnard College.
Rothman, Barbara Katz. 1986. *The tentative pregnancy: prenatal diagnosis and the future of motherhood*. New York: Viking Penguin.
Russ, Joanna. 1975. *The female man*. New York: Bantam Books.

Sacks, Karen Brodkin and Dorothy Remy, eds. 1984. *My troubles are going to have trouble with me: everyday trials and triumphs of women workers*. New Brunswick, NJ: Rutgers University Press.

Sandhu, Ruby and Joanne Sandler, comp. 1986. *The tech and tools book: a guide to technologies women are using worldwide*. New York: International Women's Tribune Center/IT Publications.

Sargent, Pamela, ed. 1975. *Women of wonder*. New York: Vintage Books.

Sargent, Pamela, ed. 1976. *More women of wonder*. New York: Vintage Books.

Sargent, Pamela, ed. 1978. *The new women of wonder*. New York: Vintage Books.

Stanley, Autumn 1988. *Mothers of invention*. Metuchen, NJ: Scarecrow Press (forthcoming).

Thompson, Dorothy, ed. 1983. *Over our dead bodies: women against the bomb*. London: Virago Press.

Tobias, Sheila, Peter Goudinoff, Stefan Leader and Shelah Leader. 1982. *What kinds of guns are they buying for your butter? A beginner's guide to defense, weaponry, and military spending*. New York: William Morrow.

Torre, Susana. 1977. *Women in American architecture: an historic and contemporary perspective*. New York: Whitney Library of Design.

Tripp, Maggie, ed. 1974. *Women in the Year 2000*. New York: Arbor House.

U.S. Congress, Office of Technology Assessment. 1985. *Automation of America's offices*. Washington, DC.

U.S. Department of Labor, Women's Bureau. 1985. *Women and office automation: issues for the decade ahead*. Washington, DC: US Department of Labor, Office of the Secretary, Women's Bureau.

Walshok, Mary Lindenstein. 1981. *Blue-collar women: pioneers on the male frontier*. Garden City, NY: Anchor Press/Doubleday.

Werneke, Diane. 1984. *Microelectronics and working women: a literature summary*. Washimgton, DC: National Academy Press.

Wertz, Richard W. and Dorothy C. Wertz. 1977. *Lying-in: a history of childbirth in America*. New York: Schocken Books.

Women and Geography Study Group of the IBG. 1984. *Geography and gender: an introduction to feminist geography*. London: Hutchinson.

Zimmerman, Jan, ed. 1983. *Technological woman: interfacing with tomorrow*. New York: Praeger.

Articles/Journals

Andrews, William D. and Deborah. 1974. Technology and the housewife in nineteenth-century America. *Feminist Studies* 2, no. 3: 309–328.

Arnold, Erik, Lynda Birke and Wendy Faulkner. 1981. Women and microelectronics: the case of word processors. *Women's Studies International Quarterly* 4, no. 3: 321–340.

Berch, Bettina, 1980. Scientific management in the home: the empress's new clothes. *Journal of American Culture* 3, no. 3: 440–445.

Bogdan, Janet. 1978. Care or cure? Childbirth practices in nineteenth century America. *Feminist Studies* 4, no. 2 (June): 92–99.

Bremner, William J. and David M. de Kretser. 1975. Contraceptives for males. *Signs: Journal of Women in Culture and Society* 1, no. 2 (Winter): 387–396.

Bruce, Margaret and Gill Kirkup. 1985. Post experience courses in technology for women: aims and processes. *Adult Education* 58, no. 1 (June): 40–50.

Bullough, Vern L. 1979. Female physiology, technology and women's liberation. In *Dynamos and virgins revisited*. ed. Martha Trescott, 233–251. Metuchen, NJ: Scarecrow Press.

Bush, Corlann G. 1982. The barn is his, the house is mine: agriciultural technology and sex roles. In *Energy and transport*, ed. George Daniels and Mark Rose, 235–259. Beverly Hills, CA: Sage Publications.

Chavkin, Wendy. 1979. Occupational hazards to reproduction: a review essay and annotated bibliography. *Feminist Studies* 5, no. 2 (Summer): 310–325.

Corea, Gena. 1980. The caesarean epidemic. *Mother Jones* V, no. VI (July): 28–35, 42.

Cowan, Ruth Schwartz. 1976. Two washes in the morning and a bridge party at night: the American housewife between the wars. *Women's Studies* 3, no. 2: 147–171.

Davies, Margery. 1974. Woman's place is at the typewriter: the feminization of the clerical labor force. *Radical America* 8, no. 4 (July–August).

Fee, Elizabeth and Michael Wallace. 1979. The history and politics of birth control: a review essay. *Feminist Studies* 5, no. 1 (Spring): 201–215.

Glenn, Evelyn Nakano and Roslyn L. Feldberg. 1977. Degraded and deskilled: the proletarianization of clerical work. *Social Problems* 25, no. 1 (October): 52–64.

Glenn, Evelyn Nakano and Roslyn L. Feldberg. 1979. Proletarianizing clerical work: technology and organizational control in the office. In *Case studies in the labor process*. ed. Andrew Zimbalist, 51–72. New York: Monthly Review Press.

Hacker, Sally. 1977. Farming out the home: women and agribusiness. *The Second Wave* 5 (Spring/Summer): 38–49.

Hafter, Daryl M. 1980. Agents of technological change: women in the pre- and post-industrial workplace. In *Women's lives: new theory, research and policy*, ed. Dorothy G. McGuigan, 159–168. Ann Arbor: University of Michigan Press.

Hafter, Daryl M. 1985. Artisans, drudges and the problem of gender in pre-industrial France. *Annals of the New York Academy of Science* 441 (April): 71–87.

Hanmer, Jalna. 1980. Sex predetermination, artificial insemination and the maintenance of male dominated culture. In *Women, health and reproduction*, ed. Helen Roberts, 163–190. London: Routledge & Kegan Paul.

Hanmer, Jalna and Pat Allen. 1980. Reproductive engineering: the final solution? In *Alice through the microscope: the power of science over women's lives*, ed. Brighton Women and Science Group, 208–227. London: Virago Press.

Haraway, Donna. 1978. Animal sociology and a natural economy of the body politic, Part I: A political physiology of dominance. *Signs: Journal of Women in Culture and Society* 4, no. 1 (Autumn): 21–36.

Haraway, Donna. 1978. Animal sociology and a natural economy of the body politic, Part II: The past is the contested zone: human nature and theories of production and reproduction in primate behavior studies. *Signs: Journal of Women in Culture and Society* 4, no. 1 (Autumn): 37–60.

Haraway, Donna. 1980. Women's place in the integrated circuit. *Radical America* (January).

Hartmann, Heidi. 1976. Capitalism, patriarchy, and job segregation by sex. In *Women and the workplace: the implications of occupational segregation*, eds. Martha Blaxall and Barbara Regan, 137–169. Chicago: University of Chicago Press.

Irvin, Helen Deiss. 1981. The machine in Utopia: Shaker women and technology. *Women's Studies International Quarterly* 4, no. 3: 313–319.

Jensen, Joan M. 1982. Churns and butter making in the Mid-Atlantic farm economy, 1750–1850. In *Working papers from the Regional Economic History Research Center* 5, nos. 2 and 3, ed. Glenn Porter and William H. Mulligan, 60–100. Greenville/Wilmington, DE: Eleutherian Mills-Hagley Foundation.

Kleinberg, Susan J. 1976. Technology and women's work: the lives of working class women in Pittsburgh, 1870–1900. *Labor History* (Winter): 58–72.

Kraft, Philip and Steven Dubnoff. 1986. Job content, fragmentation and control in computer software work. *Industrial Relations* 25 (Spring): 184–196.

Langer, Elinor. 1970. The women of the telephone company. *The New York Review of Books* XIV, 5 and 6 (12 and 26 March).

Leibowitz, Lila. 1983. Origins of the sexual division of labor. In *Woman's nature: rationalizations of inequality*, ed. Marian Lowe and Ruth Hubbard, 112–147. New York: Pergamon Press.

Levine, Susan. 1979. Ladies and looms: the social impact of machine power in the American carpet industry. In *Dynamos and virgins revisited*, ed. Martha Trescott, 67–76. Metuchen, NJ: Scarecrow Press.

Merchant, Carolyn, guest ed. 1984. Women and environmental history, special issue. *Environmental Review* VIII, no. 1 (Spring).

Murphree, Mary C. 1984. Brave new office: the changing world of the legal secretary. In *My troubles are going to have troubles with me*, ed. Karen Sacks and Dorothy Remy, 140–159. New Brunswick, NJ: Rutgers University Press.

Oliver, Sidney. 1980. Feminism, environmentalism and appropriate technology. *Quest: a Feminist Quarterly* V, no. 2: 70–80.

Olson, Margrethe H. 1983. Remote office work: changing work patterns in space and time. *Communications of the ACM* 26, no. 3 (March): 182–187.

The Politics of Reproduction. 1976. Issue theme: *Frontiers* 1, no. 2 (Spring).

Ris, Hania W. 1976. The essential emancipation: the control of reproduction. In *Beyond intellectual sexism*, ed. Joan Roberts, 85–110. New York: David McKay.

Rose, Hilary and Jalna Hanmer. 1976. Women's liberation, reproduction, and the technological fix. In *Sexual divisions and society: process and change*, ed. Diana Leonard Barker and Sheila Allen, 199–223. London: Tavistock.

Rothschild, Joan A. 1981. A feminist perspective on technology and the future. *Women's Studies International Quarterly* 4, no. 1: 65–74.

Rothschild, Joan. 1981. Technology, "women's work," and the social control of women. In *Women, power and political systems*, ed. Margherita Rendel, 160–183. London: Croom Helm.

Rothschild, Joan. 1983. Technology, housework and women's liberation: a theoretical analysis. In *Machina ex dea*, ed. Joan Rothschild, 79–93. New York: Pergamon Press.

Scott, Joan Wallach. 1982. The mechanization of women's work. *Scientific American* 247 (September): 166–187.

Stanley, Autumn. 1979. Mothers of invention. In *Proceedings: Society of Women Engineers National Conference, 1979*. New York: Society of Women Engineers.

Stanley, Autumn. 1981. Daughters of Isis, daughters of Demeter: when women sowed and reaped. *Women's Studies International Quarterly* 4, no. 3: 289–304.

Stanley, Autumn. 1983. Women hold up two-thirds of the sky. In *Machina ex dea* ed. Joan Rothschild, 3–22. New York: Pergamon Press.

Stiehm, Judith, guest ed. 1982. Women and men's wars, Special issue. *Women's Studies International Forum* 5, no. 3/4.

Thrall, Charles A. 1982. The conservative use of modern household technology. *Technology and Culture* 23, no. 2 (April): 175–194.

Tiptree, James, Jr [Alice Sheldon] 1978. Houston, Houston, do you read? In *Star songs of an old primate* [by] James Tiptree, Jr, 164–226. New York: Ballantine.

Vanek, Joann. 1978. Household technology and social status: rising living standards and status and residence differences in housework. *Technology and Culture* 19, no. 3 (July): 361–375.

Wesson, Celeste. 1981. Action from tragedy: women at Love Canal and Three Mile Island. *Heresies* no. 13, 40–43.

Women and Environments. Centre for Urban and Community Studies, Toronto, Ontario, Canada (journal).

Women's Rights Law Reporter. 1982. Symposium issue: Reproductive rights. 7, no. 3 (Spring).

Zimmerman, Jan. 1981. Technology and the future of women: haven't we met someplace before? *Women's Studies International Quarterly* 4, no. 3: 355–367.

Audio-Visual

(This list also includes films/videos appearing in the references.)

The blooms of Banjeli: technology and gender in African ironworking. 1986. South Hadley, MA:

Coalmining women. 1983. Whitesburg, KY: Appalshop Films (306 Madison Street, Whitesburg, KY 41858).

The electronic sweatshop. 1985. Les Productions du Regard et Les Productions Contre-Jour. San Francisco: California Newsreel (630 Natoma Street, San Franciso, CA 94103).

The global assembly line. 1986. Wayne, NJ: New Day Films (22 Riverview Drive, Wayne, NJ 07470–3191); also available from: Educational TV & Film Center (1947 Connecticut Avenue, Washington, DC 20009).

Hired hands. 1985. Judy Jackson, Channel 4 (G.B.). San Francisco: California Newsreel.

If you love this planet. 1982. Franklin Lakes, NJ: Direct Cinema Ltd. Library (PO Box 315, Franklin Lakes, NJ 07417); also available from: National Film Board of Canada (1251 Avenue of the Americas, 16th floor, New York, NY 10020).

The life and times of Rosie the riveter. 1980. Franklin Lakes, NJ: Clarity Educational Productions (PO Box 315, Franklin Lakes, NJ 07417).

Speaking our peace. 1985. Oley, PA: Bullfrog Films; also available from: The National Film Board of Canada (PO Box 6100, Station A, Montreal, Quebec, Canada H3C 3H5).

Terminal: VDT's and women's health. 1985. Granada Television (G.B.) San Francisco: California Newsreel.

Union Maids. 1977. Wayne, NJ: New Day Films.

Appendix

Course Syllabi

Over fifty replies were received to the questionnaire and request for syllabi, mainly from faculty in women's studies and STS programs. Of these respondents, about one-quarter reported not having relevant courses. Most of this group expressed interest in initiating such courses and thus in seeing the book. Almost another quarter forwarded syllabi that were not immediately relevant to the subject, the courses lacking feminist materials and/or focus at least in part on technology. Included in this group were proposed courses that had not been offered. More than half the respondents sent syllabi and/or course information directly relevant for preparing the book.

Twenty-two of these courses (one of which, Technology and Gender, has two syllabi) have been chosen to be printed in this Appendix as representative of the variety of approaches considered in the preceding pages. All of these syllabi are starred (*) in the text. A number of other courses, or course sequences, discussed have not been reprinted, either because the entire course was not relevant or because there was no one, representative sample of the variety of courses mentioned—as at the Open University in the United Kingdom. Of the courses included most are designed for undergraduates; two are on the graduate level only, and four are open to advanced undergraduates as well as graduate students. The courses represent 18 institutions, most of which are public. A list of student Interactive Qualifying Projects at Worcester Polytechnic Institute on women-related topics is included as the final Appendix item. Syllabi varied as to length and style. In the interest of creating a uniform and consistent appendix some information was omitted or edited. Syllabi are arranged alphabetically by course title. Each course is keyed to the chapter or chapters in which it is discussed.

COURSE TITLE: ARCHITECTURE AND PLANNING IN A FEMINIST SOCIETY: GRADUATE SEMINAR (CHAPTER 2)

Institution name: Massachusetts Institute of Technology.
Name(s) and departmental affiliation(s) of individual(s) teaching this course: Leslie Kanes Weisman, Visiting Associate Professor of Architecture.
Specific information regarding the course:
  Department(s)/Program(s) in which the course is listed: Architecture, Planning, and Women's Studies.
  Course level: Graduate and upper division undergraduate architecture majors.
  Sex ratio: Predominantly female.
  Prerequisites: None.
  Method of instruction: Lecture/seminar.

Texts:
  Heresies. # 11, Vol. 3, no. 3, 1981 and as noted on syllabus.
Methods of evaluation: Class participation, presentation and submission of term project.
Brief course description: The architectural forms and spatial arrangements of buildings, neighborhoods and cities reflect and reinforce the nature of gender, race, and class relations in society. In this seminar we will study society's buildings and spatial organization in terms of their social consequences from a feminist perspective. The disciplines of architecture and planning will be discussed in a relational analysis directed toward understanding why the acts of building and controlling space have been a male prerogative, how the built landscape shapes social experience and personal identity, and how we can begin to design and plan new housing, public buildings, communities, and urban space that challenge the patriarchal forms and values embodied in the "man-made" environment.

Special attention will be given to environments that support women's needs and enhance the quality of women's lives. Design concepts for shelters for battered and homeless women, and innovative housing and neighborhoods that support diverse households such as single person, single parent, intergenerational, dual career couples, and families of choice, will be developed through discussions about violence against women, poverty and aging, and changing conditions of work and family life. Design criteria for environments for childbirth and health care will be generated within the context of social controversies over child-bearing, reproductive freedom and practices in the male-dominated medical establishment. Schemes for buildings dedicated to women's accomplishments in fine arts, music, architecture, theater and so on, will emerge within an informed awareness of women's cultural contributions.

Other discussion topics include relationships among social values, gender roles and the Freudian characterization of architectural form and space as masculine/phallic or feminine/womblike; land use zoning as a mechanism for maintaining the social caste system; fantasy and utopian science fiction as devices for generating new environmental images and visions; and architecture as a means for social transformation.

Syllabus
Course "Text": Making Room, Women and Architecture, *Heresies, a Feminist Publication on Art and Politics.* issue 11, vol. 3, no. 3, 1981.
Articles cited below are published in *Heresies* unless otherwise noted. Other articles are available in a xeroxed reader on reserve in the library or available for purchase through me (L. K. Weisman).

	I. Architecture, Symbols, and Social Values

*February 4	Open informal talk and discussion:
	The Spatial Dimensions of Feminism
	  Introduction to my work in architecture, feminism and education
	  Course Overview
	  Reading: Leslie Kanes Weisman: "Women's Environmental Rights, A Manifesto," pp. 6–7

*February 11	Bodyscape As Landscape: Spatial Dichotomies and Social Relations
	  Reading: Mary Ellen Mazey and David R. Lee, "Her Role in Changing The Face of The Earth," Chapter 4, pp. 50–71, in *Her Space, Her Place*, Washington, DC: Association of American Geographers, 1983
	  Susan Saegert, "Masculine Cities, Feminine Suburbs," *Signs*, vol. 5, no. 3, Spring, 1980, pp. 96–111
	  Women and Geography Study Group of the BBG, "Urban

Spatial Structure," chapter 3, pp. 43–66, in *Geography and Gender*, London: Hutchinson, 1984

L. McDowell, "Towards An Understanding of the Gender Division of Urban Space," *Environment and Planning: Society and Space*, vol. 1, pp. 59–72, 1983

Leonore Davidoff, Jean L'Esperance, and Howard Newby, "Landscape With Figures: Home and Community in English Society," in Juliet Mitchell and Ann Oakley (eds.) *The Rights and Wrongs of Women*, New York: Penguin Books, 1976

February 18   NO CLASS, WASHINGTON'S BIRTHDAY

February 25   Female and Male Principles in Architecture

Reading: Diana Balmori, "Beatrix Farrand at Dumbarton Oaks," pp. 83–86

Sara Holmes Boutelle, "Women's Networks: Julia Morgan and Her Clients," pp. 91–94

Deborah Dietsch, "Lily Reich," pp. 73–76

Carol Gilligan, "Women's Place in Man's Life Cycle," pp. 224–239, in Sharon Lee Rich and Ariel Phillips (eds.) *Women's Experience and Education*, Cambridge: *Harvard Educational Review*, 1985

Margrit Kennedy, "Seven Hypotheses on Female and Male Principles in Architecture," pp. 12–13

Deborah Nevins, "Eileen Gray," pp. 68–72

Gail Price, "Cubes in the Sahara," p. 47

Jos Boys, "Is There A Feminist Analysis of Architecture?," *Built Environment*, vol. 10, no. 1, Oxford, England: Alexandrine Press, 1984, pp. 25–34

II. Spatial Dominance and Social Control

*March 4   Sexual Geography: The Territorial Imperative

Reading: Galen Cranz, "The Sharon Building," pp. 77–79

Galen Cranz, "Women and Urban Parks: Their Role as Users and Suppliers of Park Services," pp. 151–171, in Suzanne Keller (ed.) *Building For Women*, Lexington: Lexington Books, 1981

Annie Cheatham and Mary Clare Powell, "Waging Peace," chapter 11, pp. 198–218, in *This Way Day Break Comes, Women's Values and the Future*, Philadelphia: New Society Publishers, 1986

March 11   Body Boundaries and Social Trespasses: Sheltering Women From Rape and Battering

Reading: Minna Elias, "Man's Castle, Woman's Dungeon: Violence in the Home," pp. 3 and 14, in *Seventh Sister*, March, 1980

Women's Advocates and Julia Robinson *et al.*, "Women's Advocates Shelter: An Evaluation," Appendix III, pp. 69–73, University of Minnesota, July, 1983

Donna Duvall, "Emergency Housing for Women in Canada," *Ekistics* 310, January/February 1985, pp. 56–61

March 18   The Spatial Caste System

Reading: Lila Abu-Lughod, "A Community of Secrets: The Separate World of Bedouin Women," *Signs*, vol. 10, no. 4, 1985, pp. 637–657

Joan Greenbaum, "Kitchen Culture/Kitchen Dialectic," pp. 59–71

Jean E. Hess, "Domestic Interiors of Northern New Mexico," pp. 30–33

Nan Bauer Maglin, "Kitchen Dramas," pp. 42–46

Matrix Collective, "House Design and Women's Roles," chapter 5, pp. 55–80, in *Making Space, Women and the Man Made Environment*, London: Pluto Press, 1984

Nancy Lee Pollack, *Women on the Inside, Divisions of Space in Imperial China*, pp. 34–37

Anna Rubbo, "Housing Histories," pp. 39–41

March 25   NO CLASS, SPRING BREAK

April 1   Blueprint for Re-Designing Childbirth: Environments Related to Human Reproduction

Reading: Jan Bishop and Barbara Marks, "A Place of Birth," pp. 48–50

Richard W. Wertz and Dorothy C. Wertz, "Birth in the Hospital," chapter 5, pp. 132–177 and "Epilogue: The Search For The Best," pp. 234–248, in *Lying In, A History of Childbirth in America*, New York: Schocken Books, 1977

III. Housing, Communities, and Social Change

*April 8   Keeping Women House Poor: Discrimination by Design

Reading: Pat Therese Francis, "Where Do You Live?" pp. 10–11

Jacqueline Leavitt, "The Shelter Service Crisis and Single Parents," pp. 153–176, in Eugenie Ladner Birch (ed.) *The Unsheltered Woman*, New Brunswick: Center for Urban Policy Research, 1985

Susan Saegert, "The Androgynous City: From Critique to Practice," *Sociological Focus*, vol. 18, no. 2, Kent State University Department of Sociology and Anthropology, April 1, 1985, pp. 161–176

Leslie Kanes Weisman *et al.*, "Women in a Man Made Environment," in Julie Rigg and Julie Copland (eds.) *Coming Out: Women's Voices Women's Lives*, Australia: Thomas Nelson, 1985, pp. 24–34

Gerda Wekerle, "From Refuge to Service Center: Neighborhoods That Support Women," *Sociological Focus, op. cit.* pp. 79–95

April 15   Feminist Fantasies and Future Realities

Reading: Phyllis Birkby, "Herspace," pp. 28–29

Charlotte Perkins Gilman, "The Passing of the Home in Great American Cities," pp. 53–55

Dolores Hayden, "The Feminist Paradise Palace," pp. 56–58

Susana Torre, "Space as Matrix," pp. 51–52

Gwendolyn Wright, "The Woman's Commonwealth," pp. 24–27

Noel Phyllis Birkby and Leslie Kanes Weisman, "Women's Environmental Fantasies," *Heresies* 3, May 1977, pp. 116–117

Noel Phyllis Birkby and Leslie Kanes Weisman, "A Woman Built Environment, Constructive Fantasies," *Quest, A Feminist Quarterly, Future Visions*, vol. 11, no. 1, Summer 1975, pp. 7–18

Dolores Hayden, "What Would a Non-Sexist City Be Like?" *Signs*, vol. 5, no. 3, Spring 1980, pp. 170–187
Suzanne McKenzie, "Women Redesignating and Redesigning the City," *Canadian Woman Studies*, vol. 6, no. 2, 1985, pp. 5–8
Leslie Kanes Weisman *et al.*, "The Skin We Live and Work In," pp. 138–155, in Cheatham and Powell, *op. cit.*
In Ruby Rohrlich and Elaine Hoffman Baruch (eds.), *Women in Search of Utopia*, New York: Schocken Books, 1984:
  Arlene Sheer, "Findhorn, Scotland: The People Who Talk To Plants," pp. 146–156
  Batya Weinbaum, "Twin Oaks: A Feminist Looks at Indigenous Socialism in the United States," pp. 157–167
  Jan Zimmerman, "Utopia in Question: Programming Women's Needs Into the Technology of Tomorrow," pp. 168–176

April 22 NO CLASS, PATRIOTS DAY VACATION
April 29 TERM PROJECTS PRESENTED
May 6
May 13

*Designates open lecture.

* * * * *

COURSE TITLE: BODY POLITICS (CHAPTER 2)

Institution name: University of Delaware.
Name(s) and departmental affiliation(s) of individual(s) teaching this course: K. Turkel, Women's Studies.
Specific information regarding the course:
  Department(s)/Program(s) in which the course is listed: Women's Studies.
  Course level: Senior Seminar.
  Prerequisites: None.
  Method of instruction: Lecture/discussion.
Texts:
  Barbara Ehrenreich and Deirdre English, *For Her Own Good: 150 Years of the Experts' Advice to Women*, New York: Anchor Books, 1979
  Rita Arditti, Renate Duelli-Klein and Shelley Minden. *Test Tube Women: What Future For Motherhood?*, London: Pandora Press, 1984
  Wendy Chavkin, (ed.). *Double Exposure: Women's Health Hazards On the Job and At Home*, New York: Monthly Review Press, 1984
  Additional readings on library reserve.

Methods of evaluation: Three papers, group project, class participation.
Brief course description: As current controversy over birth control, abortion, and reproductive technology indicates, women's bodies are not necessarily their own. The options available to women are shaped by law, public policy, and technology. This course will examine the historical issues ranging from contraception, to reproductive technologies, to occupational health. Students will be asked to critically analyze the politics which shape these issues and the political, social, and economic implications which these issues hold for women and for the larger society.

Syllabus

	I. Introduction
February 11	Body Politics: An Overview of the Issues
	Reading: "Introduction," *Test-Tube Women*, pp. 1–8
	"Introduction," *Double Exposure*, pp. 1–19
	"Afterword," *For Her Own Good*, pp. 313–324

	II. Historical Background
February 13,	Historical Roots of Contemporary Issues
18 and 20	Reading: Chapters 1–4 in *For Her Own Good*
	Barker-Benfield, "Architect of the Vagina"
	Burnham, "Black Women As Producers and Reproducers for Profit"

	III. Gender and Science
February 25,	The Question of Scientific Objectivity
27	Reading: Fee, "Women's Nature and Scientific Objectivity"
	Bleier, "The Subordinance of Women: a Problematic Universal"
	Keller, "Introduction," *Gender and Science*
	Hubbard, "Have Only Men Evolved?"
	Gould, "American Polygeny and Craniometry Before Darwin"
	Gould, and "A Positive Conclusion"

	IV. The Politics of Reproduction
March 4, 6,	Controlling Fertility: Contraception and Abortion
11, 13, 18	Reading: Section entitled "To Have Or Not To Have A Child," in *Test-Tube Women* (all articles)
	Petchesky, "Considering the Alternatives: The Problem of Contraception"
	Luker, "Women and the Right to Abortion" and "Emergence of the Right-To-Life Movement"
	Petchesky, "Morality and Personhood: A Feminist Perspective"

	FIRST REACTION PAPER—DUE MARCH 18
March 20, 25	Technology and Expertise
	Reading: Chapters 6, 7 in *For Her Own Good*
	Kranzberg, "Technology: the Half-Full Cup"
	Florman, "Technology and the Tragic View"
	Broomfield, "High Technology: the Construction of Disaster"
	Rothman, "The Meanings of Choice In Reproductive Technology," in *Test-Tube Women*, pp. 23–33

	SPRING BREAK—March 28–April 6
March 27,	Childbirth and Reproductive Technologies
April 8, 10,	Reading: Hubbard, "Personal Courage Is Not Enough: Some Hazards of Childbearing in the 1980s," in *Test-Tube Women*, pp. 331–355
15 and 17	Holland and McKenna, "Regaining Trust," in *Test-Tube Women*, pp. 414–418
	Section entitled "Test-Tube Women," in *Test-Tube Women* (all articles)

Saxton, "Born and Unborn: the implications of Reproductive Technologies for People with Disabilities," in *Test-Tube Women*, pp. 298–312

Rapp, "Xylo: A True Story," in *Test-Tube Women*, pp. 313–328

Gallagher, "The Fetus and the Law—Whose Life Is It Anyway?"

Harrison, Excerpts from *A Woman in Residence*

April 22, 24	V. Women in the Workplace: More Than a Paycheck At Home or Away: The Varieties of Occupational Threats to Women's Health Reading: Part 1 and Rosenberg, "The Home is The Workplace," pp. 219–245 in *Double Exposure*
April 29	The Potential Mother: Exclusionary Policies in the Workplace
May 1	Reading: Part 2 in *Double Exposure*

SECOND REACTION PAPER—DUE APRIL 29

May 6, 8, 12, 15, 20	VI. Student Presentations Group Presentations by Members of the Class

May 22	VII. Possibilities for the Future Reading: Freudenberg and Zaltzberg, "From Grassroots Activism to Political Power: Women Organizing Against Environmental Hazards," in *Double Exposure*, pp. 219–245 Hanmer, "A Womb of One's Own," in *Test-Tube Women*, pp. 438–448 Schweickart, "What if ... Science and Technology in Feminist Utopias"

FINAL PAPERS DUE NO LATER THAN MAY 20, BUT MAY BE TURNED IN EARLIER

*   *   *   *   *

COURSE TITLE: CAREERS/TRENDS IN ROBOTICS (CHAPTER 3)

Institution name: Lane Community College, Oregon.
Name(s) and departmental affiliation(s) of individual(s) teaching this course: Renée LoPilato, Industrial Technology Programs and Women's Programs.
Specific information regarding the course:
   Departments/Programs in which the course is listed: Industrial Technology Programs, Community Education Division.
   Course level: Undergraduates, especially women with no entry skills.
   Sex ratio: Predominantly female.
   Prerequisites: None.
   Method of instruction: Laboratory hands on and lectures.
Texts: See syllabus.
Methods of evaluation: Completion of projects, attendance and attitude.

Brief course description: An overview of the current issues involved in the use of robots in the labor force, its effects on new careers, and identification of necessary schooling and training for these new skills. Hands on experience is stressed through actual programming and manipulating a small robot. Designed for those with no previous experience.

Other features of the course: Industrial site visits.

Syllabus

1   Definition and History—"Artificial Intelligence"
   A. State-of-the-art—flexible, reprogrammable automation applications
   B. Demonstration with HERO I—show components of stepping motor: performs various experiments; review training manual
   C. Emphasize different general areas necessary to operate robot, i.e. hydraulics, pneumatics, numerical controls, mechanics, electronics, etc

2   Robotic Applications
   A. View "Industrial Applications" videotape
   B. Discuss which fields of undersea mining, medicine, and industry utilize robot automation
   C. Identify specific kinds of training, skills, abilities, and aptitudes which are necessary for a variety of careers in robotics
   D. Where is training offered?
      1. A survey review of community colleges and four-year schools in Oregon that currently, or in the future, will offer relevant course work
      2. Review 1985 *Directory of Robotics Education and Training Institutions*, for schools with training located outside of Oregon
   E. Review relevant LCC programs and courses to determine what skills are transferable—review mechanics, electronics, computer science, software and math science courses. Have individual area counselors address academic questions

3   Industrial Site Visit
   A. Possibilities include Intelledex, Corvallis and Eckland Construction Company or Wright Communication Service, both of Eugene
   B. Each student will take notes on types of jobs seen there and description of job tasks
   C. Describe robots manufactured and their uses
   D. Describe productivity of robots

4   Class Discussion
   A. Discussion on focusing on the short and long term effects of the import of robotics on labor force in this country
   B. Handouts of articles on displaced worker estimates and need for retraining costs. Who will pay?
   C. Discuss articles on "10 Significant Breakthroughs" and project variety of high and low tech careers that will probably spawn in the next 20 years

5   Demonstration with HERO I
   A. Emphasis on voice capabilities. Handouts explaining how to program.
      1. Speech component using phoneme categories (voice synthesis)
      2. Learn Mode: each student designs a set of movements that will direct the robot to complete a task
      3. Review other 8 U.S. manufacturers of personal robots, capabilities, and costs

*   *   *   *   *

COURSE TITLE: GENDER ISSUES IN TECHNOLOGY (CHAPTER 2, CHAPTER 5)

Institution name: Washington State University.

Name(s) and departmental affiliation(s) of individual(s) teaching this course: Susan Weeks, Sociology and Women's Studies, and Jay McLean-Riggs, Women's Studies.

Specific information regarding the course:

Departments/Programs in which the course is listed: Women's Studies.

Course level: Lower division undergraduate.

Sex ratio: Predominantly female.

Prerequisites: None.

Method of instruction: Lectures, discussion, laboratory.

Texts:

Elizabeth Dodson Gray, *Patriarchy as a Conceptual Trap.* Wellesley, MA: Roundtable Press, 1982

Joan Rothschild, *Machina* Ex Dea*: Feminist Perspectives on Technology.* New York: Pergamon, 1983

Sheila Tobias, *Overcoming Math Anxiety.* New York: W. W. Norton, 1978

Packet of readings, available at Kinko's Copies, NE 1000 Colorado St.

Two floppy disks to use with Apple IIE Computer

Methods of evaluation: Examinations, short reaction papers, math and computer projects.

Brief course description: Course addresses gender issues related to technology and mathematics and helps students overcome math anxiety by understanding its causes and consequences. The course offers both theoretical understanding and practical means of alleviating math anxiety and stress. Approximately one-third of the semester is spent in learning and applying math and computer skills. Students explore their personal history with respect to math and technology, using an extensive math autobiography to gain insight into their abilities. They then establish that their conceptual grasp of math is correct by doing problems in such a way that they initially draw on their intuition, and then discover the method that they used and apply it to more formidable problems. Word processing skills are also taught, and students learn to format assignments to be turned in.

The remaining two-thirds of the course will be on the following topics and readings.

Syllabus

1 Why Study Women and Technology?

How women's experience with technology differs from men's

Underrepresentation of women in scientific fields

2 Sex Role Socialization

How socialization affects female career patterns, life choices and attitudes towards math and technology

Reading: Gray, *Patriarchy as a Conceptual Trap*

Sara Kiesler, Lee Sproull and Jacquelynne S. Eccles, "Second-Class Citizens?". *Psychology Today* 17 (March 1983): 41–48.

Film: *Pinks and Blues*

3 Math Anxiety

Research and attitudes on male/female abilities in math

Reading: Tobias, *Overcoming Math Anxiety*

H.J. McLean-Riggs, Speculations on Mathematical Literacy. Unpublished paper, Washington State University, Spring, 1985.

Film: *Math Anxiety*

4 Technology and Society

Technology's place in the larger society, especially as an instigator of social change

Reading: David Freeman, "Technology and Society: the Problem" in *Technology and Society: Issues in Assessment, Conflict and Choice.* by David Freeman (New York: Rand McNally, 1974).

Bush, "Women and the Assessment of Technology," in Rothschild

Zoe Tracy Hardy, "What Did You Do in the War, Grandma?". *MS.* (Aug 1985): 75–78.

5   Women as Antitechnocrats

Why are there so few women scientists?

The relationship between gender and science

Women scientists in history

The effect of gender on computer programming

The historical association of women with nature.

Reading: Sherry Turkle, "Women and Computer Programming: A Different Approach". *Technology Review* (Nov–Dec 1984): 48–50.

Marian Lowe, "Cooperation and Competition in Science". *International Journal of Women's Studies* (1981): 362–367.

Hypatia's Sisters: Biographies of Women Scientists, Past and Present. University of Washington Women Studies Program, (Summer, 1975).

Judy Smith, "Women and Technology: What is at Stake?". *Graduate Woman.* (Mar–Apr 1981): 8–11.

Samuel C. Florman, "Will Women Engineers Make a Difference?". *Technology Review* (Nov–Dec 1984): 51–52.

Keller, "Women, Science and Popular Mythology," in Rothschild

Merchant, "Mining the Earth's Womb," in Rothschild

6   Women as Homemakers

Household technology: men design it, women use it

1920–1980: number of hours spent on housework unchanged

Reading: Frances GABe, "The GABe Self-Cleaning House," in *The Technological Woman: Interfacing With Tomorrow.* Jan Zimmerman, ed. (New York: Praeger, 1983).

Rothschild, "Technology, Housework and Women's Liberation," in Rothschild

7   Women as Paid Workers

Impacts of technology on women in the workplace

Reading: Feldberg, "Technology and Work Degradation," in Rothschild

Judith Gregory, "The Next Move: Organizing Women in the Office," in *The Technological Woman: Interfacing with Tomorrow.* Jan Zimmerman, ed. (New York: Praeger, 1983).

Peter Calthorpe, "The Back Office: Post-industrial Factories". *Whole Earth Review* (Jan 1985): 30–31.

Joan Howe, "Housebound". *Whole Earth Review* (Jan 1985): 21.

8   Women as Bearers and Rearers of Children

Women as marginal in the labor force

Women with interrupted career patterns

Impacts of new reproductive technologies

Reading: Linda Gordon "Birth Control: An Historical Study". *Science for the People* (Jan–Feb 1977): 10–16.

Suzanne Rubin, "Reproductive Options I: A Spermdonor Baby Grows Up," in *The Technological Woman: Interfacing with Tomorrow.* Jan Zimmerman, ed. (New York: Praeger, 1983).

Karen Smith, "Reproductive Options II: An Interview With Karen Smith," in *The Technological Woman: Interfacing with Tomorrow.* Jan Zimmerman, ed. (New York: Praeger, 1983).

Hanmer, "Reproductive Technologies: The Future for Women?" in Rothschild

9   Women, Technology and the Future
    How can women gain control of the technology that affects their lives?
    Public policy issues
    Reading: Jan Zimmerman, "Technology and the Future of Women: Haven't We
            Met Somewhere Before?" *Women's Studies International Quarterly*
            4(3) (1981): 355–367.
            Patricia Huckle, "Feminism: A Catalyst for the Future," in *The
            Technological Woman: Interfacing with Tomorrow.* Jan Zimmerman,
            ed. (New York: Praeger, 1983).
            Rothschild, "Afterword: Machina Ex Dea and Future Research"

*   *   *   *   *

COURSE TITLE: MAN AND HIS IMAGE OF NATURE: GENDER-RELATED PERSPECTIVES ON SCIENCE AND TECHNOLOGY (CHAPTER 5)

Institution name: University of Sussex, U.K.
Name(s) and departmental affiliation(s) of individual(s) teaching this course: Brian
    Easlea, Science Studies Group.
Specific information regarding the course:
    Departments/Programs in which the course is listed: School of Culture and
    Community Studies.
    Course level: Undergraduates in the humanities.
    Sex ratio: Predominantly female.
    Prerequisites: None.
    Method of instruction: Seminar.
Texts:
    Joan Rothschild, *Machina ex Dea: Feminist Perspectives on Technology*
    Plus readings listed in the syllabus.
Methods of evaluation: Assessment essays.
Brief course description: The course examines the role of gender in science and
    technology, specifically through the problematic phenomenon of sexuality.
    Arguments and counter arguments are explored concerning the ways in which
    masculine images and concepts of sexuality inform our views of nature and our
    conduct of science and technology.

Syllabus
Seminar 1   The Place of Sexuality, Reproduction and Science in Feminist Utopias
            Reading: Patrocinio Schweickart, "What if . . . Science and Technology
            in Feminist Utopias," in Rothschild, chapter 12
            Marge Piercy, *Woman on the Edge of Time*, 1976; Women's
            Press, 1979
            Ursula Le Guin, *The Dispossessed*, 1975; London: Granada,
            1983
Seminar 2   Gender, Masculinity and Modern Science
            Reading: Nancy Chodorow, "Family Structure and Feminine
            Personality," in M.Z. Rosaldo and L. Lamphere (eds.),
            Woman, Culture, and Society, Stanford University Press, 1974
            Sandra Harding, "Gender Politics of Infancy," *Quest: A
            Feminist Quarterly* vol. 3, 1981, pp. 53–70
            Evelyn Fox Keller, "Women, Science, and Popular
            Mythology," in Rothschild, chapter 8

Seminar 3   Sexuality and Violence: How Gentle and Loving Can Sexuality Be?
           Reading: Lynne Segal, "Sensual Uncertainty," in Sue Cartledge and
                  Joanna Ryan (eds.), *Sex and Love: New Thoughts on Old
                  Contradictions*, Women's Press, 1983
                  Jessica Benjamin, "The Bonds of Love: Rational Violence
                  and Erotic Domination," *Feminist Studies* vol. 6, 1980,
                  pp. 144–174

Seminar 4   Modern Science and "The Masculine Birth of Time"
           Reading: Carolyn Merchant, "Mining the Earth's Womb," in
                  Rothschild, chapter 6
                  J.D. Bernal, *The World, the Flesh and the Devil: An Inquiry
                  into the Three Enemies of the Rational Soul*, 1929; Jonathan
                  Cape, 1970

Seminar 5   Thoughts on the Prolonged Death of "Mother" Nature
           Reading: *Either* David Goodman, "God and Nature in the Philosophy
                  of Descartes," in *Towards a Mechanistic Philosophy*, Milton
                  Keynes Open University Press, 1974, AMST 283, Unit 4,
                  pp. 9–42
                  or R.S. Westfall, *The Construction of Modern Science*,
                  Chichester, U.K.: John Wiley, 1971, chapters 2 and 5
                  Janna Thompson, "Women and the High Priests of Reason,"
                  Radical Philosophy no. 34, Summer, 1983, pp. 10–14
                  Jacques Monod, *Chance and Necessity: An Essay on the
                  Natural Philosophy of Modern Biology*, 1970; London:
                  Collins, 1972, chapters 1–2, 6–9

Seminar 6   Feminist Views on the Nuclear Arms Race
           Reading: Charlene Spretnak, "Naming the Cultural Forces that Push
                  Us Toward War," *Journal of Humanistic Psychology* 23,
                  1983, pp. 104–114
                  Penny Strange, *It'll Make a Man of You: A Feminist View of
                  the Arms Race*, Nottingham: Mushroom Books, 1983

Seminar 7   The Future of Reproduction
           Reading: Leon Kass, "Making Babies—The New Biology and the 'Old'
                  Morality," *The Public Interest*, Winter, 1972, pp. 18–56.
                  Peter Roberts, "The Brennan Story: A Small Miracle of
                  Creation," in W. Walters and P. Singer (eds.), *Test-Tube
                  Babies: A Guide to Moral Questions, Present Technologies
                  and Future Possibilities*, Oxford: Oxford University Press,
                  1982
                  Jalna Hanmer, "Reproductive Technology: The Future for
                  Women?" in Rothschild, chapter 11

Seminar 8   "An End to Technology" or A Possibility of Liberation
           Reading: Joan Rothschild "Technology, Housework, and Women's
                  Liberation," in Rothschild, chapter 5
                  Sally M. Gearhart, "An End to Technology: A Modest
                  Proposal," in Rothschild, chapter 10
                  Ynestra King, "Toward an Ecological Feminism and a
                  Feminist Ecology," in Rothschild, chapter 7

*   *   *   *   *

COURSE TITLE: PROGRESS, TECHNOLOGY AND GENDER, OR, IMPERATIVES OF TECHNOLOGY (CHAPTER 5)

Institution name: University of Sussex, U.K.
Name(s) and departmental affiliation(s) of individual(s) teaching this course: Brian Easlea, Science Studies Group.
Specific information regarding the course:
  Departments/Programs in which the course is listed: Science Policy Research Unit.
  Course level: Graduate students for Master of Science degree in Science, Technology and Industrialization.
  Sex ratio: Equal.
  Prerequisites: None.
  Method of instruction: Seminar.
Texts: See syllabus.
Methods of evaluation: Assessment essays.
Brief course description: The course explores, contrasts, and compares Marxist, psychosexual, and feminist perspectives on the driving forces of technology, revealing the complex gender dimension of technological imperatives.

Syllabus

Seminar 1   Marx vs Freud on the Realm of Freedom

Reading: K. Marx, *Grundrisse*, London: Penguin, 1973, pp. 161–162, 407–416, 487–488, 611–612, 705–706, 711–714

A. Gorz, *Farewell to the Working Class*, London: Pluto Press, 1980, chapters 7–9, *or*

A. Gorz, *Paths to Paradise*, London: Pluto Press, 1985, chapter 4, "A Way Out of Capitalism" and "By Way of a Conclusion," pp. 40–77

J. Schmidt and J. Miller, "Aspects of Technology in Marx and Rousseau," in T. de Lauretis et al. (eds.), *The Technological Imagination*, Coda Press, 1980

S. Freud, *Civilization and its Discontents*, 1930–31; New York: Norton, 1962, chapters 5, 6 and 8

S. Freud, "Some Psychical Consequences of the Anatomical Distinction Between the Sexes," 1925, in *On Sexuality*, London: Penguin Freud Library, 1977, vol. 7 *or* "Femininity," 1932, in *New Introductory Lectures on Psychoanalysis*, London: Penguin Freud Library, 1973, vol. 2

Seminar 2   Simone de Beauvoir and Sherry Ortner: Male Culture as Transcendence, Female Nature as Immanence

Reading: S. de Beauvoir, *The Second Sex*, 1949; London: Penguin, 1971, Part 1, chapters 2–3, Part 2, chapters 1–2, Part 3, chapter 1 and Part 7 "Towards Liberation"

M. Collins and C. Pierce, "Holes and Slime: Sexism in Sartre's Psychoanalysis," *The Philosophical Forum* 5, 1973, pp. 112–127, reprinted in C.C. Gould and M. Wartofsky (eds.), *Women and Philosophy*, (New York: Perigee Books, 1980

D. Dinnerstein, *The Mermaid and the Minotaur*, 1976, published in the U.K. as *The Rocking of the Cradle and the Ruling of the World*, London: Souvenir Press, pp. 124–134, 207–228

S. Ortner, "Is Female to Male as Nature is to Culture?," in M.Z. Rosaldo and L. Lamphere (eds.), *Woman, Culture, and Society*, Stanford University Press, 1974

H. Eisenstein, *Contemporary Feminist Thought*, London: Allen & Unwin, 1984, chapter 2 "The Public/Domestic Dichotomy . . ."

E.F. Kittay, "Womb Envy: An Explanatory Concept," in J. Trebilcot (ed.), *Mothering: Essays in Feminist Theory*, Rowman & Allanheld, 1984

Seminar 3   The Witch-hunting Imperative: Generalised Fear and Hatred of the Dangerous Feminine?

Reading: B. Easlea, *Witch-Hunting, Magic and the New Philosophy*, Brighton, U.K.: Harvester Press, 1980, chapter 1

C. Merchant, *The Death of Nature*, London: Wildwood House, 1982, chapter 5 "Nature as Disorder: Women and Witches"

G. Geiss vs H.V. McLachlan and J.K. Swales, "Lord Hale, Witches and Rape," *British Journal of Law and Society* 5, 1978, pp. 26–44 and 251–261

C. Larner, "Was Witch-Hunting Woman-Hunting?," *New Society*, 10 October, 1981, reprinted in C. Larner, *Witchcraft and Religion*, Oxford: Basil Blackwell, 1984

R. Hasted, "The New Myth of the Witch" and L. Mitchell, "Enemies of God or Victims of Patriarchy," *Trouble and Strife* no. 2, Spring, 1984, pp. 10–20

R.A. Horsley, "Who were the Witches? The Social Roles of the Accused in the European Witch Trials," *Journal of Interdisciplinary History* vol. 9, 1979, pp. 689–715

J.P. Demos, *Entertaining Satan: Witchcraft and the Culture of Early New England*, Oxford: Oxford University Press, 1982, pp. 60–64, 153–157, 197–210, 394–400

Seminar 4   The Scientific Imperative: Culture's Conquest of "Female" Nature?

Reading: W. Leiss, *The Domination of Nature*, Braziller, 1972, chapter 3 "Francis Bacon"

C. Merchant, *The Death of Nature*, London: Wildwood House, 1982, chapter 7 "Dominion over Nature"

B. Easlea, *Fathering the Unthinkable*, London: Pluto Press, 1983, chapters 1–2

E.F. Keller, "Spirit and Reason at the Birth of Modern Science," *Reflections on Gender and Science*, Yale University Press, 1985

J.D. Bernal, *The World, the Flesh and the Devil*, 1929; London: Jonathan Cape, 1970, *or*

J.B.S. Haldane, *Daedalus, or Science and the Future*, London, 1923, *or*

H.J. Muller, *Out of the Night*, London, 1936

D. Dinnerstein, *The Mermaid and the Minotaur*, "Notes towards chapter 6" and chapter 6 "Sometimes You Wonder if They're Human," pp. 88–114

I.D. Balbus, *Marxism and Domination*, Princeton University Press, 1982, chapter 9 especially pp. 334–352

Critique of Chodorow and Dinnerstein:

J.B. Elshtain, "Symmetry and Soporifics: A Critique of Feminist Accounts of Gender Development," in B. Richards (ed.), *Capitalism and Infancy: Essays on Psychoanalysis and Politics*, Free Association Books, 1984

Seminar 5   The Gestational Imperative: Replacement of the Feminine?
For a feminist overview:
Reading: Mary O'Brien, *The Politics of Reproduction*, London: Routledge & Kegan Paul, 1981, chapters 1 and 6
On new techniques such as "IVF" and "ET":
W. Walters and P. Singer (eds.), *Test-Tube Babies*, Oxford: Oxford University Press, 1982, chapter 1
For conflicting views on the moral status of the embryo:
W. Walters and P. Singer (eds.), *Test-Tube Babies*, chapter 5
In favour of, for example, limited experimentation on living human embryos:
P. Singer and D. Wells, *Reproduction Revolution*, Oxford: Oxford University Press, 1984, chapters 3–5
M. Warnock, *Report of the Committee of Inquiry into Human Fertilization and Embryology*, London: Stationery Office, 1984, chapters 1, 8, 11 and *Expressions of Dissent*, pp. 87–94, reprinted as M. Warnock, *A Question of Life*, Oxford: Basil Blackwell, 1985
Against current trends:
Reading: L.R. Kass, "Making Babies," *The Public Interest*, Winter, 1972, pp. 15–56
J. Hanmer, "Reproduction Technology: The Future for Women?," in J. Rothschild, *Machina ex Dea*, Oxford: Pergamon Press, 1983
R. Rowland, "Reproductive Technologies: The Final Solution to the Woman Question?," in R. Arditti et al. (eds.), *Test-Tube Women*, London: Pandora Press, 1984
In favour of positive eugenics and the disappearance of phenotypic gender differences, see, for example,
D. Fernbach, *The Spiral Path*, Gay Men's Press, 1981, pp. 57–58, 124–125

Seminar 6   The Weapons Imperative: Neomarxist, Psychosexual and Feminist Perspectives
Reading: D. MacKenzie, "Militarism and Socialist Theory," *Capital and Class*, Spring, 1983
M. Mann, "Capitalism and Militarism," in M. Shaw (ed.), *War, State and Society*, Basingstoke, U.K. Macmillan, 1984
W. James, "Remarks at the Peace Banquet" and "The Moral Equivalent of War," in W. James, *Essays in Religion and Morality*, Harvard University Press, 1982, and in R.A. Wasserstrom (ed.), *War and Morality*, Wadsworth, 1970
B. Easlea, *Fathering the Unthinkable*, London: Pluto Press, 1983, chapters 3–4
S. Mansfield, *The Gestalts of War*, New York: Dial Press, 1982, chapters 12 and 13
P. Strange, *It'll Make a Man of You: A Feminist View of the Arms Race*, Nottingham: Peace News/Mushroom Books, 1983, pp. 3–29
P. Parrinder, "The Prophets of Doom," *New Society*, 27 September 1984, pp. 354–355
H. Caldicott, *Missile Envy: The Arms Race and Nuclear War*, New York: William Morrow, 1984, penultimate chapter, "Missile Envy and Other Psychopathology"
S. Ruddick, "Preservative Love and Military Destruction: Some Reflections on Mothering and Peace," in J. Trebilcot (ed.), *Mothering*, Totowa, NJ: Rowman & Allanheld, 1984

Ian McEwan, *Or Shall We Die?*, London: Jonathan Cape, 1983
A. Carter, "Anger in a Black Landscape," in D. Thompson (ed.), *Over Our Dead Bodies: Women Against the Bomb*, London: Virago Press 1983

Seminar 7   Sadomasochistic Imperatives: Origins and Implications
Reading: S. de Beauvoir, *The Second Sex*, 1949; London: Penguin, 1972, Part 4, chapter 3 and Part 6, chapter 2
Ian McEwan, *The Comfort of Strangers*, London: Picador, 1982
Angela Carter, "The Bloody Chamber," in *The Bloody Chamber*, London: Penguin, 1981
P. Califia, "Feminism and Sadomasochism," *Heresies* 3, 1981, pp. 30–34
H. Eisenstein, *Contemporary Feminist Thought*, Allen & Unwin, 1984, chapter 12 "Pornography and Sadomasochism".
J. Benjamin, "Master and Slave: The Fantasy of Erotic Domination," in A. Snitow et al. (eds.), *Powers of Desire: The Politics of Sexuality* New York: Monthly Review Press, 1983, pp. 280–299 (published in the U.K. as *Desire*). This is a condensed version of Benjamin's paper "The Bonds of Love: Rational Violence and Erotic Domination," *Feminist Studies*, vol. 6, 1980, pp. 144–174, reprinted in H. Eisenstein and A. Jardine (eds.), *The Future of Difference*, Boston: G.K. Hall, 1980
D.H. George with N.A. Luce, "Toward Psychoanalytic Feminism," in M.M. Murray (ed.), *Face to Face*, Greenwood Press, 1983
R.R. Linden et al. (eds.), *Against Sadomasochism*, Frog in the Well, 1982, Introduction by R.R. Linden and articles by M. Jonel (pp. 16–22), H. Hein (pp. 83–89) and J. Stoltenberg (pp. 124–130)
Paula Caplan, "The Myth of Women's Masochism," *American Psychologist* vol. 39, 1984, 130–139

Seminar 8   Towards the Just and Peaceful Society: Insights from Science Fiction
Reading: P. Schweickart, "What if . . . Science and Technology in Feminist Utopias," in J. Rothschild (ed.), *Machina ex Dea*, Oxford: Pergamon Press, 1983
Ursula Le Guin, *The Dispossessed*, 1975; London: Granada, 1983
Marge Piercy, *Woman on the Edge of Time*, 1976; Women's Press, 1979
S. Gearhart, *The Wanderground*, 1979; Women's Press, 1985
N. Mitchison, *Memoirs of a Spacewoman*, 1962; London: New English Library, 1976
E. Callenbach, *Ecotopia*, London: Pluto Press, 1978

D. Dinnerstein, "Afterword: Toward the Mobilization of Eros," in M.M. Murray (ed.), *Face to Face: Fathers, Mothers, Masters, Monsters—Essays for a Nonsexist Future*, Westport, CT: Greenwood Press, 1983

*   *   *   *   *

COURSE TITLE: SCIENCE, TECHNOLOGY, AND HUMAN VALUES (CHAPTER 4)

Institution name: Bloomsburg University, Pennsylvania.
Name(s) and departmental affiliation(s) of individual(s) teaching this course: William Baillie, English.
Specific information regarding the course:
  Departments/Programs in which course is listed: Interdisciplinary Studies.
  Course level: Lower division undergraduate.
  Sex ratio: Predominantly female.
  Prerequisites: None.
  Method of instruction: Lecture–discussion.
Texts:
  R. Pirsig, *Zen and the Art of Motorcycle Maintenance*
  J. Rothschild, *Machina Ex Dea*
  B. Skinner, *Walden Two Revisited*
  A. Teich, *Technology and Man's Future*
Methods of evaluation: Two midterms, final exam, quizzes, group project or paper, class participation.
Brief course description: Course compares the interaction of science and technology with human values. Studies representative past, present, and future technological developments and their impact on personal and social values. Particular topics studied are different each semester.

Syllabus

	Class Topic	Readings
	1. Introduction—5 Questions	
August 29	Organization	
August 29	#1 What is a value?	
August 31	Values exercises	
September 5	#2 Where in the world are we?	Pirsig, pp. 3–57
September 7	#3 How do we know?	Pirsig, pp. 57–103
September 10	The knife of reason	Pirsig, pp. 104–164
September 12	Projects explained	
September 14	#4 What is technology?	Pytlik handout; Teich, pp. 7–28
September 17	#5 Is technology the enemy?	Teich, pp. 99–129, 40–62
	2. The Industrial Revolution	
September 19	Overview	Ashton (handout)
September 21	Project work day	
September 24	Steam engine	
September 26	Factory system (filmstrip, Industrial Revolution in America)	Lampard (handout)
September 28	Film: *Drive for Power, I, II*	
October 1	Blake, poet and prophet	Blake poems (handout)
October 3	Film: *Blake*	
October 5	MIDTERM EXAM #1	
	3. The Uncertainty Principle	
October 8	Film: *Majestic Clockwork*	
October 10	Atomic physics (15 minute film: *Conquest of Atom*)	Newell (handout)
October 12	Film: *Knowledge or Certainty I*	

October 15	Film: *Knowledge or Certainty II*	Bronowski (handout)
October 17	Uncertainty principle	
October 19	Project work day	
October 22	Scientific revolutions	Kuhn (handout)
October 24	Scientific ethics	Cohen (handout)
October 26	Women and science	Rothschild, pp. ix–xii, 99–116
October 29	Women and technology	Rothschild, pp. 5–18, 79–90
October 31	Women and work	Rothschild, pp. 59–75, 171–181
November 2	MIDTERM EXAM #2	
	4. Planning the Future	
November 5	Genetic engineering—technics	Rothschild, pp. 183–186
November 7	Genetic engineering — values	Handout
November 9	Women and genetics	Rothschild, pp. 198–210
November 12	Skinnerism	PROJECTS DUE
November 14	8:00 p.m. Rifkin lecture	
November 16	Optimism/pessimism	Teich, pp. 171–215
November 19	Technology and democracy	Teich, pp. 270–293
November 21	Discuss projects	
November 26	Skinner's Utopia	Walden, chapters 1–20
November 28	Behavior and freedom	Walden, chapters 21–36
November 30	Beyond freedom and dignity	Skinner (handout)
December 3	Intermediate technology	Teich, pp. 326–354
December 5	Thinking globally	Teich, pp. 386–418
December 7	Values clarification	
December 11	Tues. 8–10 a.m. FINAL EXAMINATION	

*   *   *   *   *

COURSE TITLE: SOCIETY, NATURE, AND TECHNOLOGY (CHAPTER 4)

Institution name: University of Delaware.
Name(s) and departmental affiliation(s) of individual(s) teaching this course: Kathy Turkel, Women's Studies.
Specific information regarding the course:
    Departments/Programs in which the course is listed: Philosophy, Sociology, The Center for Science and Culture, Honors Program.
    Course level and audience for whom it is intended: Upper division undergraduates
    Sex ratio: Equal.
    Prerequisites: None.
    Method of instruction: Lecture–discussion.
Texts:
    Marian Lowe and Ruth Hubbard, *Woman's Nature: Rationalizations of Inequality*, New York: Pergamon Press, 1983
    Michael Brown, *Laying Waste: The Poisoning of America by Toxic Chemicals*, New York: Washington Square Press, 1979
    Plus additional library materials

Methods of evaluation: Mid-term and final, both take home exams. Term paper of 15–20 pages. Class attendance and participation.

Brief course description: The course will examine a variety of perspectives toward technology and will focus on a number of issues regarding the ways in which technology has shaped human social relations and consciousness. The course will include the following issues:

The question of value neutrality in science and technology
The question of "expertise" and the layperson/expert dichotomy
Images of nature
Implications for citizenship and political participation
Rationalizations of inequality: questions of social class, race and gender

Syllabus

	I. Introductory overview
September 6, 10	Reading: Hayden, "American Identity: The Frontiers of Custer and Thoreau"
	Griffin, "The Way of all Ideology"
	Kahn and Wiener, "The Next Thirty-Three Years: A Framework for Speculation"
	II. Theories of Nature and Politics
September 13,	Reading: Hobbes, *Leviathan*, chapters 14, 15, 17, 18
18, 21	Locke, *Concerning Civil Government*, chapters 2, 3, 5
	Marx, *Economic and Philosophic Manuscripts of 1844*, Sections on "Private Property and Communism" and "The Meaning of Human Requirements"
	De Tocqueville (and Pierson), "Fortnight in the Wilderness"
	III. Ideologies of Natural Inferiority
September 20, 24	A. Scientific objectivity? Questions of class, race and gender
	Reading: Ehrenreich and English, "The Sexual Politics of Sickness"
	Barker-Benfield, "Architect of the Vagina"
	Gould, "American Polygeny and Craniometry Before Darwin"
	Burnham, "Black Women as Producers and Reproducers for Profit," in *Woman's Nature*, pp. 29–38
September 27, 30	B. From Social Darwinism to sociobiology
October 2	Reading: Gould, "The Nonscience of Human Nature"
	Gould, "Racist Arguments and I.Q."
	Gould, "Racism and Recapitulation"
	Wilson, "Man: From Sociobiology to Sociology?"
	Bleier, "Sociobiology, Biological Determinism, and Human Behavior"
	IV. Science and Technology as Authority
October 4, 9	A. Technology: definition and assessment
	Reading: Kranzberg, "Technology: The Half-Full Cup"
	Florman, "Technology and the Tragic View"
	Broomfield, "High Technology: The Construction of Disaster"

October 11,   B. Scientific management and the control of workers
16, 18   Reading: Smith, "Of the Division of Labor"
                        Taylor, "The Principles of Scientific Management"
                        Roethlisberger, "The Hawthorne Experiments"
                        Herzberg, "One More Time: How Do You Motivate
                        Employees?"
                        Braverman, "Scientific Management"
                        Braverman, "Further Effects of Management and
                        Technology on the Distribution of Labor"
                *MIDTERM TAKE HOME EXAM WILL BE GIVEN OUT
                OCTOBER 18—DUE OCTOBER 25

October 23,   C. Technology in the workplace and the question of worker
                health and safety
                Reading: Berman, "Why Work Kills"
                        Sterling, "Does Smoking Kill Workers or Working
                        Kill Smokers?"
                        Jasso and Mazorra, "Following the Harvest: The
                        Health   Hazards   of   Migrant   and   Seasonal
                        Farmworking Women"
                        Feldberg and Glenn, "Technology and Work
                        Degradation: Effects of Office Automation on
                        Women Clerical Workers"

October 30   D. Science, technology, and gender
November 2,   Reading: Fee, "Women's Nature and Scientific Objectivity," in
8, 13   *Woman's Nature*, pp. 9–27
                        Messing, "The Scientific Mystique: Can a White Lab
                        Coat Guarantee Purity in the Search for Knowledge
                        About The Nature of Women?," in *Woman's Nature*,
                        pp. 75–88
                        Harrison, *A Woman in Residence*, chapters 1, 6, 8
                        Katz Rothman, "The Meaning of Choice in
                        Reproductive Technology"
                        Corea, "Egg Snatchers"
                        Ince, "Inside the Surrogate Industry"
                        Clough and Finkelstein, "Foetal Politics and the Birth
                        of an Industry"

                V. Technology and Politics
November 15, 20 Reading: Brown, *Laying Waste: The Poisoning of America by
                        Toxic Chemicals*
                        Wolin, "The People's Two Bodies"
                        Wolin, "The New Public Philosophy"
                        Dickson, "Limiting Democracy: Technocrats and the
                        Liberal State"
                        Mumford, "Authoritarian and Democratic Technics"
                *TERM PAPERS—DUE NOVEMBER 29

                VI. Alternative Conceptions
December 4, 6, Reading: Schweickart, "What If . . . Science and Technology in
11   Feminist Utopias"
                        Roszak, "The Visionary Commonwealth"
                        Carnoy and Shearer, "A Democratic Technology"
                        New   Alchemy   Institute,   "Aquaculture,"
                        "Agriculture," "Bioshelters," "Energy"

*   *   *   *   *

COURSE TITLE: TECHNOLOGY AND GENDER (CHAPTER 2, CHAPTER 5)

Institution name: University of Lowell.
Name(s) and departmental affiliation(s) of individual(s) teaching this course: Joan
Rothschild, Political Science.
Specific information regarding the course:
  Departments/Programs in which the course is listed: Political Science, Women's
  Studies, Technology, Society and Human Values.
  Course level and audience for whom it is intended: Upper division undergraduate.
  Sex ratio: Two thirds female.
  Prerequisites: None.
  Method of instruction: Lecture–discussion.
Texts:
  Marian Lowe and Ruth Hubbard (eds.), *Woman's Nature: Rationalizations of
  Inequality*, New York: Pergamon Press, 1983
  Joan Rothschild (ed.), *Machina Ex Dea: Feminist Perspectives on Technology*, New
  York, Pergamon Press, 1983
  Conference Proceedings: Women and Technology: Deciding What's Appropriate,
  Missoula, MT: Women's Resource Center, 1979
  Vonda N. McIntyre and Susan Janice Anderson (eds.), *Aurora: Beyond Equality*,
  Greenwich, CT: Fawcett, 1976
  Plus additional materials on library reserve or distributed in class.
Methods of evaluation: Three written assignments, class presentations and
  participation.
Brief course description: This course will apply a gender analysis to the study of
  technology: for work, for invention, for technological assessment and practice,
  and for options for the future. The aim is to broaden the student's understanding
  of the issues, values and choices that confront us in the technological age.

Syllabus

September 8–15	I. Conceptual Frameworks	
	Reading:	Joan Rothschild, "A Feminist Perspective on Technology and the Future," *Women's Studies International Quarterly* vol. 4, no. 1, 1981, pp. 65–74
		Sally L. Hacker, "The Culture of Engineering: Woman, Workplace and Machine," *Women's Studies International Quarterly* vol. 4, no. 3, 1981, pp. 341–353
		Elizabeth Fee, "Women's Nature and Scientific Objectivity," in Lowe and Hubbard, 9–27
		JoAllyn Archambault, "Women: Inventing the Wheel," *Future, Technology, and Woman: Proceedings of the Conference*, March 6–8, 1981, San Diego State University
		Ruth Schwartz Cowan, "From Virginia Dare to Virginia Slims: Women and Technology in American Life," *Technology and Culture* vol. 20, no. 1, January 1979, pp. 51–63
September 19–October 6	II. Technology, Gender and Work	
	Reading:	
	Overview:	Lila Leibowitz, "Origins of the Sexual Division of Labor," in Lowe and Hubbard, pp. 123–147

Joan Wallach Scott, "The Mechanization of Women's Work," *Scientific American* vol. 247, no. 3, September 1982, pp. 166–187

Farm: Corlann G. Bush, "The Barn is His, The House is Mine: Agricultural Technology and Sex Roles," *Energy and Transport*, George Daniels and Mark Rose (eds.), Beverly Hills, CA: Sage Publications, 1982, pp. 235–259

Sally Hacker, "Farming out the Home: Women and Agribusiness," *The Second Wave*, Spring/Summer 1977, pp. 38–48

Office: Margery Davies, "Woman's Place is at the Typewriter: The Feminization of the Clerical Labor Force," *Radical America*, vol. 8, no. 4 July–August 1974

Elinor Langer, "The Women of the Telephone Company," *The New York Review of Books* vol. XIV, nos. 5 and 6, March 12 and 26, 1970

Factory: *Rosie the Riveter* (film)

Household: Susan J. Kleinberg, "Technology and Women's Work: The Lives of Working Class Women in Pittsburgh, 1870–1900," *Labor History*, Winter 1976, pp. 58–72

Ruth Schwartz Cowan, "The 'Industrial Revolution' in the Home: Household Technology and Social Change in the 20th Century," *Technology and Culture* vol. 17, no. 1, January 1976, pp. 1–23

Roslyn Baxandall, Elizabeth Ewen and Linda Gordon, "The Working Class Has Two Sexes," *Monthly Review* vol. 28, no. 3 July–August 1976, pp. 1–9

Joan Rothschild, "Technology, Housework, Women's Liberation: A Theoretical Analysis," in Rothschild, pp. 79–93.

EXAMINATION: OCTOBER 13

October 17–27   III. Technology, Gender and Invention
DEADLINE TO SELECT PROJECT FOR SECOND ASSIGNMENT: OCTOBER 17

Reading: Autumn Stanley, "Women Hold Up Two-Thirds of the Sky: Notes for a Revised History of Technology," in Rothschild, pp. 3–22.

Deborah J. Warner, "Women Inventors at the Centennial," *Dynamos and Virgins Revisited: Women and Technological Change in History*, Martha Moore Trescott (ed.), Metuchen, NJ: Scarecrow Press, 1979, pp. 102–119

Margaret W. Rossiter, "Women Scientists in America before 1920," *American Scientist* vol. 62, no. 3, May–June 1974, pp. 312–23

Autumn Stanley, "Daughters of Isis, Daughters of Demeter: When Women Sowed and Reaped," *Women's Studies International Quarterly*, vol. 4, no. 3, 1981, pp. 289–304

Helen Deiss Irvin, "The Machine in Utopia: Shaker Women and Technology," *Women's Studies International Quarterly* vol. 4, no. 3, 1981, pp. 313–19

Martha Moore Trescott, "Lillian Moller Gilbreth and the Founding of Modern Industrial Engineering," in Rothschild, pp. 23–37.

October 31–
November 7

IV. Gender Dualism and Technology
Reading: Lynn White, Jr, "Dynamo and Virgin Reconsidered," *Machina Ex Deo: Essays in the Dynamism of Western Culture*, Cambridge, MA: MIT Press, 1968, pp. 57–73
Joan Rothschild, "Introduction: Why *Machina Ex Dea?*," in Rothschild, pp. xiii–xxxiii
Carolyn Merchant, "Mining the Earth's Womb," in Rothschild, pp. 99–117.
Evelyn Fox Keller, "Women, Science and Popular Mythology," in Rothschild, pp. 130–146
Ruth Hubbard, "Social Effects of Some Contemporary Myths about Women," in Lowe and Hubbard, pp. 1–8
Shulamith Firestone, chapter 9 "The Dialectic within Cultural History," *The Dialectic of Sex*, New York: Bantam, 1971, pp. 170–191
Joan L. Griscom, "On Healing the Nature/History Split in Feminist Thought," *Heresies* #13 vol. 4, no. 1, 1981, pp. 4–9
Elizabeth Fee, "Women's Nature and Scientific Objectivity," in Lowe and Hubbard (reread, see I)

November 10–
December 8

V. Gender and Technology: Current Research and Practice

SECOND ASSIGNMENT: CLASS PRESENTATIONS AND PAPERS DUE WHEN PRESENTED
Reading:
Overview:

November 10–14

Corlann G. Bush, "To Think, to Be; to Unthink, to Free," in Rothschild pp. 151–170.
Reproduction: Rita Arditti, "Women as Objects—Science and Sexual Politics," *Science for the People*, vol. 6, September 1974, pp. 8–11, 29–32
Hilary Rose and Jalna Hanmer, "Women's Liberation, Reproduction, and the Technological Fix," *Sexual Divisions and Society: Process and Change*, Diana Leonard Barker and Sheila Allen (eds.), London: Tavistock, 1976, pp. 199–223
Jalna Hanmer, "Reproductive Technology: The Future for Women?," in Rothschild, pp. 183–197.
plus selected clippings

November 17–21 Computers/
Automation:

Sally L. Hacker, "Sex Stratification and Organizational Change: A Longitudinal Case Study of AT&T," *Social Problems*, vol. 26, no. 5, June 1979, pp. 539–557
Roslyn Feldberg and Evelyn Glenn, "Technology and Work Degradation: Effects of Office Automation on Women Clerical Workers," in Rothschild, pp. 59–78.
Race Against Time: Automation of the Office, Cleveland, Ohio: Working Women, 1980

Philip Mattera, "Home Computer Sweatshops," *The Nation*, April 2, 1983, pp. 390–393

November 28–
December 1

War and
Weapons:

Sheila Tobias and Shelah Leader, "An Intelligent Woman's Guide to the Military Mind," *Ms*, vol. XI, nos. 1 and 2, July/August 1982, pp. 118–120, 122, 252, 254, 257
Nancy Huston, "Tales of War and Tears of Women," *Women's Studies International Forum*, vol. 5, nos. 3/4, 1982, pp. 271–282
Cynthia H. Enloe, "Women in NATO Militaries—A Conference Report," *Women's Studies International Forum*, vol. 5, nos. 3/4, 1982, pp. 329–234
Lynn Stephen, "Sex and the Bomb," *Science for the People* vol. 15, no. 1, January/February 1983, pp. 37–39

December 5–8

Ecology/
Appropriate
Technology:

Ynestra King, "Toward an Ecological Feminism and a Feminist Ecology," in Rothschild, pp. 118–129.
Conference Proceedings: Women and Technology: Deciding What's Appropriate: selected articles
Celeste Wesson, "Action from Tragedy: Women at Love Canal and Three Mile Island," *Heresies* #13, vol. 4, no. 1, 1981, pp. 40–43
Manushi Collective, "Drought: God-sent or a Man-Made Disaster?", *Heresies* #13, vol. 4, no. 1, 1981, pp. 50–58

December 12–15

VI. Technology, Gender, and Future Visions
Reading:

Jan Zimmerman, "Women's Need for High Technology," in *Conference Proceedings*, pp. 19–23
Sally Gearhart, "An End to Technology: A Modest Proposal," in Rothschild, pp. 171–182
Shulamith Firestone, "Conclusion: The Ultimate Revolution," *The Dialectic of Sex*, New York: Bantam, 1971, pp. 205–242
Marge Piercy, "Woman on the Edge of Time," in McIntyre and Anderson, pp. 182–217
James Tiptree, Jr [Alice Sheldon], "Houston, Houston, Do You Read?," in McIntyre and Anderson, pp. 36–98
Patrocinio Schweickart, "What If? . . . Science and Technology in Feminist Utopias," in Rothschild, pp. 198–211
Joan Rothschild, "Machina ex Dea and Future Research," in Rothschild, pp. 213–225.

FINAL EXAMINATION

*   *   *   *   *

COURSE TITLE: TECHNOLOGY AND GENDER (CHAPTER 2, CHAPTER 5)

Institution name: University of Cincinnati.

Name(s) and departmental affiliation(s) of individual(s) teaching this course: Joan Rothschild, Visiting Professor, Center for Women's Studies.

Specific information regarding the course:

Departments/Programs in which the course is listed: Sociology, Women's Studies.

Course level: Upper division undergraduate.

Sex ratio: Two-thirds female.

Prerequisites: None.

Method of instruction: Lecture–discussion.

Texts:

Joan Rothschild, (ed.) *Machina Ex Dea: Feminist Perspectives on Technology*, New York: Pergamon Press, 1983

Race Against Time: Automation of the Office, Cleveland: Working Women Education Fund, 1980

Rita Arditti, Renate Duelli Klein and Shelley Minden (eds.), *Test-Tube Women: What Future for Motherhood?*, London: Pandora Press, 1984.

Plus materials on library reserve and/or distributed in class.

Methods of evaluation: Two exams, short paper, general level of interest and participation.

Brief course description: Course applies a gender analysis to the study of technology: for conceptual frameworks, for production and reproduction, for our environment, and for our future. The aim is to broaden the student's understanding of the critical issues, values, and choices that confront us in the technological age.

Syllabus

September 20, 25	I. Why gender and technology? The Meaning of Feminist Perspectives
	Reading:　Joan Rothschild, "Introduction: Why *Machina Ex Dea*?," in Rothschild, pp. ix–xxix
	Autumn Stanley, "Women Hold Up Two-Thirds of the Sky: Notes for a Revised History of Technology," in Rothschild, pp. 3–22
September 27	II. Women, Technology and Work
October 2, 4, 9	Reading:
	Overview:　Joan Wallach Scott, "The Mechanization of Women's Work," *Scientific American* vol. 247, no. 3, September 1982, pp. 167–187
	Sally L. Hacker, "Sex Stratification, Technology and Organizational Change: A Longitudinal Case Study of AT&T," *Social Problems*, vol. 26, no. 5, June 1979, pp. 539–557
	Office:　Roslyn Feldberg and Evelyn Glenn, "Technology and Work Degradation: Effects of Office Automation on Women Clerical Workers," in Rothschild, pp. 59–78
	Race Against Time: Automation of the Office
	Blue Collar & High Tech: "South of the Border, Down Mexico Way," in Annette Fuentes and Barbara Ehrenreich,

Women in the Global Factory, New York:
Institute for New Communications/South End
Press, 1983, pp. 27–33

Household: Ruth Schwartz Cowan, "The 'Industrial
Revolution' in the Home: Household Tech-
nology and Social Change in the 20th Century,"
Technology and Culture vol. 17, no. 1, January
1976, pp. 1–23
Joan Rothschild, "Technology, Housework, and
Women's Liberation: A Theoretical Analysis," in
Rothschild, pp. 79–93

FIRST EXAMINATION: THURSDAY, OCTOBER 11

October 16, 18   III. Dea   and   Deus   Reconsidered: Conceptual   and
Theoretical Issues
Reading: Carolyn Merchant, "Mining the Earth's Womb,"
in Rothschild, pp. 99–117
Evelyn Fox Keller, "Women, Science and Popular
Mythology," in Rothschild, pp. 130–146
Elizabeth Fee, "Women's Nature and Scientific
Objectivity," in Marian Lowe and Ruth Hubbard
(eds.), *Woman's Nature: Rationalizations of
Inequality*, New York: Pergamon Press, 1983,
pp. 9–27
Corlann Gee Bush, "Women and the Assessment
of Technology: To Think, to Be; to Unthink, to
Free," in Rothschild, pp. 151–170

October 23, 25, 30,   IV. Redesigning Human Life: Women and Reproductive
November 1, 6   Technologies
Reading:
Overview: Barbara Katz Rothman, "The Meanings of
Choice in Reproductive Technology," in Arditti
et al., pp. 23–33
Ruth Hubbard, "Personal Courage Is Not
Enough: Some Hazards of Childbearing in the
1980s," in Arditti et al., pp. 331–355

Prevention: Scarlet Pollock, "Refusing to Take Women
Seriously: 'Side Effects' and the Politics of
Contraception," in Arditti et al., pp. 138–152
Vimal Balasubrahmanyan, "Women as Targets in
India's Family Planning Policy," in Arditti et al.,
pp. 153–164
Phillida Bunkle, "Calling the Shots? The
International Politics of Depo-Provera," in
Arditti et al., pp. 165–187
Adele Clark, "Subtle Forms of Sterilization
Abuse: A Reproductive Rights Analysis," in
Arditti et al., pp. 188–212
K. Kaufmann, "Abortion, a Woman's Matter: An
Explanation of Who Controls Abortion and How
and Why They Do It," in Arditti et al.,
pp. 213–234
Marsha Saxton, "Born and Unborn: The
Implications of Reproductive Technologies for

People with Disabilities," in Arditti et al., pp. 298–312

Rayna Rapp, "XYLO: A True Story," in Arditti et al., pp. 313–328

Test-Tube
Women: Jalna Hanmer, "Reproductive Technology: The Future for Women?," in Rothschild, pp. 183–197

Betty Hoskins and Helen Bequaert Holmes, "Technology and Prenatal Femicide," in Arditti et al., pp. 237–255

Viola Roggencamp, "Abortion of a Special Kind: Male Sex Selection in India," in Arditti et al., pp. 266–277

"Test-Tube Babies and Clinics: Where Are They?," in Arditti et al., pp. 52–53

Rebecca Albury, "Who Owns the Embryo?," in Arditti et al., pp. 54–67

Jane Murphy, "From Mice to Men? Implications of Progress in Cloning Research," in Arditti et al., pp. 76–91

Shelley Minden, "Designer Genes: A View from the Factory," in Arditti et al., pp. 92–98

Susan Ince, "Inside the Surrogate Industry," in Arditti et al., pp. 99–116

Control: Robyn Rowland, "Reproductive Technologies: The Final Solution to the Woman Question?," in Arditti et al., pp. 356–369

Francie Hornstein, "Children by Donor Insemination: A New Choice for Lesbians," in Arditti et al., pp. 373–381

Carol Downer, "Through the Speculum," in Arditti et al., pp. 419–426

Jalna Hanmer, "A Womb of One's Own," in Arditti et al., pp. 438–448

Janice Raymond, "Feminist Ethics, Ecology and Vision," in Arditti et al., pp. 427–437

November 8, 13,   V. Ecology, Environment, the Fate of the Earth
15, 20

Reading: Shulamith Firestone, chapter 10 "Feminism in the Age of Ecology," in *The Dialectic of Sex: The Case for Feminist Revolution*, New York: Bantam Books, 1971, pp. 192–202

Ynestra King, "Toward an Ecological Feminism and a Feminist Ecology," in Rothschild, pp. 118–129

Celeste Wesson, "Action from Tragedy: Women at Love Canal and Three Mile Island," *Heresies* #13, vol. 4, no. 1, 1981, pp. 40–43

Carolyn Merchant, "Women and the Environment," in *Environmental Review* vol. VIII, no. 1 Spring 1984, pp. 5–6

Janice Monk, "Approaches to the Study of Women and Landscape," in *Environmental*

Review vol. VIII, no. 1, spring 1984, pp. 23–33

Elizabeth Coppinger, "Women and Appropriate Technology," in *Conference Proceedings: Women and Appropriate Technology: Deciding What's Appropriate*, Missoula, MT: Women's Resource Center, 1979, pp. 24–25

Sheila Tobias and Shelah Leader, "An Intelligent Woman's Guide to the Military Mind," *Ms* vol. XI, nos. 1 and 2, July/August 1982, pp. 118–120, 122, 252, 254, 257

Hiroshima-Nagasaki, August 1945 (film)

Guest speaker: Women poets and the threat of nuclear war

PAPERS DUE: TUESDAY, NOVEMBER 20

November 27, 29   VI. Technology, Gender and the Future

Reading: Joan Rothschild, "Afterword: Machina Ex Dea and Future Research," in Rothschild, pp. 212–225

Sally Gearhart, "An End to Technology: A Modest Proposal," in Rothschild, pp. 171–182

Patrocinio Schweickart, "What If? . . . Science and Technology in Feminist Utopias," in Rothschild, pp. 198–211

FINAL EXAMINATION: THURSDAY, DECEMBER 6

*   *   *   *   *

COURSE TITLE: TECHNOLOGY AND HUMAN VALUES (CHAPTER 4)

Institution name: University of Lowell.

Name(s) and departmental affiliation(s) of individual(s) teaching this course: Judith Pastore, English; Karl Sladek, Chemical Engineering; Joan Rothschild, Political Science; and Carol Brown, Sociology.

Specific information regarding the course:

Departments/Programs in which the course is listed: English, Chemical Engineering, Political Science, Sociology, and Technology, Sociology and Human Values.

Course level and audience for whom it is intended: Upper division undergraduates, especially engineering and science.

Sex ratio: Three-quarters male.

Prerequisites: None.

Method of instruction: Lecture and discussion.

Texts:

Thomas Dublin, *Women at Work*, Columbia University Press, 1979

Annette Fuentes and Barbara Ehrenreich, *Women in the Global Factory*, South End Press, 1983

Kurt Vonnegut, *Player Piano*, Dell, 1952

Tracy Kidder, *The Soul of a New Machine*, Avon, 1981

Steven Levy, *Hackers*, Anchor/Doubleday, 1984

Mike Cooley, *Architect or Bee?*, South End Press, 1980

Methods of evaluation: Short written assignment, quizzes, semester project or final exam.

Brief course description: The theme of Technology and Human Values this semester is Technology and Work. The course will cover the following topics: The Meaning and Impact of Work, The Industrialization of Lowell, Technology and the Global Economy, and Computers and the Electronic Age: The Second Industrial Revolution. Throughout, we will explore the interaction of changing technologies, work and human values.

Syllabus

	Topic and Instructor	Readings and Quizzes
September 4	Introduction: Technology and Human Values. Staff	
September 5, 6	Discussion Sections	
	I. The Meaning and Impact of Work	
September 9	Meaning of Work: Curse or Blessing? Brown	Dublin
September 11	Impact of Work. Brown	Dublin
September 12, 13	Discussion Sections	
	II. The Industrialization of Lowell	
September 16	Textiles as a Human Activity. Rothschild	Dublin
September 18	Craft and Technology. Sladek	Dublin
September 19, 20	Discussion Sections	
September 23	Textile Technology: Colonial America & Lowell. Sladek	Dublin
September 25	Lowell: An Ideal Community. Pastore	Kasson, chapter 2* Reading Quiz #1
September 26, 27	Discussion Sections	
September 30	Labor and City Growth. Brown	Dublin
October 2	The Immigrant Experience and Changing Values. Pastore	Dublin
October 3, 4	Discussion Sections	
	III. Technology and the Global Economy	
October 7	Slide-Lecture: Technologies, Old & New. Rothschild	
October 9	The Global Factory. Rothschild	Ehrenreich and Fuentes
October 10, 11	Discussion Sections	
October 15	Multinationals: Structure and Labor Market Segmentation. Brown	Ehrenreich and Fuentes
October 17, 18	Discussion Sections	Reading Quiz #2
	IV. From the Industrial Age to the Electronic Age	
October 21	Predestination in the Computer Age. Pastore	Vonnegut
October 23	Work and Family Life. Pastore	Vonnegut
October 24, 25	Discussion Sections	
	V. Computers and the Electronic Age: The Second Industrial Revolution	
October 28	History and Typology of Computers. Sladek	Kidder
October 30	Human Energy: The Motivation for Work. Sladek	Kidder

Syllabus	*Topic and Instruction*	*Readings and Quizzes*
October 31, November 1	Discussion Sections	
November 4	Computers and Corporate Structures. Sladek	Kidder Reading Quiz #3
November 6	The Hacker Ethic. Brown	Levy
November 7, 8	Discussion Sections	
November 13	Computer Seduction. Pastore	Levy
November 14, 15	Discussion Sections	
November 18	Computers and Communication. Rothschild	Levy
November 20	Computer Use and the Changing Structure at Work. Rothschild	Cooley
November 21, 22	Discussion Sections	
November 25	Can Computers Think? Sladek	Cooley
November 27	Architect or Bee? Rothschild	Cooley Reading Quiz #4

	THANKSGIVING RECESS	
December 2	Film	
December 4	Will We Become Robots? Pastore	
December 5, 6	Discussion Sections	

	VI. Work, Technology, and Human Values	
December 9	The Future of Work. Staff	
December 11	The Future of Work? Staff	
December 12, 13	Discussion Sections	

FINAL PROJECT/EXAM

*John F. Kasson, *Civilizing the Machine: Technology and Republican Values in America, 1776–1900*, New York: Penguin, 1977

*   *   *   *   *

COURSE TITLE: TECHNOLOGY, SOCIAL CHANGE AND THE ROLE OF WOMEN (CHAPTER 2, CHAPTER 4)

Institution name: Eastern Michigan University.
Name(s) and departmental affiliation(s) of individual(s) teaching this course: Daryl M. Hafter, Department of History and Philosophy.
Specific information regarding the course:
   Departments/Programs in which the course is listed: History, Women's Studies.
   Course level: Graduate. Required course for the Women's Studies Master of Arts in Liberal Studies.
   Sex ratio: Predominantly female.
   Prerequisites: Introductory course in Individualized Master of Liberal Arts Curriculum.
   Method instruction: Lectures, discussion.

Texts:
  John G. Burke and Marshal C. Eakin (eds.), *Technology and Change*, San Francisco: Boyd and Fraser, 1979
  Melvin Kranzberg and Carroll W. Pursell, Jr (eds.), *Technology in Western Civilization*, vol. I, New York: Oxford University Press, 1967
  Martha Moore Trescott (ed.), *Dynamos and Virgins Revisited: Women and Technological Change in History*, Metuchen, NJ: Scarecrow Press, 1979
Methods of evaluation: Research papers, exams, class participation.
Brief course description: Course explores the role of technology as it has evolved through time and its effect on human lives, concentrating on how changing technology has altered women's roles. It will show how women influenced technological change by developing new technologies themselves, or by their choice of work. Current problems growing out of modern technology will be explored against the historical development from classical to modern times in Europe and the United States.

Syllabus
  1   The Nature of Technology: An Overview and Contrasting Views
      Reading: Melvin Kranzberg and Carroll W. Pursell, Jr, "The Importance of Technology in Human Affairs," in M. Kranzberg and C. Pursell (eds.), *Technology in Western Civilization* hereafter cited as *TIWC*), chapter 1
      Jacques Ellul, "The Technological Order," in J. Burke and M. Eakin (eds.), *Technology and Change* (hereafter cited as *TAC*), pp. 13–19
      Rothschild, "Foreword," in *Machina Ex Dea*, New York: Pergamon Press, 1983
  2. The Origins of Technology and Society
      Reading: Peter Drucker, "The First Technological Revolution and Its Lessons," in *TAC*, pp. 39–46
      Nancy Tanner and Adrienne Zihlman, "Women in Evolution, Part I: Innovation and Selection in Human Origins", *Signs* vol. 1, Spring 1976, pp. 585–608
      R.J. Forbes, "The Beginnings of Technology and Man," and "Mesopotamian and Egyptian Technology," in *TIWC*, chapters 2, 3
      George Murdock and Catherine Provost, "Factors in the Division of Labor by Sex," *Ethnography* vol. 12, April 1983, pp. 203–225
      Autumn Stanley, "Daughters of Isis, Daughters of Demeter: When Women Sowed and Reaped," *Women's Studies International Quarterly* vol. 4, no. 3, pp. 289–304
  3   Pre-Industrial Technology in Society
      Reading: Reed Benamou, "Verdigris and the Entrepreneuse," *Technology and Culture* vol. 25, April 1984, pp. 171–181
      Judith Brown and Jordan Goodman, "Women and Industry in Florence," *Journal of Economic History* vol. 40, 1980, pp. 73–80
      Shepherd B. Clough, "Economic and Political Developments, 1600–1750," in *TIWC*, chapter 8
      Natalie Zemon Davis, "Women in the Crafts in Sixteenth Century Lyon," *Feminist Studies* vol. 8, Spring 1982, pp. 47–80.
      G.E. Fussell, "The Agricultural Revolution, 1600–1850," in *TIWC*, chapter 9
      Gay Gullickson, "The Sexual Division of Labor in Cottage Industry and Agriculture in the Pays de Caux: Auffay, 1705–1850," *French Historical Studies* vol. 12, 1981, pp. 177–199
      Daryl M. Hafter, "Artisans, Drudges, and the Problem of Gender in Pre-Industrial France," *Annals of the New York Academy of Sciences* vol. 441, April 1985, pp. 71–87

Daryl M. Hafter, "Agents of Technological Change: Women in the Pre- and Post-Industrial Workplace", in Dorothy G. McGuigan (ed.), *Women's Lives: New Theory, Research and Policy*, Ann Arbor: University of Michigan, 1980, pp. 159–168

A. Rupert Hall, "Early Modern Technology, to 1600", and "Cultural, Intellectual, and Social Foundations, 1600–1750," in *TIWC*, chapters 6, 7

Lynn White, Jr, "Technology in the Middle Ages," in *TIWC*, chapter 5

4   The Industrial Revolution in Europe and America

Reading: Maxine Berg, *The Age of Manufactures, 1700–1820*, New York: Oxford University Press, 1986

Melvin Kranzberg, "Prerequisites for Industrialization," in *TIWC*, chapter 13

Jean Quataert, "The Shaping of Women's Work in Manufacturing: Guilds, Households, and the State in Central Europe, 1648–1870," *American Historical Review* vol. 90, December 1985, pp. 1122–1148

Joan Scott, "The Mechanization of Women's Work," *Scientific American*, September 1982

Abbott Payson Usher, "The Textile Industry, 1750–1830," in *TIWC*, chapter 14

Susan Levine, "Ladies and Looms: The Social Impact of Machine Power in the American Carpet Industry," in Martha Moore Trescott (ed.), *Dynamos and Virgins Revisited: Women and Technological Change in History*, Metuchen, NJ: Scarecrow Press, 1979, pp. 67–76

Judith A. McGaw, "Technological Change and Women's Work: Mechanization in the Berkshire Paper Industry, 1820–1855," *Dynamos*, pp. 77–99

5   Invention as Technical and Social Act

Reading: Lynn White, Jr, "The Act of Invention," *TAC*, pp. 379–392

Deborah J. Warner, "Women Inventors at the Centennial," in *Dynamos*, pp. 102–119

Daryl M. Hafter, "The Programmed Brocade Loom and the Decline of the Drawgirl," in *Dynamos*, pp. 49–66

Eugene S. Ferguson, "Nonverbal Thought in Technology," *TAC*, pp. 400–405

John Jewkes, David Sawers and Richard Stillerman, "The Sources in Invention," *TAC*, pp. 406–416

Autumn Stanley, "Women Hold Up Two-Thirds of the Sky: Notes for a Revised History of Technology," in Rothschild, *Machina Ex Dea*, pp. 3–22

6   The Maturation of Industrialization and Women's Work

Reading: Ruth Schwartz Cowan, "From Virginia Dare to Virginia Slims: Women and Technology in American Life," *Technology and Culture* vol. 20, January 1979, pp. 51–63

Herbert Heaton, "The Spread of the Industrial Revolution," in *TIWC*, chapter 23

Susan J. Kleinberg, "Technology and Women's Work: The Lives of Working Class Women in Pittsburgh, 1870–1900," *Dynamos*, pp. 185–204

Joan Scott and Louise Tilly, "Women's Work and the Family in Nineteenth-Century Europe," *Comparative Studies in Society and History* vol. 17, January 1975, 36–64

7 Technology and the Modern Home
  Reading: Ruth Schwartz Cowan, "The 'Industrial Revolution' in the Home,"
       TAC, pp. 276–282
       Seigfried Giedion, "Engineering and the Household," *TAC*,
       pp. 273–275
       Christine E. Bose, Philip L. Bereano and Mary Malloy, "Household
       Technology and the Social Construction of Housework," *Technology
       and Culture* vol. 25, January 1984, pp. 53–81
       Joann Vanek, "Household Technology and Social Status: Rising
       Living Standards and Status and Residence Differences in
       Housework," *Technology and Culture* vol. 19, July 1978,
       pp. 361–375
       William D. Andrews and Deborah C. Andrews, "Technology and the
       Housewife in Nineteenth-Century America," *Women's Studies* vol. 2,
       no. 3, 1974, pp. 309–328
8 Technology, Leisure, and Gender
  Reading: Carroll Pursell, Jr, "Toys, Technology and Sex Roles in America,
       1920–1940," *Dynamos*, pp. 252–268
       John F. Kasson, "Coney Island: A Case Study in Popular Culture and
       Technological Change," *Journal of Popular Culture* vol. 9 Spring
       1976, pp. 960–975
       M. Kaplan and Philip Bosserman (eds.), *Technology, Human Values
       and Leisure*, Nashville, TN: Abingdon Press, 1971
9 Technological Utopias
  Reading: Howard Segal, "The Feminist Technological Utopia: Mary E.
       Bradley Lane's *Mizora* (1890)," *Alternative Futures*, vol. 4,
       Spring/Summer 1981, pp. 67–72
       Ruth Schwartz Cowan, "From Virginia Dare to Virginia Slims:
       Women and Technology in American Life," *Dynamos*, pp. 30–44
       John A. Hostetler, "Amish Society," *TAC*, pp. 168–174
       Patrocinio Schweickart, "What If . . . Science and Technology in
       Feminist Utopias," in Joan Rothschild, *Machina Ex Dea*, New York:
       Pergamon Press, 1983, pp. 198–211
10 High Technology and Women's Employment
  Reading: Joan Rothschild, "A Feminist Perspective on Technology and the
       Future," *Women's Studies International Quarterly* vol. 4, no. 1, 1981,
       pp. 65–74
       Herbert Simon, "What Computers Mean for Man and Society," in
       TAC, pp. 68–76
       Robert H. Guest, "Scientific Management and the Assembly Line,"
       in *TAC*, pp. 98–106
       John H. Broomfield, "High Technology: The Construction of
       Disaster," *Alternative Futures* vol. 3, Spring 1980, pp. 31–44
       Rebecca Morales, "Cold Solder on a Hot Stove," in Zimmerman, *The
       Technological Woman*, New York, 1983, pp. 159–168
       Barbara A. Gutek, "Women's Work in the Office of the Future," in
       Zimmerman, *The Technological Woman*, New York, 1983,
       pp. 159–168.
11 Technology vs Humanistic Goals
  Reading: Ralph Nader, "Unsafe at Any Speed," in *TAC*, pp. 290–296
       Barry Commoner, "Are We Really in Control?," in *TAC*, pp. 6–10
       Donald Marlowe, "Public Interest—First Priority in Engineering
       Design?," in *TAC*, pp. 297–301

Langdon Winner, *Autonomous Technology: Technics-out-of-control as a Theme in Political Thought*, Cambridge, MA: MIT Press, 1977

Barbara Winters, "Engineered Conception: The New Parenthood," in Zimmerman, *The Technological Woman*, New York, 1983, pp. 221–238

12   Alternative Technologies and How to Get There

Reading: Wilson Clark, "Intermediate Technology," in *TAC*, pp. 198–202

Judy Smith, "Something Old, Something New, Something Borrowed, Something Due: Women and Appropriate Technology," Missoula, Montana: National Center for Appropriate Technology, 1979, obtained from Women and Technology Network, 315 S. 4th E.; Missoula, Montana 59801; (406) 728–3941

Judy Smith, "Women and Appropriate Technology: A Feminist Assessment," in Zimmerman, *The Technological Woman*, New York, 1983, pp. 65–70

Harvey Brooks, "Technology Assessment in Retrospect," in *TAC*, pp. 465–476

David Dickson, *Alternative Technology and the Politics of Technical Change*, London: Fontana, 1974, *passim*.

*   *   *   *   *

COURSE TITLE: TECHNOLOGY, USA-STYLE: MASCULINE-FEMININE IMBALANCES (CHAPTER 4, CHAPTER 5)

Institution name: University of Detroit.

Name(s) and departmental affiliation(s) of individual(s) teaching this course: John M. Staudenmaier, S.J., History.

Specific information regarding the course:

Departments/Programs in which the course is listed: History.

Course level: Graduate and undergraduate.

Sex ratio: Equal.

Prerequisites: Technology in America: 1790–1985, recommended.

Method of instruction: Seminar, field trip.

Texts: See syllabus

Methods of evaluation: Research project, weekly essays, class presentations and participation.

Brief course description: Using primary and secondary sources (historical, sociological, psychological for secondary sources and a mix of male and female perspectives from 19th century and early 20th century authors for primary sources) the seminar discusses questions of gender in America such as the separate spheres, etiquette and impression management, contrasting lives of steel workers and their wives in late 19th century Pittsburgh, the feminist critique of technological history, etc. These seminar discussions parallel student's work on individual research projects.

Other features of the course: The course enables students to work with the staff and resources of the Henry Ford Museum and Greenfield Village complex for their major research project—to take some technology at the Henry Ford Museum or Greenfield Village and interpret its historical and social meaning. Particular attention is to be paid to the basic theme of the course "Masculine–Feminine Relationships and Values".

Syllabus

Week 1   Introduction
          Themes: 1. Syllabus and requirements
                  2. Introduction: Technological momentum vs progress talk
                  3. Gender and technology: What are the issues?

          The Edison Institute Tour
Week 2   Life Before and After Industrial Revolution
          Themes: The Industrial Revolution is a watershed of change for
                  male–female relationships and for the meaning of "technology"
                  and of human work in general. Any study of gender questions in
                  twentieth century America must begin by a study of what
                  happened in the Industrial Revolution.
          Reading: Staudenmaier, "Technology's Storytellers", chapter 5
                  Zuboff, "Work and Human Interaction in Historical
                  Perspective"
Week 3   The Myth of Progress
          Theme: The myth of progress in the West is intimately linked with the
                  Industrial Revolution and is, itself, a prime example of what
                  many call "male rhetoric" about technology and science in the
                  West. The class will aim at studying the assumptions and the
                  structure of the myth and at providing an alternative language for
                  talking about technological change in a way that is truer to
                  history and more open to questions of gender.
          CLASS BEGINS LIBRARY MEDIA CENTER FOR VIEWING OF
          "KOYAANISQUATSI"
          Reading: Beta, "Progress of Invention During the Past Fifty Years"
                  Staudenmaier, "Orwell, 1984, Technology and Faith"
          SPECIAL ASSIGNMENT: WEEKS 4 AND 5
          These two weeks focus on primary sources. We are primarily concerned
          with the "rhetoric" that men and women use about men and women.
          1. As you read each piece highlight what you consider important
             assertions IN THE TEXTS about men and women. Note that you may
             find assertions about men in the women's readings for October 25 and
             assertions about women in the men's readings.
          2. Organize those assertions into thematic clusters and score each article
             on each cluster.
Week 4   19th Century Etiquette: Women
          Theme: How did women talk about women? How did they talk about
                  men? These selections from late 19th century women's literature
                  are an excellent source for gaining familiarity with some very
                  traditional categories of female rhetoric.
          Reading: "What Can a Woman Do?"
                  C.E. Beecher and Harriet Beecher Stowe, "American Woman's
                  Home," 1869
Week 5   Male Rhetoric: 19th and 20th Century
          Theme: This is a matched set with class 4. The goal is to get a feel for the
                  contrasts between masculine and feminine rhetoric.
          Reading: Decorus, "Treatise on Etiquette and Dress", 1879
                  Taylor, "The Principles of Scientific Management"
                  "Engineering Honor" President's Address AIEE, 1906
                  Henry Adams, "The Dynamo and the Virgin"
                  A. Carnegie, "Gospel of Wealth"
Week 6   NO CLASS: RESEARCH APPOINTMENTS

Week 7   Advertising
           Theme: Historian of Advertising, Pamela Lurito will come from Boston
                   to give a slide lecture on the image of men and women and
                   technology in the late 19th and 20th centuries
           Reading: T.J.J. Lears, "From Salvation to Self-Realization: Advertising
                   and the Therapeutic Roots of the Consumer Culture,
                   1880–1930"
Week 8   18th and 19th Century Contrasts
           Theme: Cowan's chapter introduces us to the relatively balanced
                   male–female work team of a pre-industrial revolution farm
                   home. By contrast Brody and Kleinberg treat the lives of
                   working men and working women in late 19th century
                   Pittsburgh's steel mill world. These historical articles should
                   give us further information about the changing character of
                   male–female relationships.
           Reading: Cowan, "Housewifery: Household Work and Household Tools
                   under Pre-Industrial Conditions," chapter 2
                   Brody, "Sources of Stability," chapters 4–6
                   Kleinberg, "The Lives of Working Class Women in Pittsburgh:
                   1870–1900"
Week 9   20th Century Contrasts
           Theme: This is directly parallel to Week 8 but a little later. Again the
                   purpose is to introduce us to contrasts between men and women
                   as they related to technology in the early 20th century.
           Reading: Thomas, "Diesel Father and Son: Social Philosophies of
                   Technology"
                   Leach, "Transformation in Culture of Consumption: Depart-
                   ment Stores 1890–1925"
                   Cowan, "Industrial Revolution in the Home"
                   Pursell, "Toys, Technology and Sex Roles in America:
                   1920–1940"
                   Pirsig, "Zen and the Art of Motorcycle Maintenance," chapter 2
                   Ong, "Agonistic Structures in Academia"
Week 10   Gender Questions: Recent Research
           Theme: Recent questions of gender and technology have been raised
                   primarily by feminist scholars who find their parallels in the
                   works of feminist psychologists (Gilligan and Chodorow) and
                   philosophers of science (Keller). We will consider their works
                   along with another writing by Ruth Schwartz Cowan that
                   directly addresses the question of women and technology.
           Reading: Gilligan, "Woman's Place in Man's Life Cycle," Introduction
                   and chapter 1
                   Keller, "Baconian Science: A Hermaphroditic Birth"
                   Chodorow, "Family Structure and Feminine Personality"
                   Cowan, "From Virginia Dare to Virginia Slims: Women and
                   Technology in American Life"
Week 11   NO CLASS: Research
Week 12   Summary of Readings
           Theme: This summary session will be aimed at synthesis. Each student
                   will give me a 5 minute report on the two most important
                   readings (1 male, 1 female) followed by 5 minutes of questions.
                   I grade each on their presentation and handling of questions.
Week 13   PRESENTATIONS OF PROJECTS I

Week 14   PRESENTATIONS OF PROJECTS II
                    FINAL NIGHT
                    COURSE EVALUATION AT LANSING–REILLY

*   *   *   *   *

COURSE TITLE: WOMEN AND NEW TECHNOLOGY (CHAPTER 2, CHAPTER 4)

Institution name: Vassar College, Poughkeepsie, New York.
Name(s) and departmental affiliation(s) of individual(s) teaching this course: Eileen
    Leonard, Department of Sociology, Science, Technology & Society Program
    (STS).
Specific information regarding the course:
    Departments/Programs in which the course is listed: Science, Technology & Society
        Program (STS).
    Course level: Upper division undergraduate.
    Sex ratio: Predominantly female.
    Prerequisites: Two courses in STS or special permission.
    Method of instruction: Largely discussion with some lecture material and brief
        presentations by the students.
Texts:
    Jacques Ellul, *The Technological Society*, 1964
    Harry Braverman, *Labor and Monopoly Capital: The Degradation of Work in the
        Twentieth Century*, 1974
    Carolyn Merchant, *The Death of Nature: Women, Ecology and the Scientific
        Revolution*, 1980
    Barbara Ehrenreich and Deirdre English, *Complaints and Disorders: The Sexual
        Politics of Sickness*, 1973
    Linda Gordon, *Woman's Body, Woman's Right: A Social History of Birth Control in
        America*, 1976
    Rita Arditti, Renate Duelli Klein and Shelley Minden, eds. *Test-Tube Women: What
        Future for Motherhood?*, 1984
    Ruth Schwartz Cowan, *More Work for Mother: The Ironies of Household
        Technology from the Open Hearth to the Microwave*, 1983
    Dolores Hayden, *The Grand Domestic Revolution: A History of Feminist Designs for
        American Homes, Neighborhoods and Cities*, 1981
    Barbara Ehrenreich and Annette Fuentes, *Women in the Global Factory*, 1983
    Judith Gregory and D. Marschall, eds, *Office Automation: Jekyll or Hyde?*, 1983
    David Dickson, *The Politics of Alternative Technology*, 1977
    Marge Piercy, *Woman on the Edge of Time*, 1976
Methods of evaluation: Student presentation, weekly précis of reading, and term paper.
Brief course description: The course explores the relationship between women and
    technology by focusing on three types of technology of particular concern to
    women: reproductive technology, household technology and office automation.
    Ethical issues and the control of technology are discussed.

Syllabus
January 20   I. The Social Construction of Gender
                    A. The Scientific Study of Gender
                    B. Patriarchy
                    C. The Gender Division of Labor

January 27   II. Technology and Western Civilization
A. What is Technology?
B. Historical Survey of the Role of Technology in Western Civilization
C. The Acceleration of Technology in the Nineteenth and Twentieth Centuries
Reading: Edward B. Fiske, "Liberal Arts Students Meet Technology," *New York Times*, April 14, 1985
Michael Polanyi, "Science and Technology," in *Personal Knowledge: Towards a Post-Critical Philosophy*, London: Routledge & Kegan Paul, 1958, pp. 174–184
Jacques Ellul, *The Technological Society*, New York: Random House, 1964, "Note to the Reader"
Lewis Mumford, *Technics and Civilization*, New York: Harcourt, Brace and World, 1963, pp. 1–18, 105–106, 172–185, 268–284, 433–435

February 3   III. Technology and Its Relationship to Society: Mainstream, Radical, Feminist Perspectives
A. Mainstream Utopian
Reading: Daniel Bell, "Five Dimensions of Post-Industrial Society," *Social Policy*, July–August, 1973, pp. 103–110
B. Mainstream Dystopian
Reading: Jacques Ellul, *The Technological Society*, New York: Random House, 1964, Foreword, Translator's Introduction, Foreword to Revised American Edition, pp. 3–7, 22, 79–147, 429–436
C. Radical
Reading: Harry Braverman, "Machinery" in *Harry Braverman, Labor and Monopoly Capital: The Degradation of Work in the Twentieth Century*, New York: Monthly Review Press, 1974, pp. 184–235
D. Feminist
Reading: Jane Dolkart and Nancy Hartsock, "Feminist Vision of the Future," *Quest*, vol. 2, 1975, pp. 2–6

February 10   IV. Women and Technology
A. Historical and Philosophical Issues
Reading: Carolyn Merchant, *The Death of Nature: Women, Ecology and the Scientific Revolution*, New York: Harper and Row, 1980, Introduction, Chapters 1, 5, 6, 9, 12 and Epilogue
B. Contemporary Scholarship
Reading: Ruth Schwartz Cowan, "From Virginia Dare to Virginia Slims: Women and Technology in American Life," *Technology and Culture*, vol. 20, 1979, pp. 51–63
C. Technology and Values
a) Scientific Rationality
b) Feminist Holistic
Reading: C. Frankel, "The Nature and Sources of Irrationalism," *Science*, June 1, 1973, pp. 927–931
Ruth Bleier, "Patriarchal Science, Feminist Visions," in Ruth Bleier, *Science and Gender: A Critique of Biology and its Theories on Women*, New York: Pergamon Press, 1984, pp. 193–207

February 17   V. Selected Aspects of Contemporary Technology in Relation to
Women: Reproductive Technology, Household Technology and
Architecture, Office Automation
A. Reproductive Technology
a) Women and the Medical Establishment: Historical and
Contemporary Perspectives
Reading: Barbara Ehrenreich and Deirdre English, *Complaints and
Disorders: The Sexual Politics of Sickness*, New York:
Feminist Press, 1973
Linda Gordon, *Woman's Body, Woman's Right: A Social
History of Birth Control in America*, New York: Penguin,
1976, Introduction, Chapters 1, 5, 10 (pp. 249–251,
298–300), 12 (pp. 341–348, 386–390), 14
b) Technological Advances: Artificial Insemination, Embryo
Transfer, IVF, Sex 'Determination, Surrogate Motherhood,
Artificial Wombs, Cloning
c) Ramifications and Control of Reproductive Technology
Reading: Rita Arditti, Renate Duelli Klein and Shelley Minden,
Test-Tube Women: What Future for Motherhood?, Boston:
Pandora Press, 1984, pp. 1–7, 23–33, 54–67, 99–116,
165–212, 237–255, 281–355, 427–437
March 3   B. Household Technology and Architecture
a) Changing Household Technologies
Reading: Ruth Schwartz Cowan, *More Work for Mother: The Ironies
of Household Technology from the Open Hearth to the
Microwave*, New York: Basic Books, 1983
March 24   b) Feminism and Architecture
Reading: Dolores Hayden, *The Grand Domestic Revolution: A
History of Feminist Designs for American Homes,
Neighborhoods and Cities*, Boston: MIT Press, 1981
March 31   C. Office Automation
a) Theoretical Considerations
Reading: Harry Braverman, *Labor and Monopoly Capital: The
Degradation of Work in the Twentieth Century*, New York:
Monthly Review Press, 1974
b) Women's Situation
Reading: Rosalyn Baxandall, Elizabeth Ewen and Linda Gordon,
"The Working Class has Two Sexes," *Monthly Review*,
vol. 18, July–August, 1976, pp. 1–9
April 7   c) International Perspectives
Reading: Barbara Ehrenreich and Annette Fuentes, *Women in the
Global Factory*, Institute for New Communications, South
End Press, 1983
d) Policy Issues
Reading: Judith Gregory and D. Marschall, eds, *Office Automation:
Jekyll or Hyde?*, Cleveland, Ohio: Working Women
Education Fund, 1983
April 14   VI. Ethical Dimensions of Contemporary Technology
A. General Framework
Reading: Paul Goodman, "The Morality of Scientific Technology,"
Dissent, Jan–Feb, 1967, pp. 41–53
Erich Fromm. "Where Are We Now and Where Are We
Headed," in *The Revolution of Hope: Toward A
Humanized Technology* by Erich Fromm, New York:
Bantam, 1968, pp. 25–55

Melvin Kranzberg, "Technology and Human Values," *The Virginia Quarterly Review*, vol. 10, Autumn, 1964, pp. 578–592

Hyman Rickover, "A Humanistic Technology," in *The Social Impact of Cybernetics*, ed., Charles R. Dechert, Notre Dame: University of Notre Dame Press, 1966, pp. 109–128

B. Specific Technologies
Reading: R. John Buuck, "Ethics of Reproductive Engineering," *Perspectives*, vol. 39, 1977, pp. 545–547

John Elliott, "Abortion for 'Wrong' Fetal Sex: An Ethical-Legal Dilemma," *Journal of the American Medical Association*, vol. 242, 1979

George Annas, "Contracts to Bear a Child: Compassion or Commercialism?," *The Hastings Report*, April, 1981, pp. 23–24

April 21   VII. Control of Technology and Alternative Technology
Reading: David Dickson, *The Politics of Alternative Technology*, New York: Universe Books, 1977

April 28   VIII. Visions and Revisions: Fictional Treatments and Public Policy
A. Utopian Fiction
Reading: Marge Piercy, *Woman on the Edge of Time*, New York: Knopf, 1976
B. Public Policy

*   *   *   *   *

COURSE TITLE: WOMEN AND TECHNOLOGY
(CHAPTER 2, CHAPTER 4, CHAPTER 5)

Institution name: University of Washington, Seattle.
Name(s) and departmental affiliation(s) of individual(s) teaching this course: Phil Bereano, College of Engineering, Women's Studies Program.
Specific information regarding the course:
  Departments/Programs in which the course is listed: Engineering, Women's Studies, Sociology.
  Course level: An interdisciplinary course open to graduate students and advanced undergraduates.
  Sex ratio: Predominantly female.
  Prerequisites: None.
  Method of instruction: Seminar.
Texts:
  Barbara Garson, *All the Livelong Day*
  David Dickson, *The Politics of Alternative Technology*
  Barbara Ehrenreich and Deirdre English, *For Her Own Good*
  Susan Strasser, *Never Done: A History of American Housework*
  Plus extensive list in xeroxed packet and/or on library reserve.
Methods of evaluation: Term paper, class participation, presentation and leading discussion.
Brief course description: The course will investigate the interaction between technology and women. We will examine what we mean by "technology" when we use the term by discussing its role in social life and in social change. What has been

the particular impact of technology on women? And what do the women's movement and feminism contribute to our understanding of technology?
Other features of the course: Special topics include comparison of technological rationality and feminist modes of thought, development of alternative ways to assess technology and evaluate its effects, the impact of industrialization and the division of labor on the home and on the labor force, and special effects of technologies targeted at women (such as Ob/Gyn care).

Syllabus

March 27   Introduction
            Format of course, course requirements, grading system, topics covered, getting aquainted.
            Movie: *Union Maids*.

            I. Technology and Social Change
March 29   A. Technology and Society: Mainstream
            Req. Reading: Richard A. Peterson, *The Industrial Order and Social Policy*, chapter 2, "The Industrial Revolution", pp. 11–19
                           D. Bell, "Five Dimensions of Post-Industrial Society," *Social Policy*, July/August 1973, pp. 103–110
                           Thomas Kuhn, "Postscript," *The Structure of Scientific Revolutions*, 2nd ed.
            Recommended: Emmanuel Mesthene, *Technological Change*, NAL, 1970, chapter 1, "Social Change," pp. 15–44
April 3   B. Technology and Society: Radical
            Req. Reading: Harry Braverman, *Labor and Monopoly Capital*, chapter 7 "The Scientific–Technical Revolution"
                           Murray Bookchin, "Introduction," *Post-Scarcity Anarchism*, Ramparts Press.
                           David Dickson, *The Politics of Alternative Technology*, Universe, 1975, chapter 1 "The Case Against Contemporary Technology"
April 5   C. Women, Technology and Society: Pre-Industrial and Industrializing Societies
            Req. Reading: Ester Boserup, *Women's Role in Economic Development*, 1970, chapter 6 "Industry: From the Hut to the Factory," pp. 106–118
                           Marshall Shalins, *Stone Age Economics*, 1972, "Subsistence," pp. 14–32, "Elements of the Domestic Mode of Production," pp. 74–82
April 10   D. Women, Technology and Society: Industrial Societies
            Req. Reading: Ruth Cowan, "The Industrial Revolution in the Home: Household Technology and Social Change in the Twentieth Century," *Technology and Culture*, January 1976
                           Judith Blake, "The Changing Status of Women in Developed Countries," *Scientific American* vol. 231, no. 3, September 1974, pp. 137–147
                           Christine Bose, "Feminist Research in the Social Sciences," unpublished mimeograph, 1976
                           Corky Bush, "Women and The Assessment of Technology: To Think, to Be; to Unthink, to Free," in Rothschild (ed.), *Machina Ex Dea*, pp. 151–170

II. Technology and Values

April 12   A. On the Nature of Rationality

Req. Reading: Hazel   Henderson,   "Philosophical   Conflict:
Re-examining the Goals of Knowledge", *Public
Administration Review*, January–February 1975,
pp. 77–80
Theodore Roszak, "The Monster and the Titan:
Science, Knowledge, and Gnosis," *Daedalus*, Summer
1974, pp. 17–32
C. Frankel, "The Nature and Sources of Irrationalism,"
Science, June 1, 1973, pp. 927–931

April 17   B. Feminist Sensibilities

Req. Reading: Shulamith Firestone, *The Dialectic of Sex*, Bantam
Books, 1970, chapter 10, "Feminism and Ecology,"
pp. 192–202
Quest, Summer 1975: Dolkart and Hartsock, "Feminist
Visions of the Future" and Birkby and Weisman, "A
Woman Built Environment: Constructive Fantasies"
Eleanor Maccoby, and C.N. Jacklin, *The Psychology of
Sex Differences*, 1973, pp. 349–374
Susan Leigh Star, "Right and Left: An Examination of
Sex Differences in Hemispheric Brain Asymmetry,"
Paper, AAAS Meeting, Washington, DC, 1978

Recommended: L. Osen, "The Feminine Mathe-tique," 1971
John Ernest, "Mathematics and Sex," *American
Mathematical Monthly* or Pamphlet (4/76)

III. The Technological Elite

April 19   Req. Reading: Barbara Ehrenreich and Deirdre English, "Intro-
duction" and "The Rise of the Experts," *For Her Own
Good*, chapters 1–3, pp. 1–100
John McDermott, "Technology: The Opiate of the
Intellectuals," *New York Review of Books*, July 31,
1969, pp. 25–35

Recommended: Hannah Arendt, "Lying in Politics: Reflections on the
Pentagon Papers," *New York Review of Books*,
November 18, 1971
Zimmerman, et al. *Towards a Science for the People*.

IV. The Division of Labor

April 24   A. The Workforce in the 19th Century

Req. Reading: Mari Jo Buhle, Ann Gordon and Nancy Schrom Dye,
"Women in American Society; An Historical
Contribution," *Radical America* vol. 5, July–August
1971, pp. 3–66 or New England Free Press Pamphlet
Elizabeth F. Baker, *Technology and Women's Work*,
New York: Columbia, 1964, chapters 2, 3, 4, pp. 8–74
skim

Recommended: Robert Smuts, *Women and Work in America*, New
York: Columbia 1959, chapter 4.

April 26   B. Effects of Technology and Industrialization

Req. Reading: David Dickson, *op. cit.*, chapter 2 "The Ideology of
Industrialization" and chapter 3 "The Politics of
Technical Change"

M. Guilbert, Women and Work (III): "The Effects of
Technological Change," *Impacts of Science on Society*,
UNESCO, April/June 1970, pp. 85–91
Harry Braverman, *Labor and Monopoly Capital*,
chapter 5 "Clerical Workers," pp. 293–308
Working Women, "Workers Face Office Automation",
Science for the People, May–June 1981, pp. 5–9
R.L. Feldberg and Evelyn N. Glenn, "Technology and
Work Degradation: Effects of Office Automation on
Women Clerical Workers," *Machina Ex Dea*,
pp. 59–78

Recommended: Margery Davies, "Women's Place is at the Typewriter:
The Feminization of the Clerical Labor Force," *Radical
America* vol. 8, no. 4, July–August 1974.
Charlotte Perkins Gilman, *Women and Economics*,
chapters XI, XII.

May 1   C. Vignettes and Participant Observations of Contemporary Women's
Work

Req. Reading: Barbara Garson, *All the Livelong Day*, Penguin Books
Recommended: Studs Terkel, *Working*: Telephone receptionists
(pp. 57–60, 61–69), Bank teller (pp. 344–351,
Supermarket checker (pp. 374–380). [Also suggested:
Airline Stewardess (pp. 72–82), Domestic
(pp. 161–168), Cosmetics saleswoman (pp. 324–327),
Housewife (pp. 396–400), Government bureaucrat
(pp. 451–456), Government clerk (pp. 457–460),
Bread baker (pp. 607–613), Teacher (pp. 629–635),
Occupational therapist (pp. 642–646).]
Elinor Langer, "The Women at the Telephone
Company," *New York Review of Books*, March 12 &
26, 1970.
"Word Processing," *Seattle Times*, February 18, 1977,
p. H4.

May 3   D. Theories and Descriptions

Req. Reading: Rosalyn Baxandall, Elizabeth Ewen and Linda
Gordon, "The Working Class Has Two Sexes,"
Monthly Review, vol. 28, July–August 1976, pp. 1–9
Heidi Hartmann, "Capitalism, Patriarchy and Job
Segregation by Sex," pp. 137–169, in Martha Blaxall
and Barbara Reagan, *Women and the Workplace:
Implications of Occupational Segregation* (also in *Signs*,
vol. 1, no. 3, Spring 1976, Part 2)
Francine Blau and Carol Jusenious, "Economists'
Approaches to Sex Segregation in the Labor Market:
An Appraisal," pp. 181–199, in Blaxall and Reagan,
above (and in *Signs*, above)
Recommended: Elise Boulding, "Familial Constraints and Women's
Work Roles," pp. 95–117, in Blaxall and Reagan,
above (and in *Signs*, above).
Alice Cook, *The Working Mother*, NYSILR (1975),
chapter 10
Theodore Caplow, *The Sociology of Work*, 1954,
chapter 10, "Occupations of Women"

May 8, 10   E. History of Housework
           Req. Reading: Susan Strasser, *Never Done: A History of American Housework*, pp. 1–178, 224–241
                Ehrenreich and English, "Microbes and the Manufacture of Housework," chapter 5, pp. 141–182, *For Her Own Good*
                Susan Strasser, *Never Done*, pp. 179–223, 242–312
                Nona Glazer, "Housework," *Signs*, Summer 1976
           Recommended: Ann Oakley, *Women's Work: The Housewife, Past and Present*, 1974.
                Ruth Cowan, "Two Washes in the Morning and a Bridge Party at Night," *Women's Studies*, 1976, vol. 3, pp. 147–172.
                Molly Harrison, *The Kitchen in History*, Charles Scribner and Sons, New York, 1972, especially chapter 9, "The Nineteenth Century"
                Evelyn Reed, "The Productive Record of Primitive Women," chapter 5, in *Women's Evolution*, especially pp. 105–120.
                G. Wright, "Sweet and Clean: The Domestic Landscape in the Progressive Era," *Landscape*, October 1975, pp. 38–43.
                "Homemaking and Womanhood," *Dollars & Sense*, November 1979, pp. 6–8

May 15   F. Working Conditions of Housework: Time, Technology and Ideology
           Req. Reading: Ann Oakley, *The Sociology of Housework*, 1974, chapter 5 "Work Conditions," pp. 79–99 skim
                Valerie K. Oppenheimer, *The Female Labor Force in the U.S.*, Berkeley, 1970, especially pp. 29–39
                Bose, Bereano and Malloy, "Household Technology and the Social Construction of Housework," *Technology and Culture*, January 1984, pp. 53–82
                Vanek, "Time Spent in Housework," *Scientific American* vol. 231, November 1974, pp. 116–120
                Walker and Woods, *Time Use*, pp. 246–273, chapter IX "Summary"
                Pat Mainardi, "The Politics of Housework," in *Sisterhood is Powerful*, R. Morgan (ed.)
           Recommended: Scott Burns, "The Shift from a Market Economy to a Household Economy," *Co-Evolution Quarterly*, Fall 1976, 18–29
                Margaret Reid, *The Economics of Household Production*, 1934, John Wiley.
                Ruth Cowan, "A Case Study of Technological and Social Change: The Washing Machine and the Working Wife," in Hartman and Banner (ed.), *Clio's Consciousness Raised*, 245–253
                Bernheide, Berk, and Berk, "Household Work in the Suburbs, *PSR*, vol. 19, no. 4, October 1976
                Marvin Harris, *The Nature of Cultural Things*, 1964, 72–75, on episode chains in kitchen
                Joann Vanek, "Household Technology and Social Status: Rising Living Standards and Status and Residence Differences in Housework," *Technology and Culture*, Vol. 19, no. 3, July 1978, pp. 361–375

May 17   G. Wages for Housework
          Req. Reading: Brody, "Economic Value of a Housewife," U.S. Social
                        Security Administration, August 28, 1975
                        Joan Landes, "Wages for Housework," *Quest*, vol. 2,
                        no. 2, fall 1975, pp. 17–30
                        B. Ehrenreich, *New American Movement*, March 1975;
                        B. Dudley, *New American Movement*, May 1975; J.
                        Breenleaf, WIN, July 3, 1975
                        Walker and Gauger, "The Dollar Value of Household
                        Work," Bulletin no. 60, NYSCHE, Cornell
          Recommended: A. Szalai, "The Situation of Women in the Light of
                        Contemporary Time-Budget Research," UN Back-
                        ground Paper for the World Conference on
                        International Women's Year, April 15, 1975
                        Chase Manhattan Study, "What's a Wife Worth?,"
                        17–18, *Houseworker's Handbook*

May 22   H. Consumerism
          Req. Reading: Herbert Marcuse, *One-Dimensional Man*, Beacon,
                        1964, "Introduction," pp. ix–xvii and "The New
                        Forms of Control", pp. 1–18
                        Ellen Willis, "Women and the Myth of Consumerism,"
                        Ramparts, June 1970, pp. 14–16
                        Weinbaum and Bridges, "The Other Side of the
                        Paycheck: Monopoly Capital and the Structure of
                        Consumption," *Monthly Review*, vol. 28, no. 3,
                        July–August 1976, pp. 88–103

May 24   V. Women and Alternative Technology
          Req. Reading: E.F. Schumacher, *Small is Beautiful*, chapter I(3) "The
                        Role of Economics," I(4) "Buddhist Economics," I(5)
                        "Technology with a Human Face"
                        D. Dickson, *The Politics of Alternative Technology*,
                        chapter 7 "Myths and Responsibilities"
                        J. Smith, *Something Old, Something New, Something
                        Borrowed, Something Due: Women and Appropriate
                        Technology*, Women and Technology Project,
                        Missoula, Montana
                        "Appropriate Technology for Women," U.N.
                        Development Forum, June 1978

          VI. Biomedical Technologies
May 29   A. Women: Sickness and Health
          Req. Reading: Ehrenreich and English, "The Sexual Politics of
                        Sickness," chapter 4, pp. 101–140
          Recommended: "Motherhood as Pathology," and "From Masochistic
                        Motherhood to the Sexual Marketplace," Chapters 7
                        and 8, pp. 211–268, *For Her Own Good.*

June 3   B. Birthing, Birth Control and Abortion
          Req. Reading: Rita Arditti, "Male Contraception," *Science for the
                        People*, July 1976, pp. 12–15, 35
                        Linda Gordon, "Birth Control: An Historical Study,"
                        Science for the People, January–February 1977,
                        pp. 10–16; and "Birth Control and the Eugenists,"
                        Science for the People, March–April 1977, pp. 8–15
                        Adrienne Rich, "Hands of Flesh, Hands of Iron,"

chapter VI, pp. 128–155, in *Of Woman Born: Motherhood as an Experience and Institution*

June 4   VII. Architecture and Physical Spaces
            Req. Reading: Dolores Hayden, *The Grand Domestic Revolution*, "Introduction," pp. 3–29, "Feminist Politics and Domestic Life," pp. 291–305
            Susan Saegert, "Masculine Cities and Feminine Suburbs: Polarized Ideas, Contradictory Realities," pp. 93–108; Dolores Hayden, "What Would a Non-Sexist City Be Like? Speculations on Housing, Urban Design and Human Work," pp. 167–184; Gerde Wekerle, "Women in the Urban Environment," pp. 185–211, all in Catharine R. Stimpson, Elsa J. Dixler, Martha G. Nelson, and Kathryn B. Yatrakis, *Women and the American City*, (originally in *Signs*) *Heresies*, #11, *Making Room: Women and Architecture* (1981). Nunzia Rondanini, "Architecture and Social Change," pp. 3–5, Leslie Kanes Weisman, "Women's Environmental Rights: A Manifesto," pp. 6–8, and Margrit Kennedy, "Seven Hypotheses on Female and Male Principles in Architecture," pp. 12–13
            Recommended: *New Space for Women*, ed. by Gerde R. Wekerle, Rebecca Peterson, and David Morely, "Architecture: Towards a Feminist Critique," pp. 205–218, and other chapters on design of the home.

*   *   *   *   *

COURSE TITLE: WOMEN AND TECHNOLOGY
(CHAPTER 2, CHAPTER 5)

Institution name: University of Maine at Orono.
Name(s) and departmental affiliation(s) of individual(s) teaching this course: Jodi Wetzel, Women in the Curriculum Project.
Specific information regarding the course:
  Departments/Programs in which the course is listed: Sociology and Social Work.
  Course level: Upper division undergraduate.
  Sex ratio: Predominantly female, or even.
  Prerequisites: None.
  Method of instruction: Lecture, discussion, slides, flims, group projects, field work.
Texts:
  Joan Rothschild, (ed.), *Machina Ex Dea: Feminist Perspectives on Technology*
  Martha Moore Trescott, *Dynamos and Virgins Revisited: Women and Technological Change in History*
  Plus science fiction work, selected articles and monographs.
Methods of evaluation: Colloquium paper, class discussion and participation.
Brief course description: An interdisciplinary survey of the cultural effects of technology on women's lives. Topics include the evolution of domestic technology; changes in workplace technology and their relationship to women in the paid labor force; recent developments in information technology and the resulting potential for vast changes in women's lives; an historical analysis of biomedical and reproductive technology; an outline of development in architecture and design technology; and a look at the future using science fiction by women authors.

Syllabus

January 14	Introductions Course Perspective and Requirements/Discussion Group Assignments/"Good Housekeeping" Overview of the Cultural Effects of Technology on Women
January 21	Information Technology: Women's Education and Access to Power Reading: Rothschild, pp. vii–58 Trescott, pp. 1–44, 100–179 Selected journal articles
January 28	Domestic Technology: Women in the Home Reading: Rothschild, pp. 79–93 Trescott, pp. 181–232 Selected journal articles Assignment: PAPER TOPIC AND OUTLINE DUE
February 4	Architecture, Design and Planning Technology Reading: Selected journal articles Assignment: Determine which science fiction work will be read by each small group
February 11	Workplace Technology—Women in the Labor Force Reading: Rothschild, pp. 59–78 Trescott, pp. 45–99
February 18	Technology and the Third World—Women in Developing Countries Reading: Selected journal articles
February 25	Biomedical Technology and Reproduction Reading: Trescott, pp. 233–267
March 4	"Appropriate" Technology: Values "Cultural Images of Women (and Men) in Technology" (slide show) Reading: Rothschild, pp. 97–146
March 11	SPRING BREAK
March 18	SPRING BREAK
March 25	Small group meetings to discuss science fiction works and prepare presentations for April 1 and 8 Reading: Science fiction work selected by each discussion group
April 1	SMALL GROUP PRESENTATIONS
April 8	SMALL GROUP PRESENTATIONS
April 15	Forecasts of Women's Futures Reading: Rothschild, pp. 149–225 Selected journal articles
April 22	SUMMARY, REVIEW, EVALUATION
April 29	NO CLASS PAPERS DUE

Additional Required Reading

January 21	D. Bell, Five dimensions of post-industrial society, *Social Policy*, July–August 1973, pp. 103–110. A. Buchmann and W. Buchmann, You can't go home again. *Graduate Woman*, March–April 1982, pp. 17–18; 30.
January 28	C. Bose, Technology and changes in the division of labor in the American home. *Women's Studies International Quarterly*, 1979, *2*, 295–384. R. Cowan, The "industrial revolution" in the home: Household technology and social change in the 20th century, *Technology and Culture*. January 1976, pp. 1–23. D. Hayden, Home, Mom, and Apple Pie. *Redesigning the American Dream: The Future of Housing Work and Family Life*. NY: W. W. Norton, 1984, pp. 63–95

S. Kamerman, Work and family in industrialized societies. *Signs: Journal of Women in Culture and Society*, Summer 1979, *4*(4), 632–650.

February 4   J. Freeman, Women and urban policy. *Signs: Journal of Women in Culture and Society*, 1980, *5*(3) Supplement, S4–S21.

D. Hayden, *The grand domestic revolution: A history of feminist designs for American homes, neighborhoods, and cities.* Cambridge, Massachusetts: MIT Press, 1981.

D. Hayden, *Redesigning the American Dream*, pp. 3–59.

D. Hayden and G. Wright, Architecture and urban planning. *Signs: Journal of Women in Culture and Society*, Summer 1976, *1*(4), 923–934.

A. Markusen, City spatial structure, women's household work, and national urban policy. *Signs: Journal of Women in Culture and Society*, 1980, *5*(3) Supplement, S23–S44.

S. Saegert, Masculine cities and feminine suburbs: Polarized ideas, contradictory realities. *Signs: Journal of Women in Culture and Society*, 1980, *5*(3) Supplement, S96–S111.

February 11   H. Melville, The paradise of bachelors and the tartarus of maids, *The selected writings of Herman Melville.* New York: Random House, 1952, pp. 185–211.

February 18   E. Leacock, History, development, and the division of labor by sex: Implications for organization. *Signs: Journal of Women in Culture and Society*, 1981, *7*(2), 474–491.

H. Papanek, Development planning for women. *Signs: Journal of Women in Culture and Society*, 1977, *3*(1), 14–21.

I. Tinker, Women, technology, and poverty: Some special issues. *Social Education*, 1979, *43*(6), 444–445.

April 15   J. Bernard, The female world and technology in 2020. *Phi Kappa Phi Journal*, Summer 1981, *61*(3), 8–10.

E. Boulding, The coming of the gentle society, *Women in the twentieth century world.* New York: Halsted Press, 1977, pp. 211–224.

J. Dolkhart and N. Hartstock, Feminist visions of the future. *Quest: A Feminist Quarterly*, Summer 1975, *2*(1), 2–6.

S. Gearhart, Female futures in science fiction. *Proceedings of the Conference: Future, Technology, and Woman*, March 6–8, 1981, San Diego State University, pp. 41–45.

J. Zimmerman, Technology and the future of women: Haven't we met somewhere before? *Women's Studies International Quarterly*, 1981, *4*(3), 355–367.

* * * * *

COURSE TITLE: WOMEN IN INTERNATIONAL DEVELOPMENT (CHAPTER 3)

Institution name: West Virginia University.

Name(s) and departmental affiliation(s) of individual(s) teaching this course: Judith Stitzel, English & Women's Studies, Ed Pytlik, Technology Education; Kate Curtis, Technology Education.

Specific information regarding the course:

Departments/Programs in which the course is listed: Technology Education, Women's Studies.

Course level: Graduate and advanced undergraduate.

Sex ratio: Predominantly female.
Prerequisites: None.
Method of instruction: Lecture, discussion, films, guest speakers.
Texts:
K. Curtis, E. Pytlik and J. Stitzel (eds.), *Women in International Development,* readings compiled for Technology Education 280 (UND)
I. Palmer, *The Nemow Case,* Washington, DC: USAID, 1979
I. Tinker, and J. Bo Bramsen (eds.), *Women and World Development,* Washington, DC: Overseas Development Council, 1976 (WWD)
On reserve in library:
E. Bourguignon, *A World of Women: Anthropological Studies of Women in the Societies of the World,* New York: Praeger, 1980
E. Boserup, *Woman's Role in Economic Development,* New York: St Martin's Press, 1970
F. Dahlberg, *Woman the Gatherer,* New Haven, CT: Yale University Press, 1982
R. Dauber and M.L. Cain (eds.), *Women and Change in India,* New York: St Martin's Press, 1979
K. Little, *The Sociology of Urban Woman's Image in African Literature,* Totowa, NJ: Rowman & Allanheld, 1980
M.Z. Rosaldo and L. Lamphere (eds.), *Woman, Culture and Society,* Stanford University Press, 1974
A.C. Smock, *Women's Education in Developing Countries,* New York: Praeger, 1981
R.O. Whyte and P. Whyte, *The Women of Rural Asia,* Boulder, CO: Westview Press, 1982
A.M. Yohalem (ed.), *Women Returning to Work: Policies and Progress in Five Countries,* Totowa, NJ: Rowman and Allanheld, 1980
Methods of evaluation: Midterm and final evaluation.
Brief course description: Course objectives are: to examine cultural diversities and similarities in the definition of women's roles and status; to study women's contributions in the formal and informal sectors, especially in food production, food processing, household maintenance, income generation and marketing; to investigate women's access to education, health, income, credit and technology; to analyze the impact of socioeconomic development on women and to evaluate the distribution of resources not only *across* households, but *within* households: to understand how women are left out of development planning, how they can be included, and why they should be included.

Syllabus
Week 1 Introduction
Third World Development: An Overview
Reading: Bryson, pp. 1–19 (WID)
Irene Tinker, "The Adverse Impact of Development on Women," pp. 22–34 (WWD)
Week 2 Women's Studies: An Overview
Speaker: Venus Figures as More Than Fertility Symbols
Reading: Beaver, pp. 50–58 (WID)
Week 3 Film: *Kypseli*; Topic: sex stratification
Reading: Dias, pp. 20–30 (WID)
Islam, pp. 31–49 (WID)
Week 4 Speaker: Women in International Development from a Social Science Perspective
Reading: "Rural Development . . .," pp. 59–65 (WID)
Childers, "The Development Approach to Liberation: Suggestions for Planning," pp. 129–149 (WID)

Week 5   Speaker: Community Development as a Change Agent (Philippines)
           Reading: Workshop #5, Proceedings of the Seminar on Women and
                    Development, Mexico City, June 15–18, 1975, pp. 171–175
                    (WWD)
           Discussion: Impact of Colonization on Women
Week 6   Film: *The Edge of Survival*
           Reading: Olin, "A Case for Women as Co-managers: The Family as a
                    General Model of Human Social Organization," pp. 105–122
                    (WWD)
                    Palmer, *The Nemow Case*
Week 7   Speaker: Development Project Implementation and Reactions
                    (Bangladesh)
           Reading: Schumacher et al., pp. 162–214 (WID)
                    MID-TERM EXAM
Week 8   Speaker: Non-Formal Education (Bangladesh)
           Reading: Sharma, pp. 338–351 (WID)
                    Hoque, pp. 91–106 (WID)
                    Workshop #3, Proceedings, pp. 160–165 (WWD)
Week 9   Speaker: Division of Labor (Nigeria)
           Reading: Cloud, pp. 66–90 (WID)
                    Papanek, "Women in Cities: Problems and Perspectives,"
                    pp. 54–69 (WWD)
Week 10   Film Festival: Afghanistan, Bolivia, Kenya
Week 11   Speaker: Income Generation
           Reading: Dixon, pp. 215–239 (WID)
                    Hoskins, pp. 240–253 (WID)
                    Workshop #2, Proceedings, pp. 153–160 (WWD)
Week 12   SPRING BREAK
Week 13   Speaker: Agriculture and Food Production (Tanzania)
           Reading: Tinker, pp. 107–149 (WID)
                    Spring and Hausen, pp. 254–276 (WID)
Week 14   Speaker: Fertility and Family Planning (India)
           Reading: Durch, pp. 315–337 (WID)
                    Blair, pp. 277–314 (WID)
                    Workshop #4, Proceedings, pp. 165–170 (WWD)
Week 15   Speaker: Access to Technology
           Reading: Tinker pp. 150–161 (WID)
                    Workshop #1, Proceedings, pp. 147–153 (WWD)
                    EVALUATION

* * * * *

COURSE TITLE: WOMEN IN SCIENCE, TECHNOLOGY, AND MANAGEMENT (CHAPTER 3)

Institution name: Eastern Michigan University.
Name(s) and departmental affiliation(s) of individual(s) teaching this course: E. Jaynor
   Johnston, Interdisciplinary Technology, College of Technology.
Specific information regarding the course:
   Departments/Programs in which the course is listed: Interdisciplinary Technology,
   Women's Studies.
   Course level: Graduate and senior level undergraduate.

Sex ratio: Predominantly female.
Prerequisites: None.
Method of instruction: Seminar and guest lectures.
Texts:
   Coursepack available at Michigan Documents, Gallery II, McKenny Union (see
   syllabus for specific readings).
Methods of evaluation: Two papers and class participation.
Brief course description: Course objectives are to familiarize students with past and
   present concepts of "technology," "technological change" and "technological
   society"—particularly as they relate to women's issues; to probe the nature and
   probable origin of the problems (and advantages) women face in becoming
   leaders and decision-makers in a technological society and/or professional in
   technology-based fields; to give the student some concrete representations of
   women's roles, impacts, problems and problem-solving strategies in several
   non-traditional professions including telecommunications specialists, science/
   technology R&D, and industrial management.

Syllabus

	I. Women and Issues in Technology and Science
September 11	Orientation Meeting
September 18	What is Technology? Definitions and Approaches for Women
	Lecturer: Alexandra Aldridge, Ph.D.
	Reading: Carol Gilligan, "Why Should a Woman be More Like a Man?"
	Sally L. Hacker, "The Culture of Engineering: Woman, Workplace and Machine"
	Sally L. Hacker, "Mathematization of Engineering: Limits on Women and the Field"
September 24	Women and Technology: A Cultural and Historical Perspective
	Reading: Ruth Schwartz Cowan, "From Virginia Dare to Virginia Slims: Women and technology in American Life"
	Joan Wallach Scott, "The Mechanization of Women's Work"
	Joan Rothschild, "A Feminist Perspective on Technology and the Future"
October 1	Gender Differences: Implications for Industry
	Lecturer: Felix Kaufmann, President, Science for Business, Inc.
	Reading: Ruth Hubbard, "Social Effects of Some Contemporary Myths About Women"
	Felix Kaufmann, "Nonreproductive Male/Female Differences: Some Philosophical Implications and Cultural Consequences"
	C.N. Jacklin and E. Maccoby, "Sex Differences and Their Implications for Management"
October 8	The Feminist Critique of Science and Technology
	Reading: Elizabeth Fee, "Is Feminism a Threat to Scientific Objectivity?"
	Hilde Hein, "Women and Science: Fitting Men to Think About Nature"
	Corlann Gee Bush, "Women and the Assessment of Technology"
October 15	Lillian Moller Gilbreth, Engineer; Barbara McClintock, Geneticist
	Reading: Martha Moore Trescott, "Lillian Moller Gilbreth and the Founding of Modern Industrial Engineering"
	Evelyn Fox Keller, "A World of Difference" (Barbara McClintock)

	II. Women and Management Issues
October 22	The Transformation of the Workplace: Implications for Women

October 22   Lecturer: Jacqueline Scherer, Ph.D., Professor of Sociology, Oakland University

Reading: Margaret Lowe Benson, "For Women, the Chips are Down"

Mary Frank Fox and Sharlene Hesse-Biber, "Women in Professional and Managerial Occupations"

October 29   New Technologies and the Feminine Response

Reading: Ruth Hubbard, "Should Professional Women be Like Professional Men?"

Meg Wheatley, "High Tech: The Fast Tracks and Dead Ends in the Job Market of the Future"

Jan Zimmerman, "How to Control the New Technology Before it Controls You"

November 5   Working and Managing in a High Tech Environment

Reading: Barbara A. Gutek, "Women's Work in the Office of the Future"

Natasha Josefowitz, "Paths to Power in High Technology Organizations"

November 12   Some Legal Strategies and Laws Pertaining to the Discrimination Issue

Lecturers: Jean Ledwith King, Attorney-at-Law; Lana Pollack, State Senator

Reading: Mary Frank Fox and Sharlene Hesse-Biber, "Working Women: Economic and Legal Context"

Wendy Kahn and Joy Ann Grune, "Pay Equity: Beyond Equal Pay for Equal Work"

Handout: outline of Title VII, EPA, Elliot-Larsen

November 19   Women Managers in Industry—#1

Lecturer: Katherine M. Erdman, Former Vice President, Corporate Communications, Hoover Universal

Reading: Rosabeth Moss Kanter, "The Impact of Hierarchical Structure on The Work Behavior of Women and Men"

Jean Baker Miller, "Women and Power"

"Top Women Executives Find Path to Power is Strewn with Hurdles," October 25, 1984, *Wall Street Journal*

"Young Executive Women Advance Farther, Faster than Predecessors," October 26, 1984, *Wall Street Journal*

November 26   Institutional Barriers and Solutions to Their Restrictions: A Strategy Session

Reading: Cynthia Fuchs Epstein, "Institutional Barriers: What Keeps Women Out of the Executive Suite?"

Natasha Josefowitz, "Women as Leaders"

December 3   Women Managers in Industry—#2

Lecturer: Katherine Johnson, Supervisor of Product Performance, Current Product Engineering, Hydramatic Division of General Motors

Reading: Louise Bernikow, "We're Dancing as Fast as We Can"

Ruth Hubbard, "Should Professional Women Be Like Professional Men?"

"Women's Small Voice in Big 3," February 6, 1984, *Detroit Free Press*

December 10   COURSE WRAP-UP/EXAMINATION
Reading: May Frank Fox and Sharlene Hesse-Biber, "Prospects and Strategies for Change: An Institutional Perspective"

*   *   *   *   *

COURSE TITLE: WOMEN, NATURE, AND SCIENCE/TECHNOLOGY (CHAPTER 5)

Institution name: Michigan State University.

Name(s) and departmental affiliation(s) of individual(s) teaching this course: Mary Anderson, Lyman Briggs School.

Specific information regarding the course:

Departments/Programs in which the course is listed: Lyman Briggs School, Women's Studies.

Course level: Upper division undergraduate.

Sex ratio: Varies: predominantly female, and even.

Prerequisites: None.

Method of instruction: Lecture, discussion.

Texts:

Aeschylus, *The Eumenides* from *The Oresteian Trilogy*

Simone de Beauvoir, *The Second Sex* (selected chapters)

Dorothy Dinnerstein, *The Mermaid and the Minotaur*

Carolyn Merchant, *The Death of Nature: Women, Ecology, and the Scientific Revolution* (selected chapters)

Marge Piercy, *Woman on the Edge of Time*

Joan Rothschild (ed.), *Machina Ex Dea: Feminist Perspectives on Technology* (selected essays)

Recommended: Sandra Harding and Merrill B. Hintikka, (eds.), *Discovering Reality: Feminist Perspectives on Epistemology, Metaphysics, Methodology and Philosophy of Science.*

Methods of evaluation: Three essays, class attendance and participation.

Brief course description: Course focuses on the symbolic and historic association made between women and nature and the significance of that association of issues of gender and science.

Syllabus

I. Introduction: to the general issues regarding women in society and, more specifically, to the concerns that fall under the heading "gender and science".

II. Is Female to Male as Nature is to Culture?
In this unit we will explore the idea of culture as male and the dichotomy between culture and nature, with particular reference to the concept of woman as "Other".

April 2	Reading: Aeschylus, *The Eumenides*
April 4	de Beauvoir, "Dreams, Fears, Idols" and "Myth and Reality," in *The Second Sex*
April 9	Merchant, pp. 1–6; 164–190
April 11	Merchant, "Mining the Earth's Womb," in *Machina Ex Dea*
April 16	Continue with above
	Also recommended:
	Merchant, pp. 103–105; 127–132; 143–151

Sherry Ortner, "Is Female to Male as Nature is to Culture?," on reserve in the Lyman Briggs Library

III. Sex Role Arrangements and Personality Development
We will analyze feminist sociological and psychological theories of how child raising practices impact on the development of female and male personality and ultimately on the organization of society, including the organization of science and the development and use of technology.

April 18	Reading: Dinnerstein, chapters 2, 3 and 4
April 23	Dinnerstein, chapters 8, 9 and 10
April 25	Dinnerstein, continued
April 30	Continue with above

Also recommended:
Nancy Chodorow, "The Sexual Sociology of Adult Life" and "The Psychodynamics of the Family," in *The Reproduction of Mothering* (on reserve)
Jane Flax, "Political Philosophy and the Patriarchal Unconscious: A Psychoanalytic Perspective on Epistemology and Metaphysics," in *Discovering Reality*

IV. Issues in Science and Gender
We will critique the concept of scientific objectivity from a feminist perspective and we'll consider the kinds of analysis feminists undertake regarding the role of gender in scientific inquiry.

May 2	Reading: Keller, "Women, Science, and Popular Mythology," in *Machina Ex Dea*
May 7	Keller, "Feminism, Science, and Democracy" (handout)
May 9	Recommended: Kathryn Pyne Addelson, "The Man of Professional Wisdom," in *Discovering Reality*
May 14	Michael Gross and Mary Beth Averill, "Evolution and Patriarchal Myths of Scarcity and Competition," in *Discovering Reality*

V. Women in Science
Here we will look briefly at some roadblocks to women in science.

May 16	Reading: Keller, "The Anomaly of a Woman in Physics" (handout)

VI. Women and Technology
This section will serve as an introduction to some feminist perspectives on technology. We'll also analyze the impact of certain technologies on the lives of women.

May 21	Reading: Ruth Schwartz Cowan, "The 'Industrial Kevolution' in the Home: Household Technology and Social Change in the 20th Century" (handout)
May 23	Jalna Hanmer, "Reproductive Technology: The Future for Women?," in *Machina Ex Dea*

Also recommended:
Corlann Gee Bush, "Women and the Assessment of Technology: To Think, To Be, To Unthink, to Free," in *Machina Ex Dea*

VII. A Feminist Utopia

May 28	Reading: Piercy, *Woman on the Edge of Time*

May 30   Continue with above
               Also recommended:
               Patrocinio Schweickart, "What If . . . Science and Technology in
               Feminist Utopias," in *Machina Ex Dea*

*   *   *   *   *

COURSE TITLE: WOMEN, SCIENCE AND TECHNOLOGY (CHAPTER 3)

Institution name: Simon Fraser University, British Columbia.
Name(s) and departmental affiliation(s) of individual(s) teaching this course: Margaret
   Benston, Women's Studies.
Specific Information regarding the course:
   Departments/Programs in which the course is listed: Women's Studies.
   Course level: Lower division undergraduate.
   Sex ratio: Predominantly female.
   Prerequistes: None.
   Method of instruction: Lecture, discussion.
Texts:
   Sheila Tobias, *Overcoming Math Anxiety*
   Evelyn Fox Keller, *A Feeling for the Organism*
   Gene Brown, *The Friendly Computer Book*
   Xerox packet
Methods of evaluation: Mid-term, final, assignments and projects.
Brief course description: We live in a society increasingly dependent on science and
   technology. In the past few years interest has grown in investigating the different
   ways that women and men relate to these areas. In this course we will examine
   both the nature of science/technology and aspects of the above differences. Topics
   will include: barriers to women entering scientific/technical fields, "math anxiety"
   and alleged gender differences in scientific ability, science and the military, and
   the consequences of parity in the scientific workplace.
Other features of the course: Besides theoretical materials, the course will involve
   practical projects providing 'skills maps' illustrating basic principles of
   mathematical and technical areas to allow students to assess their own changing
   attitudes and reactions.

Syllabus
      I. General Considerations
 1   A. Science and Technology: the Ambiguous Legacy
      B. Women in Science and Technology: Statistics and Attitudes
      Reading: Firestone, *Dialectic of Sex*
               Gearhart, *Wanderground*
               Marcuse, Mumford, Roszak (selected parts from the above)
               Keller, "Women in Science"
               Rossi, "Women in Engineering," "Women in Chemistry"
 2   A. The Development of Modern Science and the Role of Women
      B. Technology and Automation: Some History
      Reading: Keller, "Bacon and Patriarchy in Science"
               Merchant, "The Death of Nature"
               Benston, "Women and Automation"
               Kraft, *Programmers and Managers*, chapter 2

3   A. Why Aren't Women in Science and Technology
      B. Experiences of Women in Scientific and Technical Fields
      Reading: *Report* on Science Education in B.C. Science Council Workshop on
               Women and Science Education *Proceedings*
               Stehelin, "Science, Women and Ideology
               Cole, *Fair Science* (excerpts)
               Biographies from *Conversations* and *Working it Out*
               Lowe, "Cooperation and Competition in Science"
4   A. Science and Social Issues
      Reading: Rose and Hanmer, "Reproduction and the Technological Fix,"
               Ideology of/in Natural Sciences, Rose and Rose, eds.
               Rose and Rose, "The Incorporation of Science"
               UC Collective, "Science and the Military," in *Science and Liberation*,
               Arditti et al.

      II. Barriers to the Practices of Math and Science: Practical and Theoretical
         Work
      B. Basic Approaches to Mathematics
      Reading: For the whole of Part II: Tobias, *Overcoming Math Anxiety*
5   A. Statistics: Basic Notation and Definitions
      Reading: Hill, *Statistics for Social Change*
               Beckwith and Durlin, "Girls, Boys and Math"
      B. Statistics: Basic Notation and Definitions
6   A. Statistics: Basic Notation and Definitions
      Reading: Kimball, "Women and Science: A Critique of Biological Theories of
               Sex Differences"
               Fields, *About Computers*
      B. Group Work on projects
7   A. Group work on projects
      Reading: Readings on the psychology of sex roles
      B. Introduction to Computing
      ALL DAY WEEKEND WORKSHOP (SATURDAY)
8   A. Computer Extensions of Stats Projects
      B. Computer Extensions of Stats Projects
      Reading: S. Kuhn, "Women and Computer Programming'
               Graham, *The Mind Tool* (excerpts)
               M. Benston, "Artificial Intelligence and Dehumanization," Fields,
               About Computers
9   A. Computer Extensions of Stats Projects
      B. Computer Extensions of Stats Projects
10   A. Computer Extensions of Stats Projects
      B. Sunday Math: Calculus
11   A. Sunday Math: Calculus
      Reading: Report of the Saskatchewan Women in Trades Program
      B. Women and Machine Anxiety
12   A. Women and Machines: Automobile Mechanics

      III. More General Considerations
      B. Science as a Model for Rationality
         Reading: Benston, "Feminism and the Critique of the Scientific Method"
                  Easlea, "Objectivity and Commitment in Science"
                  Gould, "Morton's Ranking of Races"
13   A. Science as a Model for Rationality
      B. Questions for the Future

Notes on the Lecture Outline

(a) The intent here is to illustrate the structure of mathematics and, additionally, to illustrate the skills and approaches necessary to practice. Statistics has been chosen because it can be used to demonstrate fundamental mathematical concepts, particularly the idea of functions, and it can be used to introduce basic notation. There are a number of problems: statistics on male/female variability, analysis of drug testing results, changes in the distribution of traits as a result of hypothetical eugenics plans, possible effects on population statistics of being able to choose the sex of children and the like, that are simple enough to be feasible and which illustrate some problem of concern in Women's Studies. Students will examine one problem in a group and a second one on their own.

(b) The computer section will involve one intensive workshop that will teach the students to write a very simple program so that they get some feeling of control over the machine and some understanding of language principles. The intent is not to teach any actual programming skills; the work on machines will involve pre-written programs that the students will be expected to read, analyze and understand before using. The work will be done using stand alone micros using BASIC.

(c) Calculus seems to be one of the major symbolic areas of difficulty in approaching math. In this section we will introduce students to numerical integration and to the reasons why one might wish to know these results (they will already have some examples from their statistics works). A careful treatment of basic concepts can lead to a comparison of their numerical results and the analytical solution.

(d) Dealing with machines is another whole area of gender difference. We will examine social and psychological barriers to women's participation in areas involving machinery. (Automobiles, for example, are not just machines; they have a major symbolic significance that is different for men and women in this society.) As a practical exercise in this section the students will do some mechanical repair or procedure—dismantling and reassembling an automobile carburetor for example on a machine that is strongly gender-typed.

* * * * *

COURSE TITLE: WOMEN, SCIENCE AND TECHNOLOGY IN EUROPE AND AMERICA: 17TH CENTURY TO THE PRESENT (CHAPTER 3)

Institution name: Stanford University.
Name(s) and departmental affiliation(s) of individual(s) teaching this course: Londa Schiebinger, Values, Technology, Science and Society.
Specific information regarding the course:
   Departments/Programs in which the course is listed: History of Science, Feminist Studies.
   Course level: Upper division undergraduate.
   Sex ratio: Predominantly female.
   Prerequisites: None.
   Method of instruction: Seminar, discussion.
Texts:
   Margaret Rossiter, *Women Scientists in America*
   Ruth Bleier, *Science and Gender*
   Evelyn Fox Keller, *Reflections on Gender and Science*

Joan Rothschild (ed.), *Machina Ex Dea: Feminist Perspectives on Technology*
Rita Arditti et al., *Test-Tube Women*
Plus books and articles placed on library reserve.
Methods of evaluation: Research project.
Brief course description: The course explores issues concerning gender, science and technology from the 17th century to the present in Europe and America. Course will examine (a) current theories of the relationship of gender, science and technology; (b) the history of women's participation in science and technology; (c) women's access to institutions of science and technology; (d) conceptions of gender in scientific texts; (e) women as the object of scientific research and technological innovation; and (f) "alternatives" in the sciences and technology proposed and/or practiced by women.

Syllabus

January 14   Introduction
               Approaches to Gender, Science and Technology
               The Profession: Statistics
               Experiences of Women Scientists: A Panel Discussion
                   Dora Goldstein (Professor of Pharmacology)
                   Elizabeth Miller (Assistant Professor of Geology)
                   Mary Sunseri (Professor of Mathematics)

January 21   Institutional Barriers to Women's Participation in Science and Technology
               Reading: A.T. Gage, *History of the Linnean Society of London*, London, 1938, pp. 86–91
                   Kathleen Lonsdale, "Women in Science: Reminiscences and Reflections," *Impact of Science on Society*, no. 1, 1970, pp. 45–59
                   Lise Meitner, "The Status of Women in the Professions," *Physics Today* vol. 13, no. 8, 1960, pp. 16–21
                   Alice Rossi, "Women in Science: Why so Few?," *Science* vol. 148, no. 3574, 1965, pp. 1196–1202
                   Barbara Reskin, "Sex Differentiation and Social Organization of Science," in *Sociology of Science*, Jerry Gaston (ed.), San Francisco, 1978, pp. 6–37
                   Sally Hacker, "Mathematization of Engineering: Limits on Women and the Field," *Machina Ex Dea*, pp. 38–58
                   Ruth Hubbard, "Should Professional Women be like Professional Men?," *Women in Scientific and Engineering Professions*, Violet Haas and Carolyn Perrucci (eds.), Ann Arbor, 1984, pp. 205–211
                   Claire Ellen Max, "Career Paths for Women in Physics," *Women and Minorities in Science*, Sheila Humphreys (ed.), Boulder, CO: AAAS, 1982, pp. 99–119

January 28   Scientific Sexism
               Reading: Robert Lowie and Leta Hollingworth, "Science and Feminism," *Scientific Monthly* vol. 2, 1916, pp. 277–284
                   Marian Lowe, "The Dialectic of Biology and Culture," *Woman's Nature: Rationalizations of Inequality*, Marian Lowe and Ruth Hubbard (eds.), New York: Pergamon Press, 1983, pp. 39–62
                   Marian Lowe, "Sex Differences, Science, and Society," *The Technological Woman*, Jan Zimmerman (ed.), New York, 1983, pp. 7–17

Janet Sayers, *Biological Politics*, London, 1982, Part I "Biological Arguments against Feminism"
Joan Burstyn, "Education and Sex: The Medical Case Against Higher Education for Women," *Proceedings of the American Philosophical Society* vol. 117, 1973, pp. 79–80
Ruth Bleier, *Science and Gender: A Critique of Biology and Its Theories on Women*, New York: Pergamon Press, 1984

February 4   Women's Contributions to Mainstream Science and Technology
Reading: Margaret Rossiter, *Women Scientists in America: Struggles and Strategies to 1940*, Baltimore: Johns Hopkins University Press, 1982
Evelyn Fox Keller, *A Feeling for the Organism: The Life and Work of Barbara McClintock*, San Francisco: W.H. Freeman, 1983
H.J. Mozans, *Woman in Science*, Cambridge, MA: 1974
Lynn M. Osen, *Women in Mathematics*, Cambridge, MA: 1974
Autumn Stanley, "Women Hold Up Two-Thirds of the Sky: Notes for a Revised History of Technology," *Machina ex Dea: Feminist Perspectives on Technology*, Joan Rothschild (ed.), New York: Pergamon Press, 1983, pp. 5–22
Autumn Stanley, "From Africa to America: Black Women Inventors," *The Technological Woman*, pp. 55–64

February 11   Feminist Theory: Science and Gender
Reading: Georg Simmel, "The Relative and the Absolute in the Problem of the Sexes," *Georg Simmel: On Women, Sexuality and Love*, trans. Guy Oakes, New Haven: 1984, pp. 102–132
Evelyn Fox Keller, *Reflections on Gender and Science*, New Haven: Yale University Press, 1985, concluding chapter
Carolyn Merchant, "Mining the Earth's Womb," *Machina Ex Dea*, pp. 99–117
Ynestra King, "Toward an Ecological Feminism and a Feminist Ecology," *Machina Ex Dea*, pp. 118–129
Corlann Gee Bush, "Women and the Assessment of Technology," *Machina Ex Dea*, pp. 151–170
Brian Easlea, *Fathering the Unthinkable: Masculinity, Scientists and the Nuclear Arms Race*, London: Pluto Press, 1983
Donna Haraway, "Class, Race, Sex, Scientific Objects of Knowledge: A Socialist—Feminist Perspective . . .," *Women in Scientific and Engineering Professions*, Violet Haas and Carolyn Perrucci (eds.), Ann Arbor: 1984, pp. 211–229
Elizabeth Fee, "Women's Nature and Scientific Objectivity," *Woman's Nature: Rationalizations of Inequality*, Marian Lowe and Ruth Hubbard (eds.), New York: Pergamon Press, 1983, pp. 9–28

February 18   HOLIDAY
February 25   Alternative Sciences Proposes and/or Practices by Women
Reading: Barbara Ehrenreich and Deirdre English, *For Her Own Good*, New York: Anchor Press 1978 Doubleday, pp. 1–140

154   *Teaching Technology from a Feminist Perspective*

Brian Easlea, *Witch-Hunting, Magic and the New Philosophy*, Brighton, U.K.: Harvester Press, 1980
Jean Donnison, *Midwives and Medical Men*, New York: 1977
JoAllyn Archambault, "Women: Inventing the Wheel," *Future, Technology and Woman*, San Diego: 1981, pp. 36–40

March 4   Sexual Division of Labor: Reality and Ideology
Reading: Rosalind Rosenberg, *Beyond Separate Spheres: Intellectual Roots of Modern Feminism*, New Haven: 1982
Karin Hausen, "Family and Role-Division: The Polarisation of Sexual Stereotypes in the Nineteenth Century—An Aspect of the Dissociation of Work and Family Life," *The German Family*, Richard J. Evans (ed.), London: 1981, pp. 51–83
Ruth Bloch, "Untangling the Roots of Modern Sex Roles: A Survey of Four Centuries of Change," *Signs* vol. 4, no. 2, 1978, pp. 237–252
Michele Rosaldo, *Women, Society and Culture*, Stanford University Press, 1974, her article
Roslyn Feldberg and Evelyn Glenn, "Technology and Work Degradation: Effects of Office Automation on Women Clerical Workers," *Machina ex Dea*, pp. 59–78
Joan Rothschild, "Technology, Housework, and Women's Liberation: A Theoretical Analysis," *Machina ex Dea*, pp. 79–93
Joan Wallach Scott, "The Mechanization of Women's Work," *Scientific American* vol. 247, 1982, pp. 167–187

March 11   Women and Power: Reproductive Technology
Reading: Jalna Hanmer, "Reproductive Technology: The Future for Women?," in *Machina ex Dea*, pp. 183–197
Barbara Katz Rothman, "Means of Choice in Reproductive Technology," *Test-Tube Women: What Future for Motherhood?*, Rita Arditti et al. London: Routledge & Kegan Paul, 1983, pp. 23–34
Rebecca Albury, "Who Owns the Embryo," *Test-Tube Women*, pp. 54–67
Ruth Hubbard, "Personal Courage is not Enough: Some Hazards of Childbearing in the 1980s," *Test-Tube Women*, pp. 331–355
Robyn Rowland, "Reproductive Technologies: the Final Solution to the Woman Question?," *Test-Tube Women*, pp. 356–370
Vern Bullough, "Female Physiology, Technology and Women's Liberation," *Dynamos and Virgins Revisited: Women and Technological Change in History*, Martha Moore Trescott (ed.), Metuchen, NJ: Scarecrow Press, 1979, pp. 236–251
Alberta Parker, "Juggling: Health Care Technology and Women's Needs," *Future, Technology and Woman*, San Diego: 1981, pp. 24–29
Alice Through the Microscope: The Power of Science over Women's Lives, Brighton Women and Science Group (eds.), London: 1980, Part Three "Technological Control"

*   *   *   *   *

COURSE TITLE:
WOMEN/SCIENCE/TECHNOLOGY (CHAPTER 3)

Institution name: State University of New York at Stony Brook.
Name(s) and departmental affiliation(s) of individual(s) teaching this course: Ruth
  Schwartz Cowan, History, Women's Studies.
Specific information regarding the course:
  Departments/Programs in which the course is listed: History, Women's Studies.
  Course level: Upper division undergraduate.
  Sex ratio: Predominantly female.
  Prerequisites: One course in either: history of science, history of technology,
    sociology of science, philosophy of science, philosophy of technology, or women's
    studies.
Texts:
  Margaret Rossiter, *Women Scientists in America*
  Ruth Bleier, *Science and Gender*
  Ruth Schwartz Cowan, *More Work for Mother*
  Evelyn Fox Keller, *Reflections on Gender and Science*
Methods of evaluation: Two papers and class participation.
Brief course description: This course considers four different aspects of the complex
  relations between and among women/science/technology: (1) the history and
  sociology of women as scientists and engineers; (2) gender-related philosophical
  issues having to do with scientific modes of thought; (3) scientific theories about
  gender; and (4) the impact of technological change on women.
Other features of the course: Guest speakers; student interviews of speakers.

Syllabus

January 23   Introduction
January 30   I. Autobiographical Accounts of Women Scientists
              Reading: "Katharine Sturgis," "Joni Magee," and "Vanessa Gamble,"
                  in Regina Markell Morantz et al. (eds.), *In Her Own Words:
                  Oral Histories of Women Physicians*, Westport CT:
                  Greenwood Press, 1982
                  "Evelyn Fox Keller" and "Naomi Weisstein," in Sara
                  Ruddick and Pamela Daniels (eds.), *Working it Out: 23
                  Women, Writers, Scientists and Scholars Talk about their
                  Lives*, New York: Pantheon Books 1977

February 6   II. Thinking about Working Women
              Reading: "Gender Differences in Labor Force Participation and
                  Occupational Distribution," in Patricia A. Roos, *Gender
                  and Work: A Comparative Analysis of Industrial Societies*,
                  Albany: SUNY Press, 1985
              OUR GUEST WILL BE: PATRICIA ROOS, ASSISTANT
              PROFESSOR OF SOCIOLOGY

February 13   III. Is there Discrimination Against Women in the Sciences?
              Reading: Alice Rossi, "Women in Science: Why So Few?," *Science*
                  vol. 148, 1965, pp. 1196–1202
                  Martha S. White, "Psychological and Social Barriers to
                  Women in Science," *Science* vol. 170, 1970, pp. 413–416
                  "Women's Place in the Scientific Community," in Jonathon
                  R. Cole, *Fair Science: Women in the Scientific Community*,
                  New York: Free Press, 1979, pp. 51–89

OUR GUEST WILL BE: DR ROSEANNE DISTEFANO,
ASSISTANT PROFESSOR OF PHYSICS, NEW YORK IN-
STITUTE OF TECHNOLOGY AND RESEARCH ASSOCIATE,
INSTITUTE FOR THEORETICAL PHYSICS

February 20   IV. Historical Perspectives on Women in Science
Reading: Margaret Rossiter, *Women Scientists in America: Struggles
and Strategies to 1940*, Baltimore: Johns Hopkins
University Press, 1981, chapters 1–6

February 21   V. Historical Perspectives on Women in Science
Reading: Margaret Rossiter, *Women Scientists in America*, chapters
7–11
OUR GUEST WILL BE: DR MONICA RILEY, PROFESSOR OF
BIOCHEMISTRY

March 6   VI. Is there Discrimination Against Women in the Sciences?
There is no reading assignment because YOUR PAPERS ARE DUE
TODAY. We will devote our class time to discussion of them.

March 13   VII. Gender and Science
Class will meet for only one hour today for discussion of topics for
final papers. All students are expected to attend lecture by Sandra
Harding, "The Science Question in Feminism" at 4:00, Room 249,
Old Physics. If possible you might also find it interesting to attend the
Dean's Conversations in the Disciplines, tonight at 8:00, Javits
Conference Room; at this time Dr Harding will engage in a debate on
the question, "Is Science Gender Neutral?"

April 4   VIII. Biology Constructs the Female
Reading: Ruth Bleier, *Science and Gender: A Critique of Biology and
its Theories on Women*, New York: Pergamon Press, 1984,
chapters 3 and 4
OUR GUEST WILL BE: DR BARBARA BENTLEY,
ASSOCIATE PROFESSOR, ECOLOGY AND EVOLUTION

April 10   IX. Biology Constructs the Female
Reading: Ruth Bleier, *Science and Gender*, chapters 2 and 5
OUR GUEST WILL BE: DR SHERYL SCOTT, ASSOCIATE
PROFESSOR, NEUROBIOLOGY

April 17   X. Why are there so Few Women Engineers?
Reading: Sally Hacker, "The Culture of Engineering: Woman,
Workplace and Machine," *Women's Studies International
Quarterly* vol. 4, no. 3, 1981, pp. 341–353
Samuel Florman, "Engineering and the Female Mind,"
Harper's, February, 1978, pp. 57–64
"Women in Technology: Why the Door is Opening
(Slowly)," special issue of *Technology Review*, November,
1984, *passim*

April 23   XI. Women, Machines and Work
Reading: Ruth Schwartz Cowan, *More Work for Mother: The Ironies
of Household Technology from the Open Hearth to the
Microwave*, New York: Basic Books, 1983, chapters 1, 4, 7

Diane Werneke, *Microelectronics and Working Women: A Literature Summary*, Washington, DC: National Academy Press, 1984

April 30 DISCUSSION OF STUDENT PAPERS
May 8 DISCUSSION OF STUDENT PAPERS

* * * * *

COURSE TITLE: WOMEN, TECHNOLOGY AND SOCIAL CHANGE (CHAPTER 2)

Institution name: Portland State University, Oregon.

Name(s) and departmental affiliation(s) of individual(s) teaching this course: Jane Peters, Urban Studies.

Specific information regarding the course:

Departments/Programs in which the course is listed: Urban Studies, Women's Studies, and Sociology.

Course level: Upper division undergraduate.

Sex ratio: Predominantly female.

Prerequisites: None.

Method of instruction: Lecture and discussion.

Texts:

Joan Rothschild (ed.), *Machina Ex Dea: Feminist Perspectives on Technology*, Pergamon Press, 1983 (MED)

Margaret Llewelyn Davies (ed.), *Life as We Have Known It: by Cooperative Working Women*, Norton Press, 1931, reprint 1975 (Life)

Rita Arditti, Renate Duelli Klein and Shelley Minden (eds.), *Test-Tube Women: What Future for Motherhood?*, London: Pandora Press, 1984 (TTW)

Reading Packet (P); selections from:

Christine E. Bose, Philip L. Bereano and Mary Malloy, Household Technology and the Social Construction of Housework. *Technology and Culture* vol. xxv, 1984, pp. 53–82

Harry Braverman, *Labor and Monopoly Capital; The Degradation of Work in the Twentieth-Century*, New York: Monthly Review Press, 1974

John G. Burke and Marshall C. Eakin (eds.) *Technology and Change*, San Francisco: Boyd & Fraser, 1979

Gena Corea, *The Hidden Malpractice: How American Medicine Mistreats Women*, New York: Harper Books, 1977, rev. 1985

Roslyn Dauber and Melinda L. Cain (eds.), *Women and Technological Change in Developing Countries*, Boulder, CO: Westview Press, 1981

Zillah Eisenstein (ed.), *Capitalist Patriarchy and The Case For Socialist Feminism*, New York: Monthly Review Press, 1979

Dolores Hayden, *The Grand Domestic Revolution*, Cambridge, MA: MIT Press, 1981

Sheryl Ruzek, *The Women's Health Movement: Feminist Alternatives to Medical Control*, New York: Praeger, 1979

Martha Moore Trescott, (ed.), *Dynamos and Virgins Revisited: Women and Technological Change in History*, Metuchen, NJ: Scarecrow, 1979

Joann Vanek, "Time Spent in Housework," *Scientific American* vol. 231, November 1974, pp. 116–120

Methods of evaluation: Three short papers, and a take home final.

157

158   *Teaching Technology from a Feminist Perspective*

Brief course description: The course is structured to enable students to leave the class with the ability to ask questions about technology—to assess the effects on their lives and others. To do this we first focus on the fundamental policy issues of the technology 'triumph, threat, neutral' debate and develop a feminist critique of this. Then we apply this analysis to 3 technological areas, workplace (with the focus on clerical work), domestic (with a spatial focus) and reproductive (looking at new technologies).

Syllabus

I. Introduction and Overview

January 7	Introduction
January 9	Views of Technology

Reading: (P) Commoner, "Are We Really in Control?," Mumford, "The Technique of Total Control," Ellul, "The Technological Order," Florman "In Praise of Technology" (MED) King, "Toward an Ecological Feminism and a Feminist Ecology," chapter 7

January 14   Industrial Revolution

Reading: (P) Braverman, chapters 2 and 3 "The Origins of Management" and "The Division of Labor" (Life) "Memories of Seventy Years," pp. 1–55 Choice of two other memories between pp. 56–108

January 16   Reading: (P) Braverman, chapters 7, 8 and 12 "The Scientific–Technical Revolution," "The Scientific–Technical Revolution and the Worker," "The Modern Corporation"

January 21   Feminist Views of Technology and Technology Assessment

Reading: (MED) Stanley, "Women Hold Up Two-thirds of the Sky: . . .," chapter 1, Merchant, "Mining the Earth's Womb," chapter 6, Bush, "Women and the Assessment of Technology . . .," chapter 9

January 23   Reading: (MED) Trescott, "Lillian Moller Gilbreth . . .," chapter 2 Hacker, "Mathematization of Engineering . . .," chapter 3

II. Workplace Technologies

January 28   Reading: (P) Braverman, chapter 15 "Clerical Workers"
January 30   Reading: (P) Davies, "Woman's Place is at the Typewriter . . ."
February 4   Reading: (P) Zimmerman, (a) "Technology and the Future of Women . . .," (b) "Women in Computing," Gutek, "Women's Work in the Office of the Future" (MED) Feldberg and Glenn, chapter 4 "Technology and Work Degradation . . ."

February 6   Reading: (P) Srinivasan, "Impact of Selected Industrial Technologies on Women in Mexico," Lim, "Women's Work in Multinational Electronics Factories"

III. Domestic Technologies

February 11   Reading: (P) Kleinberg, "Technology and Women's Work . . .," Cowan, "The 'Industrial Revolution' in the Home . . .," Hayden, chapter 1 "The Grand Domestic Revolution"
February 13   Reading: (P) Vanek, "Time Spent in Housework" (MED) Rothschild, chapter 5 "Technology, Housework, and Women's Liberation . . ."
February 18   Reading: (P) Hayden, chapters 9, 10, 11 and 13 "Domestic Evolution . . .," "Community Kitchens . . .," "Homes without Kitchens . . ." and "Madame Kollontai . . ."

February 20   Reading: (P) Bose et al., "Household Technology and the Social Construction of Housework"

IV. Reproductive Technology

February 25   Reading: (P) Ruzek, "The Rise of the Women's Health Movement," Corea, chapter 7 "The History of the Birth-Control Movement"

February 27   Reading: (P) Corea, chapters 8 and 9 "Modern Birth Control," "Male Contraception"

March 4   Reading: (TTW) pp. 23–116, 153–187, 213–234, 281–312

March 6   Reading: (TTW) pp. 331–370, 427–448

V. Synthesis

March 11   Reading: (P) Carr, "Technologies Appropriate for Women . . ." (MED) Keller, chapter 8 "Women, Science and Popular Mythology"

March 13   A Feminist Technology Assessment Wheel

March 21   9:30 a.m. TAKE HOME FINAL DUE

* * * * *

INTERACTIVE QUALIFYING PROJECTS, WORCESTER POLYTECHNIC INSTITUTE, WORCESTER, MA

Students at Worcester Polytechnic Institute, Worcester, MA, must complete a unique degree requirement, called the Interactive Qualifying Project (IQP). The IQP challenges students to define, research, and report on a topic that relates science and/or technology to some social need or issue.

The following is a list of IQPs related to Women and Technology, 1978–86. Further information is available from the Projects Office, Interdisciplinary Affairs, Worcester Polytechnic Institute, Worcester, Massachusetts.

Women in Business (1978)
Women and Engineering: WPI Women and Fear of Success (1978)
Women in Nontraditional Careers (1978)
Women at WPI: A Profile (1978)
Employment of Housewives (1978)
Women in Engineering: A Study of WPI Graduates (1979)
Women in Engineering: Comparison of Britain and U.S. (1979)
Effects of Technology on Egalitarian Role Norms (1980)
Work-Related Problems of the WPI Alumnae (1980)
You've Got to Have a Sense of Humor (interviews with 8 women engineers) (1980–1981)
WPI Women: A Survey of Attitudes (1981)
Nurse Scheduling Considerations (1981)
Alternatives in Nursing Education—A Quantitative Evaluation (1981)
Women's Health Education (1981)
Sexual Politics at WPI (1982)
Women in the Skilled Trades (1982)
Visual Display Terminals and Health Effects (1982)
A Study of the Controllability of Nursing Turnover (1982)
Design and Implementation of a Nurse Staffing Study (1982)

Employer Supported Child Care Services (1982)
Present Day Options in Childbirth Location (1982)
Women Career Handbook (1982)
Human Research—DES (1982)
Kitchens in the 1830s (1982)
Oral Contraception (1983)
Topics in Medical Technology (in vitro ferilization) (1983)
Rape Prevention Workshop (1982)
Technology and Childbirth (1983)
Women in Medieval Life (1983)
History of the Pill (1983)
Women, Marriage and Engineering: A Decade of Change (1983)
History of the Birth Control Pill (1984)
Advertising and the Professional Woman (1984)
Office Automation (1984)
Health Effects of Video Display Terminals (1984)
Technology and Childbirth (1984)
Childbirth and Technology: Doctors and Modern Alternatives in Childbirth (1985)
Stress and College Women (1986)
Office Automation Stress (1986)
Potential Radiation Hazards from VDTs (1986)
Modern Alternatives in Childbirth (1986)
The Patriarchal Power of Medicine and Religion (1986)
Technology in Pregnancy and Childbirth (1986)
Sex Differences in Nuclear Opinion on Four Campuses (1986)

Name Index

Subject Index

"add women and stir," 30, 31, 36, 40, 43

architecture and design, feminist perspectives, 9, 16–17

attitudes toward science and technology, gender-based differences. *see* gendered attitudes toward science and technology; learning approaches

audio-visual materials, 18–19, 35, 51, 70, 78–79, 93
  feminist critique of, 70
  need for, 78–79
  use in teaching, 18–19, 35, 51

Bloomsburg University, 36, 39, 42, 111

Bolter, J.D.
  Turing's Man critiqued, 59–66, 68–69

Bulletin of Science, Technology, and Society, 3, 81. *see also* Pennsylvania State University

Bush model of technology assessment, 13, 54–55. *see also* feminist technology assessment; Technology Effects Assessment Wheel

class, race and gender, 4, 32, 39, 41, 69, 75

classroom format and atmosphere. *see* teaching methods

computers
  as defining technology, 60
  as evocative object, 61
  male culture of, 62, 65, 76
  overcoming resistance to, 24, 29

conceptual frameworks. *see* feminist conceptual frameworks; gender conceptual frameworks

curriculum integration. *see* feminist curricular integration; McIntosh developmental model; women's studies and technology studies

demystification of science and technology, 23–24, 27–29, 75–76. *see also* empowerment; technological literacy; Women's Computer Literacy Project

Eastern Michigan University, 2, 15, 26, 37, 76, 124, 144

empowerment
  of women 75
  of liberal arts students, 75–76
  see also Open University

experiential approach. *see* feminist research method

faculty development, 79

feminine, as a gender category, 33–34, 45–46. *see also* gender; masculine

feminist analysis, 3, 7, 41, 69, 70, 71. *see also* gender analysis

feminist conceptual framework(s), 39, 40–44, 45–55, 74
  need for, 42, 45
  problems in creating, 45–47
  use of feminist technology assessment, 48, 54–55
  women/technology courses as models, 41–42
  see also gender conceptual framework(s)

166   *Subject Index*

of language, 58, 68–69. *see also*
Bolter; language, gendered usage
of technology literature, 58, 70–71,
72
of traditional scholarship, 3–4,
30–31, 40–41, 69, 72
feminist curricular transformation, 4, 6,
30–44 *passim*, 54
McIntosh developmental model, 4,
31, 38–44, 74
feminist research method, 3–4, 53–55,
66, 67–70
experiential approach, 3, 40, 67–68,
69
interactive and connected, 54, 59,
67, 69
"objectivity," 54, 66, 67
The Second Self as model, 67–69
feminist resource materials for
technology studies, 45–56, 57–72,
74, 80–93
criteria for, 58, 69–71
feminist technology assessment, 13, 48,
54–55, 74.
as conceptual framework, 48, 54–55
see also Bush model; Technology
Effects Assessment Wheel
feminist theories of sex and gender
difference, 45–46
films. *see* audio-visual
Future, Technology and Woman
Conference, 89

gender
and language, 58–69. *see also*
language, gendered usage
and sex, 45–46
and sex difference, 45–46, 48
as a category of analysis, 45, 51, 54,
67, 69
defined as a category, 45
see also gender analysis
gender analysis, 45, 51, 69, 71, 74. *see
also* feminist analysis
gender, class and race, 3–4, 32, 39, 41,
69, 75
gender conceptual framework(s), 7, 45,
47–48, 49–50, 51, 52, 74
masculinist-feminist conceptual
framework, 47–48, 49–50, 51–52
philosophical and sociological
critique, 48, 49–51

philosophical, psychological,
woman-nature critique, 48, 51–53
social science critique, 48–49
see also feminist conceptual framework
gender dualism, 38, 45, 46, 47–48, 52,
54, 63, 65
gendered attitudes toward science and
technology, 24, 28–29, 36–37,
75–76. *see also* learning approaches
gendered language. *see* language,
gendered usage
"ghettoization", 34–35, 41
guest lecturers, use in teaching, 18, 25,
26, 38

"hands on" courses, 13, 14, 22, 23–24,
27, 29, 50, 75. *see also* Open
University
history of technology
courses, 2, 15–16, 24–26, 32–34, 37,
40–41, 42–43, 49–50, 74, 76,
124–31, 151–57
curriculum development, 2–3
history of discipline, 1–2
impact of feminist perspectives, 5–6
and technology studies, 1–2, 5–6
see also Society for the History of
Technology; *Technology and Culture*
household technology, 9, 11, 15, 25,
34–35, 78
humanist man, 66. *see also* Bolter
humanities, and feminist curricular
integration, 4

integration of feminist materials
general, 4–5
McIntosh model, 4, 31, 38–44, 74
"mainstreaming", 4, 31
into technology studies courses, 6–7,
30–44, 73–74
resistance to, 32, 35–36, 38, 43, 44
integrative courses, 31–32, 32–33,
33–34, 34–36, 36–37, 37
interdisciplinary approaches
in courses, 8–20 *passim*, 22–27
passim, 31–38 *passim*, 48–53
passim
in technology studies, 1–2, 31–37
passim. see also STS; team teaching
Interactive Qualifying Projects,
Worcester Polytechnic, 19–20

Lane Community College, 27, 101
language
feminist critique of, 58, 68–69
gender inclusive, 31, 61–62, 68
gender-neutral, 65–66, 68, 69, 70
gender-neutral usage by Turkle, 59,
65–68
and gender awareness, 59–60,
65–66, 67, 68, 69, 70
and gender bias, 58, 60, 61, 65, 68
gendered usage, 58–60, 61–66, 68
gendered usage by Bolter, 58–65, 68
artificial procreation, 64–65
computers, 58–63, 65–69
creation, 64–65
man, 58, 62–63, 66
nature, 63
learning approaches, gender-based
differences, 24, 28–29, 36–37,
45–46, 75–76. *see also* gendered
attitudes toward science and
technology; Women's Computer
Literacy Project
Lehigh University
STS program, 2
*Science, Technology and Society
Curriculum Newsletter*, 2, 85

McIntosh developmental model of
curriculum integration, 4, 31,
38–44, 74
applied to technology studies courses,
31, 38–44, 74
Phase 1, 4, 38–39, 40
Phase 2, 4, 39, 40
Phase 3, 4, 39, 40, 41
Phase 4, 4, 40, 41, 42, 43
Phase 5, 4, 40
The Machine in the University, 2–3,
81, 85, *see also* STS curriculum
"mainstreaming," 4, 31
Stimpson, "both/and," 4
see also feminist curricular
transformation; McIntosh
developmental model
male hostility to feminist perspectives,
10, 11, 32, 35–36, 38, 42–44, 74. *see
also* teaching methods
man. *see* language, gendered usage; *see
also* nature
masculine
as a gender category, 45–46

contrasted with feminist as conceptual
framework, 45, 47–48, 49–50,
51–52
cultural perspective, 52, 66, 68
see also gender; feminine
masculinist-feminist conceptual
framework, 47–48, 49–50, 51–52
Massachusetts Institute of Technology,
16, 95
mathematics, overcoming resistance to,
14, 23–24, 50
methods of teaching. *see* teaching
methods
Michigan State University, 53, 147
museum facilities, use in teaching,
33–34

National Endowment for the Humanities
curriculum development grant, 35
National Women's Studies Association,
3, 5, 30, 44
Task Force on Science and
Technology, 5
nature
images of, 32, 37–38, 51, 53
man and, 38, 51, 52, 53, 54, 63
New Liberal Arts
courses and programs, 2, 3, 15, 75,
77, 79
NLA News, 3, 84
see also technological literacy
NLA News, 3, 84
Non-traditional courses. *see* "hands on"
NWSA. *see* National Women's Studies
Association

office technologies, 11, 15
Open University, U.K.
"hands on" courses, 27–28
and feminist technology assessment,
28, 55
"Other," women as, 69, 70, 71, 75

pedagogy. *see* teaching methods
Pennsylvania State University
*Bulletin of Science, Technology, and
Society*, 3
STS program, 3
Portland State University, 13, 157

About the Author

Joan Rothschild is professor of political science at the University of Lowell (Mass.) and visiting scholar at the Philosophy and Technology Studies Center of Polytechnic University (Brooklyn, NY), and was recently visiting scholar at the Center for the Study of Women and Society, Graduate Center, The City University of New York. She holds a B.A. in English Literature from Cornell University, and an M.A. and Ph.D. in politics from New York University. Her other publications include *Machina Ex Dea: Feminist Perspectives on Technology* (Pergamon 1983), *Women, Technology and Innovation* (Pergamon 1982), and numerous articles and review essays in feminist theory, politics, and gender and technology.

A former research associate at the Harvard University Program on Technology and Society, Professor Rothschild has been associated with interdisciplinary programs and curriculum development in technology studies and women's studies for over a decade: at the University of Lowell, the Wellesley Center for Research on Women, the University of Cincinnati, and the Technology Studies and Education group of the Society for the History of Technology. Her current research focuses on the new reproductive technologies and the ideology of human perfectibility.